Radical Narratives of the Black Atlantic

THE BLACK ATLANTIC

General Editor: Polly Rewt, The Open University and University of Stirling

Series Advisers: Caryl Phillips, novelist; David Dabydeen, Centre for Caribbean Studies, University of Warwick; Vincent Carretta, Professor of English, University of Maryland; Angus Calder, writer

The cultural and theoretical parameters of the Black Atlantic world are explored and treated critically in this timely series. It offers students, scholars and general readers essential texts which focus on the international black experience. The broad scope of the series is innovative and ambitious, treating literary, historical, biographical, musical and visual arts subjects from an interdisciplinary and cross-cultural perspective.

The books address current debates on what constitutes the Black Atlantic, both geographically and theoretically. They include anthologized primary material and collections of seminal critical value to courses on the African diaspora and related subjects. They will also appeal more widely to a readership interested in biographical and other material that presents scholarship accessibly.

In the series:

Madge Dresser, *Slavery Obscured: The Social History of the Slave Trade in an English Provincial Port*

Paul E. Lovejoy (editor), *Identity in the Shadow of Slavery*

Nancy Priscilla Naro, *A Slave's Place, a Master's World: Fashioning Dependency in Rural Brazil*

Alasdair Pettinger (editor), *Always Elsewhere: Travels of the Black Atlantic*

James Walvin, *An African's Life: The Life and Times of Olaudah Equiano, 1745–1797*

James Walvin, *Making the Black Atlantic: Britain and the African Diaspora*

RADICAL NARRATIVES OF THE BLACK ATLANTIC

ALAN RICE

continuum
LONDON • NEW YORK

Continuum
The Tower Building, 11 York Road, London, SE1 7NX
370 Lexington Avenue, New York, NY 10017–6503

First published 2003

British Library Cataloguing-in-Publication Data
A catalogue record for this book is available from the British Library.

ISBN 0–8264–5606–5 (hardback)
    0–8264–5607–3 (paperback)

Library of Congress Cataloging-in-Publication Data
Rice, Alan J., 1960–
    Radical narratives of the Black Atlantic / Alan Rice.
        p. cm. — (The Black Atlantic)
    Includes bibliographical references and index.
    ISBN 0-8264-5606-5 — ISBN 0-8264-5607-3 (pb.)
    1. African Americans—Intellectual life. 2. African Americans—
History—To 1863. 3. Africans—America—History. 4. African
diaspora. 5. Slavery—America—History. 6. Slave trade—
America—History. 7. American literature—African American
authors. 8. Slavery in literature. 9. Slaves' writings, American.
I. Title. II. Series.

E185. R49 2002
973'.0496073—dc21   2002071583

Typeset by YHT Ltd, London

CONTENTS

ILLUSTRATIONS

ACKNOWLEDGEMENTS

This book is dedicated to the memory of my grandfather Fred Rice, who taught me the value of stories and that knowledge is far wider than that found in books. All of my family have given unstinting support to this project over the last five years. In particular, my partner Lizzie, who gave me space to write, my daughters Amy and Kezia for putting up with Daddy's 'working' and my father Tony, whose survival to see it finished defied doctors' logic.

My principal pragmatic vote of thanks goes to the Arts Humanities Research Board whose financial support in the form of a leave award meant that the book could be completed. Also, the Department of Cultural Studies at the University of Central Lancashire supported the project by granting leave, which enabled me to attend numerous conferences. Of course, such support is reliant on the flexibility of individual colleagues and particularly on those in my American Studies section. Additionally, Eithne Quinn and George McKay made helpful suggestions and comments throughout the writing of the manuscript. Will Kaufmann and Heidi Macpherson provided transatlantic nuances despite their base in Preston. Encouragement and intellectual support also came from Richard Hinchcliffe, John Joughin, Anne Wichmann, Alizon Brunning, Stuart Hampton-Reeves, Anne Woodward, Daniel Lamont and Michael Hayes, even though their fields were hardly (if at all) black Atlantic. My undergraduate students on the course 'Narratives of the Black Atlantic' provided a laboratory for many of the ideas presented here and the book would have been more pedestrian without them. I have presented the work at a variety of venues over the last five years and would like to thank the audiences for their input.

The work for the project preceded my entry into academia by a decade and I would like to thank friends who helped me form these ideas long before I was paid for doing it. Principally, Nigel Robson Smith who got me into jazz, Kubi Tchackarov who helped me escape suburban mundanity and Ewan Davidson who provided the necessary ironic commentary. Also worthy of thanks are Trevor Leat and Becky Wood, while Alasdair Pettinger helped with dole-time fraternity and black Atlantic intellectual encouragement from an early stage. Thanks must also go to Jack Fuller, Susan Hogan, Paul and Kim Tebble, Mark Holding, Keith Davidson, Paul Baker, Helen Chandler and Pauline Mullin for similar support.

The community of black Atlanticists have helped in so many ways. In particular, all my good friends at the Collegium for African American Research (CAAR) – Sabine Broeck, Maria Diedrich, Justine Tally, Judith Wilson and Alison Goellen – and in the African American Literature and Culture Society (AALCS) – Wilfred Samuels, Richard Blackett, Sam Shepperson, Cindy Hamilton and Gloria Cronin. Vin Carretta, Sarah Meer, Fionnghuala Sweeney, Lee Jenkins and Frank Faragossa provided Douglass fellowship, while Melinda Elder, Suzanne Schwarz and Frances Wilkins showed the value of local north-western histories to the full black Atlantic story. Tony Tibbles and Gary Morris from the Merseyside Maritime Museum, and Nigel Dalziel from the Lancaster Maritime Museum, as well as Richard Crownshaw, helped refine my work on memorialization. Angela Leonard, Michelle Wright and Carol Smith have offered much help and useful comments from their own multiple expertise. Some of the initial work on this project began in the nurturing environment of American Studies at Keele University, where the support of my supervisor Mary Ellison was crucial to my development as an interdisciplinary animal. Keelites David Adams, Richard Godden, Martin Crawford, Tim Lustig, Oliver Harris and fellow PhD candidates, Tony Mann and Sam Hitchmough, nuanced my thoughts and kept me on the straight and narrow. Friends in the British Association for American Studies (BAAS) have been supportive in many ways. In particular, Maria Balshaw, Judie Newman, Dick Ellis, Susan Castillo, Jude Davies, Deborah Madsem and Mick Gidley.

Some portions of the manuscript have appeared in print before. A shorter version of Chapter 5 appeared in *Research in African Literatures*. Elements of Chapter 6 appeared in Deborah Madsen (ed.), *Postcolonial Literatures: Expanding the Canon* (Pluto, 1999) and in Saadi Simawe (ed.), *Black Orpheus: Music in African American Fiction from the Harlem Renaissance to Toni Morrison* (Garland, 2000). Chapter 7 incorporates some short passages from the introduction to Alan Rice and Martin Crawford's *Liberating Sojourn: Frederick Douglass and Transatlantic Reform* (1999). Individual chapters have benefited from specific help. Rosemary Archer corresponded with me about Pompey and my mother Alison Gomez took her mind off the horses in the Crabbett books to keep an eye out for mentions of the African major-domo. Michael McCaughan from the Ulster Folk and Transport Museum provided invaluable information about the *Titanic*. Lubaina Himid was an inspiration and opened my eyes to a whole new visual world which made the fine art sections of the book more contemporary than I had at first envisaged. Graham Lock's work showed me how to bring Sun Ra into the argument of the book, while Peter Hulme delineated the importance of cannibalism without being sensationalist. Thanks too to Muriel Burns for the information about the Culzean connection, and to Rochdale Art Gallery for information on their 1992 exhibition 'Revenge'.

The team at Cassell (now Continuum) have been extremely supportive of this project. In particular, I would like to thank Polly Rewt, who recognized the possibilities of this project when it was mere scribbling on the back of envelopes. Janet Joyce and Valerie Hall were the ultimate professionals and proved most understanding as deadlines were pushed back. The final word goes to my daughter Amy (aged four at the time) who in the midst of the project told me to remember that 'Africa is next to America, Dad'.

In memory of Fred Rice (1905–95)

═ 1 ═
UPROOTED AND RE-ROUTED

ACTUAL AND IMAGINATIVE BIOGRAPHIES
OF THE BLACK ATLANTIC

Do not all records of human accomplishment document the
motions of bodies? (Susan Foster, quoted in Roach, 1996: 27)

Yeah, I think one day Worth'll be just one mass of houses and
nobody will ever know what happened in Worth. There is a lot
of history to it, I know. It goes back beyond me, but I try to
explain to people what it was like ... There were three pubs in
the village of Worth, there were two blacksmiths worked in the
village, there was wheelwrights in the village, four huge
estates ... I always thought it was the loveliest little village in the
world. (Rice, 1993: 10)

This idyllic description of a Sussex village at the turn of the century comes
from the oral narrative of a non-literate agricultural labourer who spent his
whole life in its environs. Quintessentially a nostalgic paean to rural England,
Fred Rice's memory of turn-of-the-century Worth evokes a history which is
being hidden by the march of progress. However, the backward gaze of Fred
(1905–95), my grandfather, is, like the modernity he constantly condemns, an
occluding one. His account of his white, rural, working-class life on one of
those country estates, the Crabbet Park House and Arabian Stud, has no space
for the memory of a most interesting figure who had served as major-domo to
Wilfred Scawen Blunt from 1870 to 1885, a Cape Verdean who came to be
known as Pompey. Like many black presences in rural Britain, Pompey has
been virtually forgotten, his grave unknown and his fascinating biography
reduced to a footnote in the life of a famous white poet, traveller, politician
and dilettante. His path would have crossed those of Fred's grandfather, great-
uncles and great-aunts, and he would surely have created quite a stir as the
only African for miles around. Yet, Fred never mentioned Pompey to me. He,
like other Worth residents, designated the 1960s as the arrival date for non-
white presences in West Sussex, with the large influx of New Commonwealth
immigrants to the burgeoning new town of Crawley. Pompey's presence leaves

hardly a trace: some photographs in the collections of Blunt and his wife Lady Anne, diary entries which relate his dutiful attention to the family and a marriage record that details his short-lived betrothal to Annie, another servant at the house and, to the intense interest of all on the estate, a white woman.

In setting out to narrate a cultural history of the black Atlantic, I had always assumed it was my very distance that created the frisson of intellectual excitement in tracing these putative strangers' histories. My lineage, which could be traced back to rural Sussex, surely gave me the most Anglo-Saxon roots. I based my regional Anglocentric chauvinism (such as it was) on the tongue of my grandfather who, the family boasts, exhibited one of the last recorded genuine rural Sussex dialects in the homogeneous Estuary-English-speaking suburbia of late-twentieth-century Crawley. My grandfather's story, and the ellipses it contains, in fact shows how African lives impacted on even the most English of biographies. Pompey's grave remains undiscovered but in country churchyards up and down the land, black graves tell a story of lives lived in the most obscure corners of the country, from Culzean Castle in Scotland to Douglas on the Isle of Man, from Poulton and Sunderland Point in Lancashire to Whitehaven in Cumbria and Culworth in Northamptonshire. It is little wonder that there are such black presences in Britain, for the nation played a leading role in the transatlantic slave trade that transported over eleven million Africans to the New World. That some of them, both slave and free, came to the homeland of their oppressors is unsurprising. I shall return to these graves in the final chapter of this study, but for now it is not memorial markers that concern me but the lived existence of a black boy in a white world miles from his homeland. How did Pompey get to Sussex and what can his wandering life tell us about the biographies of Africans in what Paul Gilroy has appropriately called the 'black Atlantic'? The lives of Pompey and other uprooted Africans in the period from 1600 to the present delineate the ways in which 'routes' rather than the populist term 'Roots' (after Alex Haley) designate most appositely the trajectory of so many individuals caught up in the maelstrom of the black Atlantic, where home, in Fred D'Aguiar's neatly coined phrase, is 'always elsewhere' (Pettinger, 1998: 280).

In a sense, Pompey represents a throwback to an eighteenth-century pattern of black servitude in Britain. His service in an aristocratic family is reminiscent of the many hundreds of black servants who were fashionable accessories in Georgian and Regency Britain. Pompey, however, represented something new too: an exoticism that Blunt and his circle cultivated, an avant-gardism that included a penchant for sexual liberation, foreign travel and a besottedness with Arab culture and horses. Having an African personal servant was merely the icing on a cake, and showed a wilful disdain of provincial Victorian mores. Blunt had literally bought the boy at the coaling station in the Cape Verde Islands (then a Portuguese colony off the coast of Africa) during a trip to Argentina in 1865. Encountering a large group of starving mothers with boys for sale, he took a shine to one of them and bought ten-year-old Felipe Pedro da Cruz, naked but for his shirt, for just four shillings. There is no record of when he renamed him with the imperial soubriquet 'Pompey', but his ascent was so rapid that by the time he reached his maturity he was Blunt's most

Figure 1 The staff at Crabbet *c*. 1885 (including Pompey), Add. 54–085. Reproduced by permission of the British Library.

trusted personal servant. As Elizabeth Longford, Blunt's biographer, contends: 'Pompey proved to be the best of all majordomos, following his adoptive family all over the world and becoming the head of Blunt's household in Britain' (Longford, 1979: 66). We shall never know how Pompey felt to be sold by his own mother to a complete stranger, but his faithful service to the Blunt family for the next nineteen years shows he possessed a strength of character to withstand a brutal loss of familial relations at such a formative time. His centrality to the Crabbet household is attested to most strikingly in a photograph of the staff taken in 1885. He is pictured in the front row, smartly turned out, while many of the lesser employees stand behind him and the other privileged house servants (Figure 1).

I would like to freeze-frame Pompey's life at this point, as he provides us with evidence not only for survival despite massive odds but also for a successful assimilation to Victorian Britain that places him in a relatively privileged situation *vis-à-vis* his working compatriots on the estate. As propertyless rural labourers, they would be unable to vote (indeed it would not be until the legislation of 1921 that all males would be enfranchised). On the other hand, Pompey, as a man with personal property, could potentially have gained the right to vote. Enfranchisement was based on class and gender position, and was not (at least as far as the law was concerned) based on race. His privileged position is shown in that he had almost limitless access to the chambers of his master, an access which was denied to most other workers on the estate. Likewise, he had ascendancy, as head of the household, over all the working-class whites at Crabbet, and we can only guess at the kinds of jealousies that this exotic servant's privilege aroused. Such an interesting biography should warn us against easy clichés concerning the hierarchical relations between the races. In the Crabbet household, Pompey would give orders to lesser servants, however white they were. My great-grandfather, a non-literate gardener on the estate, would hardly have merited a second glance from the privileged Pompey. My intention here is not to downgrade the suffering of a boy of 10 sold into servitude to a country an ocean and several climate zones away, rather to interrogate an attitude about the black Atlantic which would interpret it in purely Manichean terms of black victims and white oppressors. White working-class agricultural labourers in Victorian England had their overrated 'freedom' (and not much else) to distinguish them from the overworked black brethren in a slave system that had only recently (1838) been fully disbanded in the colonies. Mercifully for Pompey, his conditions of service for the Blunts were not as draconian as those suffered by the agricultural labourers on the estate. It was not only his race that defined his role on the estate but also his elevated status in what was still an intensely rigid class system.

His relatively privileged status is confirmed by diary entries made by Blunt and his wife which show an easy familiarity with their favoured servant. When Lady Anne miscarried on one of their frequent trips to Arabia in 1874, it was Pompey who made tea, coffee and soup and provided companionship for her in their tent while her husband negotiated their passage through the country with passing Arabs (Longford, 1979: 98). In accompanying them on their trips to Arabia, Pompey shared their adventures, including stand-offs with hostile tribes (*ibid.*: 116). His travels far beyond the confines of the estate contrasted with the static life of those left behind (like my Great-Uncle Alf), who would have to wait for the horrors of the Great War before they left Sussex. Pompey had already crossed the Atlantic to South America and back as a boy before landing in England; now, following his travels to Arabia, his biography could be seen as symptomatic of a life lived beyond 'discrete national' boundaries. From beginnings which would indicate a life of penury, he was to become an archetypal figure in the black Atlantic. 'Lodged between the local and the global' by virtue of a life lived out in the black diaspora, Pompey, like other black travellers before him such as Olaudah Equiano, cannot be explicated by a history which is confined to describing national dynamics (Gilroy, 1993a: 6). While we have no autobiography to shed light on Pompey's own narrative of an extraordinary life, in reconstructing a life history we can begin to identify the limitations imposed on him by rigid chauvinistic nationalism and how he transcended them, in part at least, through a lived and dynamic internationalism. His life could be described as essentially 'routed' rather than 'rooted'.

Pompey's intimacy with the Blunts is attested to by Wilfred's implicit trust in him. Thus in 1874, when Wilfred organizes a debaucherous outdoor revel at the heronry on the estate, it is Pompey who is entrusted as chief cook, keeping vigil through the night as his master sleeps between his wife and his paramour (Longford, 1979: 110). When the family hawk goes missing in 1882, it is

Pompey who leads the futile search party, only to discover that the bird has been shot dead by a farmer's gun (Blunt, 1986: 469). These sideways glimpses at Pompey's life are all that we have, because it is all mediated through the narratives of the Blunts, who consistently portray him in the role of favoured servant. The Blunts' affection for Pompey is obvious; but, as ever with the master–servant relationship, especially when complicated by race, there are dynamics at work which preclude us from getting a clear view of the black servant's life. Despite Blunt's liberal political and social views, his opinions on the status of blacks betrayed a Victorian racism that directly impacted on Pompey's opportunities under his tutelage. Blunt had a great interest in 'the colored races of mankind', especially his beloved Arabs, but his admiration did not extend to a belief in their equal intellectual attainment with Europeans. He was especially scathing about the intellectual capability of 'negroes' in general, and had forthright views about the schooling of Pompey:

> I would not allow him to be taught his letters though Alice would have done so, but I believed then and I still think rightly that the negro is happier in life without them. What is valuable about the black man is that his race is a distinct one with instincts and ways of thought apart from ours and less divergent from the general animal type, and so much the happier. It is doing him no benefit to place him by education in our white groove of discontent and restless ambition. (quoted in Longford, 1979: 66)

Despite Blunt's refusal to educate Pompey, he learnt excellent English and Spanish apart from his native Portuguese, undermining somewhat Blunt's contentions about 'negro capabilities'. If Wilfred Blunt's attitude can be described as 'anti-assimilationist', his wife Lady Anne betrays a simplistic racism in her description of an African she met on her travels in Arabia. In *Pilgrimage to Nejd* (1881), in a diary entry of 11 January 1879, she comes across Johar, who 'is a perfectly black negro with repulsive African features: tall and very fat ... It struck me as eminently absurd to see this negro who is still a slave, the centre of a group of adulous white courtiers' (Blunt, 1881: 143–4).

The Blunts' affection for their black servant does not extend to educating him or to a tolerance of the physical differences in other Africans they meet. The African encountered by Lady Anne is particularly offensive because he assumes a superior social role, while Pompey is acceptable as he occupies the traditional black role of servant. Pompey was attending to Lady Anne's every need as she penned such thoughts about repulsive Africans, yet she would probably not have included him as a Negro like this alien other, both because he was inferior socially (and so not offensive) and also because, paradoxically, he had become a member of her household in this designated inferior place.

As a trusted servant he gradually became integrated into the community, a fact that is confirmed when the Blunts grant him permission to marry the servant girl Annie in 1884. Despite Blunt's belief in the separation of the races, he was happy for Pompey to achieve what estate gossip described as his 'highest ambition' – to marry a white woman (Longford, 1979: 66). Pompey, then, even in his personal life, is confined by the stereotypes imposed by the overwhelming white society about him. His marriage is dismissed as the lust of the black man for the white woman and his desire for the status a white wife would bring (though how he could find anyone other than a white wife in 1880s Sussex is not indicated). Despite his privileged position on the estate and the contribution he has made to its upkeep, Pompey is reduced to a cipher for ideas about race then prevalent in imperial Victorian Britain. That Pompey is much more than a black servant who found his 'white groove' with a housemaid can only be reconstructed by a discussion of his life in the context of the black Atlantic, a context of forced and voluntary travel and of triumph over the adversity of being abandoned by his natural parents at such an early age. His death in 1885 as a mere servant with no known progeny has meant that until now his life has not attracted the interest it deserves, despite its dynamic internationalism.

Pompey's enforced servitude after the abolition of slavery reveals how exploitative racial interactions persisted throughout the Victorian imperium. However, as I indicated earlier, the black slave/servant had been a constant feature in British society, most noticeably in the eighteenth century. Hogarth and other artists of the period attest to a significant black presence that David Dabydeen's incisive study *Hogarth's Blacks* (1985) describes as crucial to our understanding of artists, from society portrait painters to caricaturists. Black servants, usually bought as slaves in the Caribbean, were important status symbols for aristocrats and the nouveau riche and were already entering the domain of a nascent popular culture. Early advertising, as discovered and set forth briefly by Norma Myers in her book *Reconstructing the Black Past* (1996), used the relationship between the master and servant/slave to sell new products. In a November 1794 advertisement in the *Morning Chronicle* headlined 'A Dialogue between a Merchant and his Black Servant', the intimate relationship that develops while the 'black servant' shaves his master is portrayed as idealistic and unproblematically familiar (and familial). The advertisement is framed as a conversation between 'a merchant and his black servant'. Even the designation of the black as 'servant' is problematic here, as many blacks kept as servants in England, well into the nineteenth century, were actually slaves, despite court cases such as the Somerset case of 1772, which had undermined the institution of slavery in the home country but had not, as many contemporary and historical commentators regularly assert, actually made it illegal. As F. O. Shyllon states, the peer who had handed down the judgment, Lord Mansfield, had 'made it clear that his ruling was not a declaration of emancipation' (Shyllon, 1974: 221).

In the advertisement, at first the merchant chastises Scipio for occasions in the past when he had 'tore the skin from my face'. He wonders at Scipio's happy mood despite this rebuke:

S: Yes, Massa, I ave got good news this morning, Massa.

M: Have you got that long-looked-for letter from your Father and Mother?

S: No, Massa, good to you, not to me Massa, I was no thinking of my
Fader nor Moder. ('Packwoods Superior Razor Strop', 1794)

Scipio is portrayed here as totally beholden to his master, happy because of his
new-found ability to shave his master efficiently. His own mother and father
are displaced by his fidelity and attention to his master's needs which, thanks
to a new product, he is able to satisfy fully. The creators of the advertisement
play on Scipio's fidelity, which stands in for the consistent worth of the product they are promoting. Scipio now performs his function so much better that
his master believes he must be using hot water; however, his newly acquired
skill is due to technological advances, as he explains:

S: I ave no hot water Massa – dis is an old razor you throw away Massa,
above twelve mont ago, because was good for noting, I ave stropped it
on de butler's new razor strop, he bought dis morning, he say it would
take out notches, he praise it so much, I taught me would try it on dis
old razor, and I find it please you Massa, dis is de good news, Massa.
(*ibid.*)

The magical transformation of the old razor by the new strop immediately
restores the master–servant relationship, reducing it to mere dependence on
the proper working of a piece of barber's equipment rather than the operation
of a debauched intercontinental racial economy. The foundation of this
economy on imperial trade is stressed by the master's aside that the new strop
'will be a fine article, to form part of my cargo in the next ship that goes out'
(*ibid.*). It is Scipio who has outlined the use of the strop and knows where it
can be obtained, but his master who will benefit financially from its exploitation by exporting it to planters abroad. While the advertisement apparently
stresses the everyday nature of the slave economy, it actually portrays its
extraordinary exploitation of human resources for the comfort of the planters
and their supporters who benefit in the Atlantic economy. Such depictions of
diasporic Africans in the pictorial advertising of personal hygiene products
such as soap and shaving equipment become commonplace in the nineteenth
and twentieth centuries, where the dark skin of the African serves to highlight
the whiteness of their masters, as numerous examples in Anne McClintock's
Imperial Leather (1995) and Jan Nederveen Pieterse's *White on Black* (1992)
illustrate. Scipio and his master's extraordinary dialogue provides an early
example of the potency of such mercantile narratives and illustrates how the
reduction of the diasporic African to a mere prop to aggrandize the white
master occurred well before advertising became a sophisticated and all-
pervasive visual element of Western capitalist culture.

Sophisticated eighteenth-century portrait paintings would often portray
black servants or slaves gaudily dressed alongside their masters to display the
transatlantic wealth of British merchants and aristocrats. The arrival of similar
imaginary scenarios in the relatively unsophisticated advertisements of the late
eighteenth century outlines the potency and familiarity of such narratives in
the emergent popular culture too. Such comforting narratives are dependent

on a trust between master and slave/servant that is based on the unyielding fidelity of the latter. However, the 1790s witnessed the gradual erasure of that bond through the ongoing abolitionist struggle against slavery and the conflagration of the major slave revolt in San Domingo (James, 1963). At this point, when master–slave relations are at their most volatile, narratives like the 'Packwood Superior Razor Strop' advertisement present a comforting utopian vision of domestic harmony that remains unaffected by the realities of slave revolt or political opposition to the slavocracy. Sixty years later, Herman Melville, in his short story 'Benito Cereno' (1856), will use a similar scene to show the threat posed to a white man by the valet who is apparently shaving him zealously, but who is in fact the leader of a slave revolt which has the white man totally in his power. Homi Bhabha illustrates how shaving scenes continue to be duplicitous into the colonial era, describing the wily mimicry of the colonial barber who, as he picks his clients' pockets, cries out, ' "How the master's face shines!" and then, in a whisper, "But he's lost his mettle" ' (Bhabha, 1986: 161). In the unequal power relations of colonialism and slavery, Africans learnt to use their master's vulnerability to their advantage. However, this earlier manifestation of the everyday toilet scene promotes an imperial fantasy of white power and holds no danger for the master, whose control is only strengthened through the loyalty of his servant/slave. He offers Scipio a reward but is rewarded himself with the fawning reply that 'if I am continued in your service, dat will be ample reward for Scipo' ('Packwoods Superior Razor Strop', 1794). This fantasy of imperial power and voluntary servitude is in stark contrast to the actual lives of contemporary figures in the metropolis such as Robert Wedderburn, who lived beyond the control of the British imperium in a radical counter-culture that brooked no compromise with the slave power.

Such black figures in the diaspora are never fleshed out fully by a purely national history (whether an English, Scottish, British, Caribbean, African-American or African narrative). Thus, Robert Wedderburn (1761–1830), of Scots ancestry, lives much of his life in Britain, but is best framed in the context of the black Atlantic. His scurrilous pamphlet *The Horrors of Slavery*, written in 1824, regales against the institution that still exists in his home colony of Jamaica, and describes how Britain remains tied to it in a nexus of blood and abuse exemplified by his own life as the mulatto son of the Scottish slave trader and plantation owner, James Wedderburn. As Iain McCalman says, Robert Wedderburn was a 'direct product, witness and victim of the Jamaican slave system' (McCalman, 1991: 3). However, his political activism was not confined to condemning the evils of that 'peculiar institution' alone, but was directed at ending a domestic British abuse of power he regarded as equally antediluvian: namely, wage slavery. His remarkably prescient acknowledgement of the interplay between race and class in capitalism highlights the limitations of a dogmatic insistence on the overwhelming primacy of race as the determining factor in the creation of Atlantic personalities. In critiquing Paul Gilroy's concept of the black Atlantic, Neil Lazarus contends that 'indenture, wage labor, forced migration, colonization etc ... are as inextricably conducive of the modern world as slavery is' (Lazarus, 1994:

334). Wedderburn's radicalism, forged in the wake of many of these other oppressive systems, shows the importance of foregrounding the multi-layered, complex nature of personalities in the black Atlantic in order to avoid over-easy generalizations about lives lived in that modernizing world. Wedderburn attracted notice from the authorities not so much because of his racial politics, but rather on account of his radical critique of capitalism throughout the British Empire.

Thus, Wedderburn's linkage of the two horrors of wage and chattel slavery and the activism designed to end them brought him into a conflict with the authorities, which differentiated him from those black British liberal reformers of the period like Olaudah Equiano who did not take such a consistently radical class-based position or display his same class loyalty (McCalman, 1991: 6). Wedderburn's working-class Jacobinism was probably developed, in part at least, during his service in the British navy aboard HMS *Polymethus* in the late 1770s and later as a privateer. Paul Gilroy identifies such service at sea as foundational for the development of an internationalist radicalism in black activists of the period and links Wedderburn with the radical William Davidson (also from Jamaica) who would be executed for trying to blow up the cabinet in the 1820 Cato Street Conspiracy:

> both Wedderburn and his sometime associate Davidson had
> been sailors, moving to and fro between nations, crossing
> borders in modern machines which were themselves micro-
> systems of linguistic and political hybridity. Their relationship
> to the sea may turn out to be especially important for both the
> early politics and poetics of the black Atlantic world that I wish
> to counterpose against the narrow nationalism of so much
> English historiography. (Gilroy, 1993a: 12)

Ironically, then, Wedderburn's dynamic internationalism is learnt in the service of British imperial power in the Royal Navy. However, the ships represent a microcosm of radical politics, demonstrated by the later mutinies at Nore and Spithead in 1797. Jesse Lemisch has outlined how sailors often framed their experiences in the language of enslavement, regarding impress-ment as tantamount to the imposition of chattel slavery, being cruelly whipped and having themselves described in naval law as 'not fully adult', just like slaves in the Americas (Lemisch, 1993: 115). The linkage of slaves to seamen by the authorities was accompanied by collaboration between these disen-franchised and oppressed sections of the circum-Atlantic world, leading to what Marcus Rediker and Peter Linebaugh have called 'a history of interracial cooperation that underlay the joint protests of sailors and slaves against impressment and other measures during the revolutionary era' (Rediker and Linebaugh, 1993: 140). A seaman's life in the late eighteenth century thus afforded radical companionship for sailors, but not without draconian slave-like conditions at the service of Empire. Such contradictory experiences moulded Wedderburn's internationalist vision, which does not flinch from attacks on all forms of slavery. In *The Axe Laid to the Root* (1817), he links the crime of slavery to other crimes of the privileged against the poor, and addresses his fellow Jamaicans using his experiences at the centre of the belly of the beast of Empire in London to frame an internationalist vision which sides with blacks across international boundaries. Talking of the British government, he says:

> at the same time they make it right that hundreds of thousands of Africans may be stolen and sold, like cattle on the market; in truth they can do what it is impossible for God to do ... You will have need of all your strength to defend yourself against those men, who are now scheming against the blacks of St. Domingo. (Wedderburn, 1991a: 90)

His accusation of British collusion in the slave trade comes a decade after its abolition, while his warnings about the dangers to the nascent black nation of San Domingo show a developed vision of an international movement for black autonomy in the colonies and the dangers it faced from the European powers. In speeches, too, he linked oppression against Africans abroad to that waged against a home proletariat by capitalists who controlled the political machine. For instance, at a speech witnessed by the government spy Sd. J. Bryant at the Hopkins Street chapel he made the link clear:

> They would employ blacks to go and steal females – they would put them in sacks and would be murdered if they made an alarm Vessels would be in readiness and they would fly off with them This was done by Parliament men – who done it for gain – the same as they employed them in their Cotton factories to make slaves of them to become possessed of money to bring them into Parliament. (Bryant, 1991: 114)

Here, the slave trade is linked directly as oppressive praxis to the exploitation of labourers at home, and the guilty parties are identified as the most powerful in the land. Wedderburn believed that an alliance of rebels across racial divisions would create a class-based revolt against international capitalism in all its manifestations. As well as the writing and dissemination of pamphlets and contributions to radical periodicals, Wedderburn preached sedition at political meetings to the radical working class. Ironically, we only have access to these rhetorical delights through the good offices of government spies, who repeatedly reported how Wedderburn stressed the importance of the global context in his radical ideology, using Caribbean revolt to urge on the working class in Britain. The Reverend Chetwode Eustace reported on a speech in August 1819 where

> One of those men who appeared to be the principal in their concern is a Mulatto and announced himself as the Descendant of an African Slave. After noticing the insurrections of the Slaves in some of the West India Islands he said they fought in some

instances for twenty years for 'Liberty' – and he then appealed to Britons who boasted such superior feelings and principles whether they were ready to fight now but for a short time for their Liberties – He stated his name to be Wedderburn ...
(Eustace, 1991: 116)

Inspired by the rebellion on San Domingo and the activities of rebellious maroons in Jamaica, Wedderburn uses a black Atlantic discourse of radicalism to incite revolution on the streets of the imperial capital. While access to the speechifying, vernacular rhetoric of Wedderburn comes mainly through his enemies, his performative power shines through the perfunctory narrative of the straight-laced Reverend's discourse. These official narratives cannot drown out the authentic voice of black Atlantic radicalism which the imperial state apparatus seeks to neutralize. In fact, they provide a window on black involvement in these movements which rescues these seminal figures in British radicalism from marginalization. The accent on the vernacular by a figure like Wedderburn dramatizes his identification with a multiracial Atlantic working class that has only recently been fully identified by historians as pivotal in the struggles for liberty in the late eighteenth and early nineteenth centuries. This 'many-headed Hydra', as described by Marcus Rediker and Peter Linebaugh, was instrumental in creating radical movements throughout the circum-Atlantic region:

> The circulation of working-class experience, especially certain forms of struggle, emerges as another theme, linking urban mobs, slave revolts, shipboard mutinies, agrarian risings, strikes and prison riots, and the many different kinds of workers who made them – sailors, slaves, spalpeens, coalheavers, dockworkers, and others, many of whom occupied positions of strategic importance in the international division of labor. That much of this working-class experience circulated *to the eastward*, from American slave plantations, Irish commons, and Atlantic vessels back to the streets of the metropolis, London, cannot be overemphasised. This interchange within a predominantly urban portside proletariat took place over, around, beneath, and frequently against the artisans and craftsmen who are generally credited with creating the early working-class movement. (Rediker and Linebaugh, 1993: 150–1)

If Wedderburn is placed in this radical, multicultural and solidly working-class context, the logic of his rhetoric is unassailable. He should be identified not only as a black radical or even merely as a proletarian revolutionary, but also as a key intellectual figure in the circulation of a new vernacular discourse. Wedderburn's language, learnt in his struggle against the plantocracy in Jamaica, honed in his travels aboard ship, before being unleashed in the metropole where the chapel and the prison both contributed their specific discourses to what became a unique and splendidly polyglot transatlantic dialect, frames a new counter-hegemonic ideology that challenges the imperial polity. His is the logical outcome of a truly 'routed' experience that transcends the national boundaries of traditional historiography. As Jeffrey Bolster in his wonderful paean to African diasporan sailors, *Black Jacks*, asserts: 'By setting blacks in motion, maritime slavery not only provides them with perspectives denied to island-bound slaves, but contributed to the embryonic antislavery movement in London' (Bolster, 1997: 20). Wedderburn's biography is testament to this mobile radicalism. However, his plaguing by government spies bears witness to a firebrand orator whose internationalist vision is tempered by a realistic understanding of his own hazardous position as a black man in a racist world order which limits his freedom in the metropolis and in which he is unable even to countenance a visit to his birthplace. As he says, in the conclusion to *The Horrors of Slavery*:

> I should have gone back to Jamaica, had I not been fearful of the planters; for such is their hatred of any one having black blood in his veins, and who dares to think and act as a free man, that they would most certainly have trumped up some charges against me, and hung me. With them I should have had no mercy. (Wedderburn, 1991b: 61)

Home, then, is not unproblematic for Wedderburn: in a sense it is 'always elsewhere', because his past as a barely free mulatto in the colonies means Jamaica is as unwelcoming as a London replete with government spies who demonize him as foreign and as an alien other because of his skin colour and radicalism. All is not negative, however, as Wedderburn turns his doubled national allegiance, what Du Bois would later call 'double-consciousness', to his political advantage, combining a vernacular Caribbean perspective with a demotic metropolitan dynamic to create a truly unique political discourse. Even the English language must make room for this new kind of voice, which is demonstrated by the way his written discourse is littered with 'italic, bold, and upper-case characters from the typographer's case' as he attempts to bend the King's English to his oral mode and distinctive vernacular dialect (Linebaugh and Rediker, 2000: 403). For instance, in *The Horrors of Slavery*, Wedderburn describes the harshness of his upbringing in Jamaica, for which plain type is shown as wholly inadequate:

> I being a descendant of a Slave by a base Slave-Holder, the late JAMES WEDDERBURN, Esq. of Inveresk, who sold my mother when she was with child of me, HER THIRD SON BY HIM!!! She was FORCED to submit to him, being *his Slave*, THOUGH HE KNEW SHE DISLIKED HIM! ... I have seen my poor mother stretched on the ground, tied hands and feet, and FLOGGED in the most indecent manner, though PREGNANT AT THE SAME TIME!!! her *fault* being the not acquainting her mistress that her master had *given her leave to go and see her mother in town*! (Wedderburn, 1991b: 50–1)

Here, Wedderburn manipulates the King's English to tell a new story from the colonies: one from its subterranean reaches that literally inscribes what Gayatri Spivak would later term a 'subaltern' perspective. In order to do so, he imbricates his voice through the use of various typographical estrangements so that the plain discourse of written English is, as Homi Bhabha would term it, hybridized. *The Horrors of Slavery* cannot be related in the plain prose of normal typography; the enormity of the horror must be challenged with a vernacular discourse that lies outside the traditional literary language. Such hybridization 'reverses the effects of the colonialist disavowal, so that other denied knowledges enter upon the dominant discourse and estrange the basis of its authority' (Bhabha, 1986: 156). Bhabha's description accurately delineates the power of Wedderburn's vernacular discourse to 'unmask' the innocence of the master–slave relationship, revealing the perverted and violent relations it perpetuates and, in a florid publication of its evils, challenging its hegemonic power in transatlantic discourse. However, it was not only in the realm of the printed word that Wedderburn challenged the imperial polity; his unique brand of political radicalism used counter-hegemonic discourse as a motor for physical action too.

As Linebaugh and Rediker describe in their meticulously researched chapter on his life in *The Many-Headed Hydra: The Hidden History of the Revolutionary Atlantic* (2000), Wedderburn was a 'linchpin' in the transatlantic revolutionary movement linking different radical movements chronologically and geographically. Most particularly, 'He linked the trumpet of jubilee in the enclosed commons of England with the "shell-blow" of jubilee of Jamaica' (Linebaugh and Rediker, 2000: 326). The 'shell-blow' is a reference to the rebellious maroons of Jamaica who communicated with conch shells. Wedderburn, following on from the revolutionist Thomas Spence, reinvigorated the biblical idea of jubilee as liberation and sought to apply it in the present, vigorously asserting its relevance to both wage and plantation slaves. As Linebaugh and Rediker attest, 'Robert Wedderburn, a Methodist and Spencean, was perfectly situated to understand and advance the Atlantic revolutionary tradition of jubilee' (*ibid*.: 300), as it enshrined a dualism particularly relevant for his politics based in opposition to slavery and to the evils of capitalism: felicitously 'the biblical jubilee [Leviticus] authorized the call for an end to bondage and for the return of the commons to the dispossessed' (*ibid*.: 11–12). Like the white radical Harriet Martineau, Wedderburn understood the class dimension of any discussion of revolutionary change and the exploitative nature of capitalism at home as well as slavery abroad. He recognized that a politics which just concentrated on slavery ran the risk of complacency once abolitionism had succeeded. In answer to abolitionist demands for the primacy and singularity of the fight against slavery, Martineau asserts in 1838:

> We have a population of our manufacturing towns almost as
> oppressed, and in our secluded rural districts also as ignorant as
> your negroes. These must be redeemed. We have also negroes in
> our dominions, who though about to be entirely surrendered as

property, will yet we fear, be long oppressed as citizens, if the
vigilance which has freed them be not as active as ever.
(Martineau, quoted in Ferguson, 1992: 302)

Such prescient commentary was rare in bookish radical circles, but can be
related to Wedderburn's advancement of a radical inclusive agenda which
related the problems of the diasporan African to those of the nascent British
working class. Martineau expresses, albeit in less vernacular mode, Wedderburn's multiracial, geographically diverse and radical class-infected politics.

Wedderburn's agenda, though marginalized, was not completely lost at his
death. In fact, Wedderburn could be seen as an exemplary figure of the black
Atlantic (like Pompey, only with greater implications for his fellow diasporan
Africans), in that he uses the possibilities inherent in the apparent geographical
and economic straitjacket of that ocean's race and class interrelationships to
fashion a life which is ultimately liberating. His latest literary critic, Helen
Thomas, agrees and in her *Romanticism and Slave Narratives* (2000) she
articulates this paradox most felicitously:

> Wedderburn's work establishes an astonishingly vivid model of
> consciousness in the black diaspora. For Wedderburn the
> oceanic emptiness of the Atlantic functions not only as a
> demarcation of absence, or 'nothingness', in which black
> subjects were 'erased' and redefined as cultural 'voids', but as a
> simultaneous and paradoxical signifier of infinite possibilities
> and transformations. (Thomas, 2000: 10)

The institution of slavery, in which rigidity is a defining feature, is effectively
challenged by a movement away from its geographical borders. The ocean
stands both as marker of slavery's harsh alienating and dehumanizing realities
and of the possibility of mobility to freedom. As Paul E. Lovejoy discusses:
'The general movement of people was indeed from Africa to the Americas, but
ideas moved in many directions around the Atlantic, as did some people'
(Lovejoy, 2000: 8).

Not all journeyings among these dichotomies are as dynamically liberating,
however. If Robert Wedderburn's radicalism exemplifies how the black
Atlantic is instrumental in creating a particular brand of worldly, fiery per-
sonality, then the biography of Robert Adams displays the paradoxes of being
a black wayfarer on those choppy waters. In his semi-autobiographical *Narrative* (1816), he relates how, born in Hudson, NY, in 1785, 'he was brought
up to the seafaring line and made several voyages to Lisbon, Cadiz, Seville and
Liverpool' (Adams, 1999: 214). His life as a free-black sailor in the circum-
Atlantic region up to this moment is typical to the point of mundanity.
However, it is his 1810 voyage to Gibraltar and its consequences that establish
his biography as one of the most interesting of the early nineteenth century
and expose some interesting fault-lines along the colour-line that complicate
the binary oppositions which too often determine academic discourse about
blackness in the Atlantic. These fault-lines are further complicated by the

publication history of the *Narrative*, which was successful enough to be published in London, Boston, Paris, Stockholm and Amsterdam. As he was non-literate, Adams relied on his amanuensis, Samuel Cook, from the British African Company, to transcribe his story; hence the rather strained third-person narrative form. Like many eighteenth- and nineteenth-century black narrators, Adams's *Narrative* 'was shaped and told by a white narrator' (Baepler, 1999: 207) who had his own agenda that highlighted what interested him: in this case, the travelogue with its revelations about the fabled Timbuktu rather than Adams's 'personal experiences as a captive' (*ibid.*: 21). However, as is usually the case with such texts, reading between the lines to discover Adams's perspective is not impossible.

Adams and his companions are shipwrecked off the coast of North Africa and enslaved by 'indigent' Moors. Being sailors from the maritime powers, they offer the prospect of handsome profits if they can be ransomed. Adams's narrative of his capture and travels is unique, being the only Barbary captivity account written by an African American. There are ironies aplenty in his *Narrative*: most pointedly in his return to the continent of his free forebears that ends in his enslavement, while his eventual release is brokered by the nation that still enslaves its black population in the Caribbean, Great Britain. For his captors, Adams's arrival in the company of European Americans almost literally colours him white, a status that is confirmed when he is captured by black villagers and marched to Timbuktu, where he is identified as white and becomes a local curiosity. The 'one-drop' rule which would designate him black in America has no equivalent in North Africa, where his almost-white pigmentation (at least in the eyes of the darker natives) defines him as white. As such, he is regarded almost as a freak of nature in the heart of the African continent, as his *Narrative* relates: 'For a considerable time after the arrival of Adams and his companion, the people used to come in crowds to stare at them; and afterwards he understood that many persons came several days' journey on purpose' (Adams, 1999: 221).

On the coast he had been kept as a slave, but here he has a great deal more freedom and is able to take in enough of the sights to witness the dynamics of this important trading city. Adams's journey to Timbuktu is an amazing story, because he had achieved what many white men had died attempting to do and reached the fabled city. This led to his claims being hotly disputed on his return. As Paul Baepler asserts, 'Timbuctoo' to an early nineteenth-century European readership

> was a town where no white man had traveled and that many
> well-outfitted explorers had died trying to find. That the black,
> illiterate Adams did not set out to discover Timbuktu but had
> simply been dragged there against his will as part of a slave
> caravan, and that he also refused to confirm the glittering
> majesty of the town – popular speculation that would not be
> disproved until a few years later by a white explorer – only
> added fuel to criticism of Adams' account particularly in the
> United States. (Baepler, 1999: 20)

The African-American sailor Robert Adams makes his greatest physical discovery on dry land in the deserts of North Africa, but is denied credit by a scepticism that refuses to give plaudits for black achievement. But he makes another philosophical discovery too, namely that the hierarchical edifice of race which has constructed him as inferior in America and to an extent throughout the circum-Atlantic region is not absolute but relative. Viewed as a freakish white in Timbuktu, Adams even begins to see himself as such, and his *Narrative* dances 'chameleon'-like between the various identities of 'white', 'Arab' and 'black' (*ibid.*: 21). In part, this is because his identity is destabilized by his status as a traveller from a so-called civilized country which, at least to a certain extent, whitens him in the eyes of the amanuensis who helps him construct his narrative, as well as in those of the natives he encounters. By talking of black others, he more fully Americanizes and whitens himself. In seeking to understand his friendly reception in Timbuktu, Adams even unselfconsciously designates himself white:

> In short, they never experienced any act of incivility or unkindness from any of the Negroes, except when they were taken prisoners in company with the Moors engaged in stealing them. Adams could not hear that any white man but themselves had ever been seen in the place; and he believes, as well from what he was told by the Moors, as from the uncommon curiosity which he excited (though himself a very dark man with short curly black hair), that they never had seen one before. (Adams, 1999: 229)

Of course, this self-designation, what would later be called 'passing for white', will not survive his reabsorption into life in the *civilized* American polity, but the *Narrative*'s proposition that racial identity can be constructed differently through travel dramatically destabilizes the certitudes of racial stratification. Or as Langston Hughes was later to assert, 'What a difference a border makes' (Hughes, 1993: 399). Pilloried for his colour in America, the black traveller can sometimes escape the confines of racism through travel as Alasdair Pettinger explains: 'Crossing borders involves not only a change of social status, but often a change of *colour* too. As different countries have different systems of racial classification one may be "Black" in one country and not in another' (Pettinger, 1998: xiv). Robert Adams's *Narrative* relates how such an occurrence, which was to become a commonplace of African-American travel writing, was apparent even at the beginning of the nineteenth century. Slavocracies and plantocracies in the colonies and their imperial home countries had established a hegemony through seemingly rigid and unyielding systems that brooked no argument, particularly from African slaves and hirelings. If these were, however, in fact culturally specific and confined to distinct geographical regions, then the ubiquity they relied on to establish power was based not on natural law but on the mere operation of polity. Black Atlantic travellers and activists were in a unique position to challenge such widely accepted ideological frameworks, whether like Wedderburn they did so through activism or like Adams almost inadvertently.

Challenges to Anglocentric racial designations, to slavery and the racism that followed occurred in popular culture as well as in written texts, and nowhere is this more apparent than in the prevalence of sea shanties throughout the circum-Atlantic region. The derivation of these folk songs sung by sailors while undertaking their varied tasks is complex; however, one of the major sources is black folk song, which supplied the form's characteristic strong call and response patterns. One of the first accounts of shantying describes black workers in Jamaica unloading the *Edward* in 1811:

> They beguiled the time by one of them singing one line of an English song, or a prose sentence at the end of which all the rest join in a short chorus. The sentences which prevail with the gang we had aboard were as follows:
>
> Two sisters courted one man
>   Oh, huro my boys,
> And they lived in the mountains
>   Oh, huro boys O. (Hugill, 1984: 8)

The African diasporan origin of the tradition of shantying is confirmed by black contributions to the enhancement of the form, such as the development of core techniques like 'wild falsetto yells', which Hugill confirms black men performed 'much better than white men' (*ibid.*: 29). Although Hugill does not make the connection, such yells are almost certainly related to the field cries which were such a feature of life on Southern and West Indian plantations. Such high yelps at the end of solo lines were a distinctive feature of shantying technique and attest to the significant black contribution to the tradition. The lyrics, as they developed, also exemplify a significant black American and Caribbean input to the development of the form through the nineteenth century. The songs literally relate the tale of black movement and its contribution to the development of a black Atlantic tradition of routed freedom. W. T. Lhamon Jr calls such vernacular forms 'lore cycles' (his own example is minstrel song), which he describes as 'gather[ing] momentum in improvised cycles. As their gestures winnow into repeated narratives, they help people understand themselves as a distinct group' (Lhamon, 1998: 75). A song like 'Roll the Cotton Down' relates the move from labouring for poor pay in the racist cotton South to an escape to sea, where the rewards were greater. Sung by cotton stowers in such towns as Mobile, Alabama, and expressing a wished-for liberation out to sea, it became what Hugill calls a 'halyard and capstan song', performed at sea to celebrate the move away from the South:

> 2. Was ye ever down in Mobile Bay,
>   Screwin' Cotton by the day?

> 3. Oh, a black man's pay is rather low,
>   To stow the cotton we must go.

4. Oh, a white man's pay is rather high,
   Rock an' shake 'er is the cry.

5. Oh, so early in the mornin', boys,
   Oh, afore the day is dawnin', boys.

6. Five dollars a day is white man's pay,
   So bring yer screws an' hooks this way ...

10. Oh, tier by tier we'll stow 'em neat,
    Until the job is made complete.

11. Oh, Mobile Bay's no place for me,
    I'll pack my bags an' go to sea [I'll sail away on some other
    sea] ... (Hugill, 1984: 153)

These songs were not only sung by blacks but were also part of an inter-racial tradition of shantying that allowed white sailors who had similar nar-ratives of displacement to sing them with feeling too, despite the obvious dichotomies caused by the racial inequality highlighted in the lyrics. According to Hugill, 'the wharves of Mobile and such places were the meeting ground of white men's songs and shanties and Negro songs and work songs' (*ibid.*: 17). In this 'work song exchange' (*ibid.*) or 'shanty mart' (*ibid.*: 258) in the Gulf ports, such songs as 'Roll the Cotton Down' gained a currency beyond their black origins. However, the lyrics of the song attest to these origins in a strictured life on shore and the importance of sea travel to transcending them. The shanties reveal a black tradition of song-making which delights in a movement away from the slave South (despite the occasional regret for the loss of lovers, family and a familiar home). Shantying reveals the life experiences of diasporan Africans literally on the move. As Bolster describes the phenom-enon: 'Sailors linked far-flung black communities and united plantations with urban centers' (Bolster, 1997: 6), and one of the ways they achieved this was through cultural forms such as song. Unaccounted for in traditional histories, the songs these black seafarers have passed down reveal the enhanced freedom they discovered in travelling the circum-Atlantic. They reveal biographies which traditional historiography has omitted and point to a rich cultural heritage of intercontinental and interracial musical exchange that predates the export of minstrelsy to Britain in the mid-nineteenth century and its con-tinuance well into the twentieth century. As with Lhamon's example of minstrelsy (but thankfully without that tradition's endemic racism), shanties reveal the development of a new, more mobile transatlantic proletariat that is not as hidebound as in previous eras but enabled to negotiate

the inbetween problem of licensed-but-enforced roaming. Slaves and other workers forced to middle passages without their families for war, for sugar or for canalling were characteristically caught in this quandry. What too often has seemed like sentimental nonsense and childish rhyming is really a way of declaring ... the terrible exhaustion, loneliness and

privation forced onto the lowest workers of the Atlantic.
(Lhamon, 1998: 66)

Lhamon's commentary has implications beyond minstrelsy, as the cross-racial shantying tradition that has many of its roots in black song shows. Its vernacular resonances reveal the routed nature of proletarian and sometimes specifically black proletarian life in the early nineteenth century. Their sentimentality has often made them easy to dismiss as simplistic but, as Lhamon shows in relation to minstrelsy, this merely reflects the privations endured and overcome and should not blind us to their power to reveal the consciousness of this new class of mobile proletariat with diasporan Africans at its heart. These black workers are both part of this roaming population and responsible for core elements of the cultural form which communicates their hopes and desires, the shanty. The ship, and its role in ever-more complex communication and trading technologies, was responsible for the effective dispersal of the shanty throughout the trading world. The shanty is, of course, only one of the many manifestations of influence of African diasporan musical forms on popular music. Paul Gilroy discusses later forms such as 'hip-hop, reggae, soul and house' as displaying a similarly profound influence and mobility, though now reliant on new technologies for their dispersal (Gilroy, 2000: 251). His commentary relates equally to the shanty and helps to explain how its longevity is due partly to its diasporic mobility which gives it relevance to people throughout the circum-Atlantic region:

> itinerant cultures are propagated by unforeseen means and
> proceed by unknown routes to unanticipated destinations.
> Traveling itself contributes to a sense of multiplicity for which
> utopian – technically placeless – patterns of cultural use
> constituted around popular music provide the most pertinent
> examples. Chaotic cultural dissemination in more and more
> elaborate circuits itself enjoys a complicated relationship to the
> technologies that have conquered distance, compressed time,
> and solicited novel forms of identification between the creators
> of cultural forms, moods and styles and various groups of users
> who may dwell far from the location in which an object or event
> was initially conceived. This art is dispatched in provisional and
> unfinished forms that anticipate further input and flow in a
> communicative economy in which creative recycling rather than
> immoral disposability is the regulative norm. (*Ibid.*: 251–2)

The improvisational nature of the shanty tradition and its changing forms as it is dispersed through the early nineteenth century world by sailors is an uncanny precursor of the dissemination of reggae and hip-hop by migrating workers in the later twentieth century (albeit the means of transmission are usually more technically sophisticated for these later songsters). The numerous versions of shanties sung over wide geographic regions anticipate Amiri Baraka's (1963) 'changing same' or 'creative recycling' that is a feature of most black Atlantic music. Originating in the Caribbean, in the American Southern states and at sea on the wild Atlantic, shanties are the prototype of a mobile, sea-chopped, African diasporic music.

Many of these shanties were love songs to women left on the shore. However, this should not lull us into an oversimplified dismissal of the role of black women in the development of the black Atlantic as merely marginalized or domestic. Female sailors are hard to detect because they invariably had to cross-dress to be able to work in such a masculine profession. Occasionally, though, contemporary documents attest to their presence on board ship. Suzanne J. Stark discovered one such character, a sailor in the British navy, whose case was highlighted in a London newspaper of 1815:

> Amongst the crew of the Queen Charlotte, 110 guns, recently paid off [31 August 1815], it is now discovered was a female African who had served as a seaman in the Royal Navy for upwards of eleven years, several of which she had been rated able on the books of the above ship, by the name of William Brown. [She] served for some time as the captain of the foretop, highly to the satisfaction of the officers ... her features are rather handsome for a black ... (Stark, 1999: 10)

The Edinburgh-born Brown exemplifies how a sailor's life was not only liberatory for black males, but for adventurous females too. Her life, lived in the liminal zone of the sea, allows her freedoms which her double burden of race and gender would have militated against on land. Her skills are more important and define her status in the 'shipboard democracy' that existed on ships that plied the ocean (Costanzo, 1987: 76). Like Wedderburn, Equiano and Davidson before her, Brown discovers a liberation here among her sea-faring companions, despite the despotic rule of the merchant and military captains.

Another black woman who countered her perceived role as passive victim in the economics of the circum-Atlantic was Mary Prince, whose 1831 narrative described a transatlantic sojourn which reversed a middle-passage enslavement and led to emancipation. Her narrative is the first African-British slavewoman's autobiographical account and, as Moira Ferguson asserts, it not only joins issue with the plantocracy but also with sentimental abolitionist discourses on the position of black women in society: 'Mary Prince inaugurates a black female counter-offensive to pro- and anti-slavery Anglo-Africanism and refuses a totalizing conception of black women as flogged, half-naked victims of slavery's entourage' (Ferguson, 1992: 298). This counter-offensive outlines a life lived amidst the worst deprivations of Caribbean slavery. For, as Hilary Beckles discusses, 'An understanding of the "enterprise of the Indies" as a project of modernity therefore requires the development of a knowledge of gender as a socially constructed relation of domination' (Beckles, 2000: 180).

As a black woman, Prince was at the bottom of the social pile. But, like many before and after her, it was a transatlantic sojourn which was to lead to her emancipation. Born into slavery in Bermuda around 1788, Prince's early life was relatively happy until the death of her mistress, Mrs Williams, led to her sale. As related by another white woman, the reasons were plain and, in the context of the plantocracy, financially justifiable: 'Mary you will have to go home directly; your master is going to be married, and he means to sell you and two of your sisters to raise money for the wedding' (Prince, 1986: 50).

Prince juxtaposes these preparations for a wedding in the white family with the funereal death of her black family, who will be separated to provide the capital for the melding of the reconstructed white family. She does this by revealing the words of her own mother as she prepares her children for the sale: 'See, I am *shrouding* my poor children; what a task for a mother!' (*ibid.*: 51; emphasis in original). This funereal imagery shows how the fecundity of the white society is based on the disavowal of black rights to family life (in fact, the literal extinction of them), and is re-emphasized by Prince's mother's use of mercantile imagery that reduces her children to property. 'I am going to carry my little chickens to market ...' she says in despair (*ibid.*). Having been sold 'like sheep or cattle' (*ibid.*: 52), Prince then endures privations under various masters which enable her to reveal the institution of slavery in all its manifold ugliness, including habitual floggings, frequent sadistic sexual abuse and commonplace murder. Her own suffering included a stint in the salt works of Turks Island, where the physical hardships and sense of isolation were extreme. The sexual abuse she endured is glossed over in her narrative, but the hints she drops testify to a life lived as the constant prey of white men. Mr D, for instance,

> had an ugly fashion of stripping himself quite naked and
> ordering me then to wash him in a tub of water. This was worse
> to me than all the licks. Sometimes when he called me to wash
> him I could not come, my eyes were so full of shame. (*Ibid.*: 68)

Her reference to his 'ugly fashion' and her shame is redolent of an abusive sexual relationship, which is further emphasized by her declaration that he had 'no shame for his own flesh' (*ibid.*). Although written in language designed not to offend a middle-class British readership, Prince is able subtly to point to the abuse she and other slave women were forced to endure.

Her final owners, the Woods, took umbrage at her marriage and whipped her for such an insolent attempt at asserting her right to choose a partner. As a result, she determines to gain her freedom by raising money to manumit herself. Mrs Wood refuses, but even during this most demeaning of events in her narrative, Mary Prince employs subtle description to undermine the traditional power relationship of white dominance and black subservience. Prince's wilful independence begins to unravel the certainties of the slave system:

> I was earnest in the request to my owners; but their hearts were
> hard – too hard to consent. Mrs Wood was very angry – she
> grew quite outrageous – she called me a black devil, and asked

> me who had put freedom into my head. 'To be free is very
> sweet,' I said: but she took good care to keep me a slave. I saw
> her change colour and leave the room. (*ibid.*: 75–6)

Mrs Wood's 'change' of 'colour' after her outburst is a physical representation of a diminution of her whiteness that has up to this moment connoted her power. The strong black woman standing up for her rights begins to undermine the relationship between enslaved and enslaver. This undermining, of course, is relatively ineffective in the belly of the beast of slavery in the Caribbean where the slave polity is strong, but as soon as Prince arrives in Britain, she is able more easily to make her escape. Once free, her publication of the vices of slaveholders like the Woods 'reverse[s] the power relationship', allowing her to 'expose their barbarity' (Ferguson, 1992: 292). Mrs Woods is literally 'coloured' differently by Mary Prince's revelations, which use the subtleties of language to interpret anew the potential power relationships in the black Atlantic. She carries out a kind of verbal guerrilla warfare in retaliation for the extreme oppression she suffered at their hands. Standing up to the forces of oppression and expressing a different reality undermines the power of whiteness, revealing it to be a chimeric construction rather than a fact of nature. If 'whiteness produced – and was reproduced by – the social advantage that accompanied it' (Harris, 1998: 116), then Prince's outburst and its colour-changing effect on her mistress undermines this teleology. For, if her mistress can be made to change colour by her revelatory outburst, then the slavocracy, like colour difference, becomes open to challenge. Such an 'active moment of challenge against a dominant power' (Homi Bhabha, quoted in Young, 1995: 23) introduces dialogue into a relation where hitherto hierarchical monologue had seemed to be the primary mode of discourse.

Mary Prince's powerful (yet subtle) discourse reflects a women's radical tradition which has often been neglected in traditional historiography but which has nevertheless been played out through contestatory language. A flavour of it is revealed by a British West Indian government official's lament in 1823 that women were more prone to use 'that powerful instrument of attack and defence, their tongue' (Ferguson, 1992: xi). Prince's autobiography is testimony to the strength of women in the black Atlantic whose stories have been hidden by a patriarchal historical discourse. Revelation changes the power dynamics. Her narrative subtly repositions her both in relation to the plantocracy which had abused her and just as importantly in relation to the abolitionists who had provided safe refuge. Moira Ferguson notes how, as a result of the proliferation of texts about her that accompany and follow the publication of her *Narrative*, 'she establishes an autonomous domain of her own ... [which] ... signifies visible public victory for a self-motivated subject. She attains authorship while simultaneously conforming and subversively erupting (consciously and unconsciously) out of that conformity' (*ibid.*: 298). Mary Prince's black female voice is seen here as originating a tradition of texts which reinterpret the transatlantic through a hitherto silenced (at least within majority discourse) black female lens.

This chapter has sought to reveal numerous silenced voices. Some have been teased out before, but their juxtaposition allows a new interrogation of such narratives of the black Atlantic. Paul Gilroy, in his epochal 1993 study *Black Atlantic*, advances a different litany of names to represent the complexities of the many dynamic African diasporan lives which have all too often been lost in traditional histories of the circum-Atlantic. However, his monograph attempted more than a discovery of such hitherto marginalized figures, indicating a paradigm shift beyond the narrow nationalisms of much African diasporan history to posit an interconnected internationalist narrative that, by focusing on 'routes' rather than 'roots', actually unravels the multivarious reality of lives lived in the diaspora. As he explained, 'cultural historians' should 'take the Atlantic as one single, complex unit of analysis in their discussions of the modern world and use it to produce an explicitly transnational and intercultural perspective' (Gilroy, 1993a: 15). Such an assertion challenges the nationalist approach to history with its search for a univocal purity of expression linked inexorably to a single defined point of origin. Thus, it problematizes imperial histories and their legacies and likewise interrogates Afrocentric historical paradigms. With its positing of an inbetween space of encounter and meaning, Gilroy's theory designates new spheres of cultural activity that exhibit 'an inescapable hybridity and intermixture of ideas' (*ibid.*: xi). More recently, Srivinas Aravamudan's idea of *Tropicopolitans*, imbricated in imperial/colonial struggles, yet contesting such European rule through actual and textual encounters, fits many of the exemplary biographies I have traced here, particularly those of Mary Prince and Robert Wedderburn who, while subjected to the 'politics of colonial tropology ... correspondingly seize agency through contesting language, space and the language of space that typifies justifications of colonialism' (Aravamudan, 1999: 6). The biographies I have documented here illustrate this movement away from cultural purity to a more complex and culturally entangled reality for many in the black Atlantic. Black Atlantic personalities are formed through encounters on the move with social movements and intellectual currents that are intermixed among the cultures of three continents. The process and product of these encounters are not racially, culturally or nationally pure. Peter Linebaugh and Marcus Rediker, following a similar model to Gilroy, literally retrieve lives left behind by such stifling purities that create a 'violence of abstraction in the writing of history, the severity of history that has long been the captive of the nation-state, which remains in most studies the largely unquestioned framework of analysis' (Linebaugh and Rediker, 2000: 7). To move beyond the national in our analysis does not mean a descent into abstraction, as ideas such as the transnational, the diasporic and the oceanic provide equally rigorous geographies of analysis. In fact, moving away from concerns with national origins allows the cultural historian to be intrigued rather than disturbed by Vincent Carretta's scrupulously researched revelations that Olaudah Equiano might have been born in the Carolinas rather than Nigeria. The possibility that his minutely observed discussion of African mores could be in part the product of a transmitted oral memory from his unacculturated background in Low-country, South Carolina, could provide yet more evidence to support the survival of African culture despite the harsh rigours of chattel slavery

(Carretta, 1999). Such people carried their culture in their heads, which meant that even in America, Africa was part of their existence. Africans in the diaspora are crucially routed as well as rooted.

It is in such 'contact zones' (Pratt, 1992: 6–7) between cultures that men like Olaudah Equiano, Robert Adams, Pompey and Robert Wedderburn, along with women like William Brown and Mary Prince, constructed lives in negotiation with European race, class and gender ideologies. Mary Pratt's phrase is redolent for my study here, as it illuminates 'the space of colonial encounters, the space in which people geographically and historically separated come into contact with each other and establish ongoing relations, usually involving conditions of coercion, radical inequality and intractable conflict' (ibid.: 6). These dynamic lives, though, warn us against an over-deterministic reading of diasporan Africans as victims, as the 'term "contact" foregrounds the interactive, improvisational dimensions of colonial encounters so easily ignored or suppressed by diffusionists' accounts of conquest and determination' (ibid.: 7). In talking back, the diasporan African dynamically destabilizes homogeneous narratives of Anglo-American imperial conquest and white racial dominance or purity. But what does it create in its stead? Reconstructed biographies can speak to delving historians, but what of permanent legacies?

Pierre Nora's notion of 'lieux de mémoire' helps us to establish the meaning of such cultural exchange within defined spaces and encourages us to locate these legacies in various forms throughout the diaspora. In Nora's conception, 'memory attaches itself to sites, whereas history attaches itself to events' (Nora, 1994: 298). Although we might want to complicate such an oversimplistic binary notion, it does have its uses: for example, in discussing African diasporan culture, with its continual reliance on oral narratives and ceremonials for remembering itself to itself, such a concept liberates. The Atlantic becomes 'un lieu de mémoire' wherein diasporan Africans create cultural modes that transcend national boundaries and intersect dynamically with such representation of Anglo-European culture as the shanties I described earlier. These sea-based forms speak of and to a mobile proletariat that has diasporan Africans at its core. They 'become a form of counterhistory that challenges the false generalizations in exclusionary "History"' (Werner Sollors, quoted in Fabre and O'Meally, 1994: 8). Such oral forms help to create a new version of transatlantic history that moves us beyond the narrowness of traditional historiography. Sabine Brock has talked about the 'ethical and political need for a far reaching restoration of Western cultural memory to the effect of re-inscribing, foregrounding a crucial cultural lack by way of what Bhabha has called the "supplement" of memory of oppressed cultures' (Brock, 1999: 23).

Cultural forms forged in the black diaspora provide this necessary counter-memory that challenges international Western (white) amnesia. Nowhere is this more true than in African-American oral narratives constructed about the Atlantic during slavery in the South and later in the post-emancipation Northern and Southern ghettoes, and it is these I would like to explore now.

=== 2 ===

'I HAD A CORK IN MY ASS AND I COULDN'T GO DOWN'

SURVIVING THE MIDDLE PASSAGE – A COUNTER-HISTORICAL READING OF ORAL NARRATIVES OF THE BLACK ATLANTIC

The cultural memory inscribed in the hegemonial 'writing' of Western documents, imperial monuments, colonial rituals, trade records, and individual – fictional or autobiographical – recollections have as a general rule not contained the 'words' of colonial or enslaved subjects; their visceral experiences, their memories of oppression and resistances have become left 'behind' by Western historiography, prose, and poetry. Those 'obscurities' now, in keeping with a continuing history of social and economic decolonization and cultural reorientation, need to be displaced by way of artistic recuperation of the colonial and imperial past from the point of view of those previously muted subjects. This recuperation is by necessity an artistic act and challenges, since in most cases, 'chronicles' of the dates and facts of colonization – coherently figured from that subaltern perspective – do not exist. The pervasive ellipses of Western historiography will only be pointed out and filled by way of the (literary) imagination. (Brock, 1999: 24)

There was no such thing as the sinking of the Titanic. It was just a movie, an omen, an hallucination. (Hans Magnus Enzensburger, quoted in Foster, 1999: 309)

If nothing else, the scholarship of the last thirty years has repeatedly under-lined how Africans, far from being merely hamstrung victims of the awful conditions of the transatlantic slave trade, have been agents in their own history even during the most extreme periods of repression. Many scholars of the black Atlantic have stressed shipboard revolts or liberational shipboard slave narratives as key indicators of an autonomous African impulse despite the hegemonic control of brutally strong slave polities whose tentacles encompass the three continents of the triangular trade (see Jones, 1986;

Carretta, 1996; Sale, 1997; and Linebaugh and Rediker, 2000, etc.). The urge to rewrite these polities' repressive narratives, either through actual revolt or transformative written narratives, merely represents the tip of a slumbering volcano of responses which help to refigure the Atlantic middle passage, albeit sometimes in a more allegorical mode. Even the plantation narrative of 'Ole Massa and John', which at first glance betrays no specific materials of relevance to the black Atlantic, contains a trickster tale which displays a revaluation of the Atlantic from death scene to site of triumph:

> **The Swimming Contest**
> The master and his wife were leaving on a ship – probably for the Old Country, since they were going away from this country. So the slave stowed away, and when they got nearly to land he began to call out, 'Oh Massie George, Oh Missie George.' At first it sounded faint, and then it kept getting louder. They said, 'That must be John,' but they couldn't believe it. He slipped out and began swimming toward the boat. So they pulled him aboard, all dripping and asked him how he got there. 'Well I swim all the way here; I wasn't going to let you leave me.'
> (quoted in Roberts, 1989: 55)

Here, John desires to expand his horizons in a transatlantic direction towards America, where the opportunities for personal and economic advancement would be much greater. By voluntarily stowing away on a transatlantic ship and transporting his labour power to a destination of his choice, he undermines the hegemony of the slave power and alters the power relationship between himself and his master. Gaining for himself several days without labour, he reconstructs the ship as sign of forced transportation into an arena for his libidinal transformation from chattel to free agent. His stowage on board ship exemplifies Paul Gilroy's concept that ships were more than vessels of transportation in the economy of the Atlantic, frequently acting as active modes of transformation: 'ships ... were something more – a means to conduct political dissent and possibly a distinct mode of cultural production' (Gilroy, 1993a: 17). Shipboard, the slave's trickery has greater implications for freedom than it ever could at home on the plantation site of the Southern slave power.

Despite his position in mid-Atlantic, John knows that if his master realizes he has stowed away he will be in trouble. Thus, he devises the hyperbolic subterfuge that he is a superhuman swimmer. In his dream-heroic mode, the Atlantic is merely a river to swim across. This elaborate trickery chimes with African-American folk belief that the ocean is only a river which can be symbolically crossed to return to the land of their ancestors. John's subterfuge merely panders to the ego of his white master, who believes so implicitly in the loyalty of his slave that he is tricked into believing his ridiculous tale of heroism. Pulling John out of the water represents a reversal of the commonplace act of throwing slave bodies (both alive and dead) into the sea during both the legal and illegal slave trades. A symbolic refiguring of transatlantic death is thus enacted in a humorous tale that seeks to undermine the claims of mastership enshrined in the peculiar institution. John de-masters his master by being in control even when he is awash in mid-Atlantic. His baptism in the water transforms him from controlled chattel to a player in the perverted economics of bodily accomplishments. The story continues:

> So he went along with them, and his master was bragging about how he had the best swimmer in the world. There was a white swimmer parading around, and they made a date with him to have a contest. The day of the contest he was waiting on the beach, until finally the colored man came, puffing and making a lot of noise, with a cookstove and provisions on his back. He said, 'Where's that white fellow who's goin' to swim with me?' (in a big voice). The white man said, 'Here I am' (in a little voice). John said, 'Man, ain't you carrying nothing to eat with you?' He answered 'No.' 'Well you'd better, for I'm a-fixing to stay.' The white man ran away. (quoted in Roberts, 1989: 55–6)

Now John's economic value, enhanced by his swimming prowess, is seen as a boon by his master, who seeks prestige and money by exploiting his chattel's talents for his own gain. The putative swimming contest is all about the ego of the master, whose presumed power over his athlete is based on the debauched racial economy of the Atlantic, where the talents of the black body benefit the slave-owning plantation class.

John must extricate himself before his trickery is exposed, and as with all tricksters he improvises another subterfuge to ensure that his deception is never revealed . This time, to outwit the obviously superior white swimmer, he apparently makes preparations for a ridiculously long swim. This undermines the confidence of the white swimmer, who backs down before the race even begins. John's quick-wittedness ensures his status as an uncontested champion without having to demonstrate any prowess in swimming. The illusion of superhuman accomplishment fools not only his master but the white swimmer too. The Atlantic, the scene of degradation and tragedy for African Americans, is here refigured in the world of the vernacular as a scene of tricksterism triumphant. That this triumph is achieved through trickery and illusion does not undermine it, for as J. W. Roberts contends the trickster tradition 'offered a model of behaviour for equalizing conditions between masters and slaves by breaking the rules of the system that gave the slavemasters a clear economic, political and social advantage. It, in essence, functioned as an outlaw tradition within the value system of slavery' (*ibid.*: 185).

The concept of trickery works particularly well as an allegory of the slaves' position in the slave economy because it is based on a truism about African-American survival in the middle passage. John's supposed prowess is not in the sprints but in the long distances, and the emphasis he places on the value of perseverance by preparing (if only that) for a marathon swim parallels his people's doughty survival through the nightmare of a long and arduous middle passage. Despite John's triumph, however, he and his body remain beholden to the slave power (even if he has gained advantages which mean he is more valued under that burden). His pre-emancipation triumph is thus only partial, in accordance with the realities of being an owned body in the intricate network of the Atlantic while slavery was still a powerful, if challenged, reality. With the advent of freedom, more adventurous comic heroes began to appear. Foremost of these in a black Atlantic context was the apocryphal stoker from the doomed *Titanic*, Shine. He was lionized in a sequence of extended oral poems which have become known as the '*Titanic* Toasts'. Developed in the aftermath of the *Titanic* disaster of 1912, these poems were still being recited a full half-century later, when folklorists began to collect them in earnest. They continue to be told into the twenty-first century. Discussing the toast, which he uses as a key exemplar of African-American vernacular praxis, Larry Neal, the black nationalist writer and activist, said, 'It is part of the private mythology of black America. Its symbolism is direct and profound' (Neal, 1989: 7).

The provenance and meaning of the toast has been very well delineated within the context of folklore, comic history and sociology by distinguished scholars such as Roger Abrahams, Bruce Jackson, Lawrence Levine, William Labov *et al.*, Larry Neal, Daryl Cumber Dance and Mel Watkins. However, I want to widen the parameters of the discussion by tracing a variety of black vernacular responses to the disaster and moving beyond the USA to discuss the manifold versions of the toast in the context of the black Atlantic, illustrating their relevance not only to the *Titanic* disaster itself but also to the middle-passage experience of previous centuries. Preliminary work has already been undertaken by Steven Biel in his cultural history of the sinking of the ship, *Down with the Old Canoe* (1996), but the ramifications of the toasts and other African-American imaginative reactions to the disaster are wider and more profound than his brief discussion allows for. As he says of the event, 'What deeply engaged white Americans did not affect African Americans in the same way; what seemed universal to some was actually a matter of perspective' (*ibid.*: 108).

What gives perspective to this Atlantic disaster and its horrendous loss of life are twin concerns of Africans in the diaspora: first, the tragic lives lived by so many Africans in the diaspora because of racism, and then, of course, that earlier (too often forgotten in Anglo-American discourse) transatlantic journey, the middle passage. It blighted the lives of over eleven million transported Africans, as well as the 'uncounted millions' lost on the journey to embarkation points in Africa and then at sea. These perspectives mean that the disaster is apprehended differently in African-American communities from the way it is encoded within majority Anglo-American discourse. Paul Oliver, in discussing blues ballads about the sinking (which on the whole preceded the toasts), highlights this duality in reactions to the disaster in terms of different racially charged moral perspectives:

> For whites the scale of the disaster and its cruel involvement of
> the weak and innocent could only be accounted for in human
> error or folly; for blacks, the sinking assumed a somewhat
> different significance, indicating the inevitability of God's

judgement on the arrogance of those who believed themselves invincible. (Oliver, 1984: 223)

Oliver's discussion of numerous *Titanic* ballads shows that this was a common African-American response to the disaster, and was often characterized by a distinct class agenda that condemned the separation of the poor from the wealthy and the implications for the survival of the latter. In foregrounding this class dimension throughout my discussion in this chapter, I want to respond to Laura Chrisman's critique of Paul Gilroy's perceived over-culturalist approach. It is her recommendation

> that Gilroy's analysis be supplemented by an analysis which holds on to the utility of economic analysis in conceptualizing black cultural productions, one which postulates these cultures as voicing a working relationship between labour and play. (Chrisman, 2000: 455–6)

This relationship is one that I follow throughout the chapter as a means of rescuing African-American responses to the black Atlantic from a narrow ethnic nationalism (a charge against Gilroy which I think is overstated anyway). It is the interrelationship of race and class which makes reactions to the *Titanic* disaster particularly potent and ensures a dynamic multi-layered black Atlantic reading. For instance, Blind Willie Johnson's 1929 version, *God Moved on the Water*, outlines how the disaster impacted on numerous poor victims (Oliver, 1984: 224). Such responses were not uncommon in the years after the disaster and produced some elegiac forms, but it was the perceived racial exclusion on the *Titanic* which enabled the satiric mode to come to the fore in African-American vernacular responses. Hence, a different narrative form other than the tragic is developed. As Biel puts it, 'some consumers of the conventional narrative became active producers of alternative narrative, defying its tone as well as its content. Some even made it into a joke' (Biel, 1996: 118). This comic narrative is given impetus by the social context surrounding the *Titanic* and its ramifications for African peoples in the diaspora, which would become a prime concern of the later toasts. For instance, the socialist magazine *Appeal to Reason*, published in Kansas, commented:

> The *Titanic* rushed headlong to her terrible fate in pursuit of profit. So much space had to be given to the private promenades, golf links, swimming pools for the plutocrats aboard that there was no space left for lifeboats when the crash came. ('A Capitalist Disaster', 1999: 166)

The golf links might have been an exaggeration, but Turkish baths, electric elevators, a squash court, a gymnasium and elaborately tiled reception rooms meant that the first-class suites on the liner exhibited a conspicuous opulence beyond the imaginings of those crammed below decks in the third-class accommodation. While the spectacle of the 'unsinkable ship', a floating palace where rich people indulged in conspicuous consumption beyond the imaginings of poor diasporan Africans was bad enough, the rumours of black exclusion from the voyage on account of colour alone meant there was less sympathy for *all* the victims when the ship went down.

Early African-American vernacular responses to the disaster countered such exclusion by boasting of their own presence on the *Titanic*. Butler 'String Beans' May's 'Titanic Blues' of 1913 shows how quickly irreverent responses to the disaster were penned and performed. Here can be identified the seed-corn of the *Titanic* toasts which were to follow as String Beans cavorted about the stage moving his hips in so-called 'Elgin movements', a kind of 'horizontal grind which would make today's rock and roll dancers seem solid citizens' (Abbot and Seroff, 1996: 436), while boasting the following:

> I was on dat great Titanic
> De night dat she went down
> Ev'ybody wondered
> Why I didn't drown –
> I had dem Elgin movements in ma hips,
> Twenty years' guarantee! (Niles, 1928: 290–1)

His superhuman prowess is linked to black vernacular dance with its wild hip movements. This imaginative salvation through dynamic black movement links the song to the toasts I will discuss later, as does his wholly imagined presence on the fabled whites-only ship. The rumour that even boxing world champion Jack Johnson's money and fame had not bought him a passage merely confirmed the contention of many African Americans that the lily-white ship deserved its fate. This legend (for there is no proof that Johnson was denied passage) was the spur to Leadbelly's (Huddie Ledbetter's) famous *Titanic* song. In it, Captain Smith refuses passage to Johnson with the refrain 'I ain haulin' no coal', thus confirming a history of exclusionary racial practices on transatlantic ships which scholars such as Alasdair Pettinger have recently traced (Pettinger, 1999). When Johnson hears of the disaster from his safe berth on land, Leadbelly has him 'doin' th' eagle rock', dancing for joy in a fashion reminiscent of String Beans. The final stanza describes the happy moral for Africans in the diaspora:

> Black man oughta shout for joy,
> Never lost a girl or either a boy.
> Cryin', 'Fare thee Titanic, fare thee well!' (Leadbelly, 1998: 815)

This ironic refrain of leave-taking is a calculated revisioning of the tragic mode, highlighting the racial dynamic which makes the sinking of the ship an occasion for African-American celebration of survival. This trope, linking African-American pugilist triumph to the sinking of the great white hope, is continued in Bill Gaither's song 'Champ Joe Louis' which celebrates Joe Louis's victory over Max Schmeling in a world title defence of his heavyweight crown in 1938. In their first fight in 1936, Schmeling had been triumphant.

The German press heralded the victory as proof positive of the superiority of the white race, but also of the importance of keeping the 'Negro' in his place. *Der Weltkampf*'s racialized view was typical:

> The Negro is of a slave nature, but woe unto us if this slave nature is unbridled, for then arrogance and cruelty show themselves in the most bestial way ... these three countries – France, England and white North America – cannot thank Schmeling enough for his victory, for he checked the arrogance of the Negro and clearly demonstrated to them the superiority of white intelligence. (quoted in Vasili, 1998: 193)

The rematch was crucial to exploding such racial myths of black inferiority and transcontinental white racial solidarity. Furthermore, the importance of this event in puncturing German claims to Aryan superiority was highlighted by Louis himself:

> I even heard that when the Germans learned how badly I was beating Schmeling, they cut the radio wires to Germany. They didn't want their people to know that just a plain old nigger man was knocking the shit out of the Aryan Race. (quoted in Gilroy, 2000: 169)

In Gaither's song, Louis's first-round knockdown of Schmeling, who was promoted by Hitler as the acme of Anglo-Saxon physical superiority, is linked to the mythical unsinkability of the *Titanic*, which, of course, had been promoted as the pre-eminent technical achievement of white civilization. Both examples of white hubris, the *Titanic* and Schmeling, suffer an ignominious fate:

> I came all the way from Chicago to see Joe Louis and Max
>   Schmeling fight.
> Schmeling went down like the *Titanic* when Joe gave him just
>   one hard right. (Gaither, 1998: 811)

As Alan Lomax contends, 'The unsinkable *Titanic* is just another white folks' brag' (Lomax, 1994: 53), and Schmeling's invincibility is inexorably linked by Gaither to the doom-laden ship and its eventual demise. The connection is established further by a hyperbolic take on Schmeling's reaction to the knockdown, as Gaither has him react cravenly to his fate:

> It was only two minutes and four seconds poor Schmeling was
>   down on his knees,
> He looked like he was praying to the Good Lord to 'Have mercy
>   on me, please!' (*ibid.*)

Like the *Titanic*, Schmeling's fate is sealed surprisingly swiftly, and just like the poor survivors he is forced to resort to prayer in the face of his inevitable fate. There are echoes of the singing of 'Nearer My God to Thee', the final signature tune of the *Titanic* disaster, in Schmeling's last prayer, which shows him to be as vulnerable to the 'Black Bomber' as the *Titanic* had been to the white Atlantic iceberg. The hubris of imperial fantasists promoting their unsinkable marvel of Anglo-Saxon technical superiority is linked by Gaither's song to the white supremacists in Nazi Germany, and both groups suffer the same ignoble fate.

If Gaither's song is true to the emotional symbolics of an event it utilizes as an extended metaphor, Leadbelly's triumphalism is less honest about his facts; and not only in the hyperbole of Johnson's exclusion. Recent scholarship has unearthed a black victim of the *Titanic* disaster whose presence rather punctures the legend of total black exclusion. This Haitian passenger, Joseph Laroche, boarded with his wife and two daughters in Cherbourg and went down with the ship. His black presence on board was never commented on by contemporary chroniclers and has only now been fully documented in a *Titanic* exhibition at the Musuem of Science and Industry in Chicago. Designated a French passenger, his racial origins were not revealed by either the black or white press in the aftermath of the disaster. This was despite the fact that middle-class black commentators were desperate for a sable hero to emerge from the debris so they could attach themselves to the tragic/heroic narrative that was being written all around them by Anglo-American journalists. For instance, the *St Paul Appeal* wistfully commented: 'And when in the last day the sea gives up its dead' the black hero 'like the others will come into his crown of glory' (Biel, 1996: 113). The black hero would indeed 'come into his crown of glory', but not quite as the *Appeal* had hoped for. The only heroism delineated until Laroche's story was recently uncovered was encapsulated by the character of the bad-mouthed, cynical Shine, to whom I shall turn, in detail, shortly. Meanwhile, the Southern plantocracy press could not resist an antithetical imaginative racial spin on the disaster, with the *Savannah Tribune* quoting, as if true, an apocryphal story of a black stoker 'shot because he was about to stab a wireless operator' (*ibid.*: 113). According to this jaundiced account, in the midst of white heroism, the nefarious black badman emerges as the bogeyman of white civilization.

In fact, there were no African-American crewmen on the rosters of the *Titanic*, not even among the stokers, where diasporan Africans and other non-whites were legion throughout the world's merchant marine. In a segregationist move, blacks had been literally 'relegated to the stokehold' in the later nineteenth and early twentieth century, as the job could be designated as unskilled. Also, according to received opinion, they possessed the 'natural attributes' for the work, as their tropical origins 'made them better suited to stand the heat than Nordic specimens' while performing a job that required 'the brute force of a gorilla' (quoted in Tabili, 1996: 184). Flying in the face of such logic, the White Star Line (the *Titanic*'s owners) had obviously made a conscious decision to keep the crew rosters as lily-white as possible, as lily-white in fact as the passenger rosters were in mythology. Even where they could not be seen, deep in the bowels of the ship, the crew was decidedly and uncharacteristically white.

The *Titanic* toasts are not only a rejection of such racist praxis, they are also a response to the myth that the *Titanic* represented the acme of transatlantic Anglo-American technological prowess, the virtual embodiment of the utopian possibilities of white civilization. The control of the White Star Line had already passed from British into American hands through the machinations of the American financier J. P. Morgan, so that despite its appearance as a British ship manned by British officers and flying a British flag, it was entirely under American financial control. As owners and builders talked of the great triumph of the white race which the *Titanic* epitomized, they could not help lauding a transatlantic relationship 'of British technology and American capital' which foreshadowed the transfer of world leadership from Britain to America (Davie, 1999: 7–9). At the official launch of the RMS *Titanic* in 1911, the language of Anglo-Saxon triumphalism was pervasive. First, Mr J. Shelley, representing the owners of the ship, commented:

> It seemed to him that as the year passed and the conditions of life changed, the Anglo-Saxon nations became more closely united as a result of such co-operation as was indicated by the building of ships like the *Titanic* and the *Olympic*, which promoted intercourse between the mighty Republic in the West and the United Kingdom. ('The Genius of the Anglo-Saxon', 1999: 254)

In reply, for the shipbuilders, Harland and Wolf, Mr Saxon J. Payne went even further, promoting a white transatlantic racial alliance whose exclusionist racialist dynamic is proudly promoted. According to the *Belfast Telegraph*:

> he did not recognise any distinctions between the various sections of the Anglo-Saxon race, and they looked upon the building of the *Titanic* and the *Olympic* as a great Anglo-Saxon triumph ... The two vessels were pre-eminent examples of the vitality and the progressive instincts of the Anglo-Saxon race, and he did not see anything which need give them alarm for the future. As a race they were young and strong and vigorous, and by what it had done in assisting the White Star line in its great and commendable enterprise Belfast could lay claim to no small share in the prosperity of the British Empire. (*ibid.*: 255)

Such grandiosity was designed to establish Anglo-Saxons as pre-eminent over other European races such as the Teutonic Germans at a time of tremendous power rivalry. However, it also served to exclude non-whites from a position at the top table with the Anglo-Alliance. It was not only at the launch that the promoters of the *Titanic* let their enthusiasm run riot. Promotional literature distributed by the White Star Line continued to heap praise on their Leviathan ships, which embodied 'the latest developments in modern propulsion' (quoted in Foster, 1999: 256) as symbolic of Anglo-Saxon inge-nuity and mercantile and technological achievement:

> The *Olympic* and *Titanic* are not only the largest vessels in the World; they represent the highest attainments in Naval Architecture and Marine Engineering; they stand for the pre-eminence of the Anglo-Saxon race on the Ocean; for the 'Command of the Seas' is fast changing from a Naval to a Mercantile idea, and the strength of a maritime race is represented more by its instruments of commerce and less by its weapons of destruction than was formerly supposed.
> Consequently these two Leviathans add enormously to the potential prosperity and progress of the race … (*ibid.*: 256–7)

Through such material, the White Star Line seek to inculcate their own commercial needs as central to the promotion of white imperial hegemony on both sides of the Atlantic. Out of their own mouths, both the manufacturers and owners of the *Titanic* establish its launch and its subsequent promotion as key to the development of a racialist, imperialist ideology based at the inter-face of transatlantic travel and technology. This ideology becomes central to the creation of the *Titanic* myth, so that the creators of the toasts feel free not only to highlight the way personal vices such as greed, hypocrisy and over-confidence are displayed but also to foreground such public vices as institu-tional, transcontinental racism, racial imperialism and an overweening belief in technology as panacea. Control might be passing from Britain to the United States as modernity gains pace at the start of the twentieth century, but the same or similar racial dynamics apply around the whole circum-Atlantic region. As Paul Gilroy characterizes, in talking elsewhere about black ver-nacular forms in the diaspora, the toasts provide 'dissident assessments of modernity's achievements' (Gilroy, 1993a: 71) which challenge widespread notions about the benefits of such progress. The black stoker hero, Shine, draws attention to these as he first warns the complacent captain about the danger of believing the ship to be unsinkable:

> 'Captain, captain, I can't work no more.
> Don't you know there's forty foot a water on the boiler room
>   floor.'
> Captain say, 'Shine, Shine, that can't be a fact,
> I got four hundred pumps to keep that water back.
> Go back and hit another blow.'
> Shine said, 'Captain, captain, can't you see,
> this ain't no time to bullshit me!
> I'd rather be out on that ocean going 'round and 'round
> than be on this big motherfucker slowly sinkin' down.'
> (Jackson, 1974: 187)

Shine's preference for the ocean over the sinking ship shows his levelheadedness in contrast to the blinkered white command of the ship. Far from keeping the ship afloat, the belief in the intrinsic merits of technological progress is contributing to its sinking. The contestation of the captain and Shine is played out through language where the captain's voice of authority is undermined by what Robert Young, following Mikhail Bakhtin, calls an intentional hybridity. This 'hybridity ... has been politicised and made contestatory ... as the two points of view are not mixed but set against each other dialogically' (Young, 1995: 21). This 'active moment of challenge and resistance against a dominant power' (*ibid.*: 23) reveals the text to be defiantly political and quintessentially postcolonial, as Shine's common-sense rebuttal of the captain's overweening power is tantamount to 'depriv[ing] the imposed imperialist culture, not only of the authority that it has for so long imposed politically, often through violence, but even its own claims to authenticity' (Bhabha, 1991: 57–8). This is seen most clearly in Shine's renaming of the *Titanic* in the black vernacular as a 'big motherfucker', and in his radical claim that the captain, hitherto source of all shipboard authority, is in fact 'bull-shitting' him. Shine's mid-ocean revolution should alert us to the manifold diasporan valencies of his toast. Hence, the way that some commentators have come to discuss the ship as an allegory of America – a ship of state endangered by its crew's hubris and racist praxis 'symboliz[ing] African Americans' plight in America' which Shine, as a militant black, refuses to help (Watkins, 1995: 468) – should be seen as a limiting of Shine's political vision. Such a view restricts the meaning of the toast to domestic American politics when the narrative itself fishes in more profound diasporan waters.

As the narrative develops, Shine's choice of murky (natural) depths rather than failing white technology is immediately justified as the pumps fail and the ship sinks. Roger Abrahams comments astutely on Shine's choice:

> Shine undergoes a real transformation, is reborn. His act of jumping overboard is a conscious rejection of white commands, followed by a rejection of status symbols. He undergoes a symbolic slaying of himself to be reborn in the ocean (not a surprising place to be reborn) ... Turning his back on white people ... Shine made it to the shore and the whites, the oppressive yet less strong did not. (Abrahams, 1970: 80–1)

Shine's rebirth in the Atlantic, though, does not only speak to twentieth-century racial realities of inequality and racism but is also a fundamental refiguring of the Atlantic as a 400-year burying ground for black bodies. The ocean is not a watery grave but a repository of libidinal possibilities in comparison to the drudgery of boiler-room work in a doomed ship. Even the most frightening of middle-passage myths are domesticated in Shine's reworking of the narrative of Atlantic passage. Apocryphal and actual tales of slavers would always include a pursuing school of sharks eager for the dead (and sometimes the living sick) to be thrown overboard, yet here Shine, far from being easy meat, is portrayed as a super-heroic figure well able to deal with the ravenous fish both verbally and physically:

So Shine began to swim, runnin' with a shark.
Shark say, 'Shine, oh, Shine you better swim fast,
I got thirty two teeth in the crack of your ass.'
Shine say, 'I outswim the white man, I outswim the Jew,
I know motherfucken well I can outswim you.'
(Jackson, 1974: 191–2)

Shine's verbal dexterity here and elsewhere in the toast shows the importance of quick-wittedness to his triumph. In his dealings with both the captain and the shark, Shine has to have his answer ready. If anything, there is a surfeit of words as the black subject compensates for the muteness of centuries of enforced silence with both an excess of speech and a sudden switch from inaction to swift mobility that transfigures a sinking body into a swimming one. He uses what Henry Louis Gates and other critics of the African-American vernacular would call a 'Signifyin(g)' retort to the dominant narratives of the sinking of the *Titanic*. The Manichean realities of black slaughter and white indifference are literally reversed as the sharks find the white bodies present them with easy meat. There occurs what Gilroy would call 'a utopian transformation of racial subordination' (Gilroy, 1993a: 71) literally in mid-ocean. In keeping with the cynical and contestatory nature of the toast, there is none of the sentimentality so prevalent in majority culture narratives about the sinking. What in Anglo-American narratives are employed as key exemplars to enhance the tragic narrative are used in the toast as mere joke props to its subterranean view:

Folks on the land were singin' 'Nearer my God to Thee,'
The Sharks in the ocean were singin', 'Bring your ass to me.'
(Jackson, 1974: 188)

Note here how it is not the victims on the *Titanic* who are singing the immortalized hymn but those at home. In fact, as the junior wireless operator Harold Bride's eyewitness account confirms, the ship's band played mostly ragtime tunes in the ship's final minutes (Bride, 1999: 130). The narrator of the toast could well be speculating that the heroic tale of hymn singing was of more comfort to myth-makers at home than to those trapped on the ship at sea. In keeping with such a realistic reading, the sharks are seen as respecters of no sentimental or financial appeal, consuming millionaires and white women alike. In the cruel but 'natural' world of the ocean, away from the Anglo-American hegemony shipboard with its perverted monetary values, native wit and physical endurance are the qualities needed for survival. On this level playing field, Shine, the putative bottom-of-the-ladder stoker, is transformed into a trickster-hero *par excellence*. Such dichotomies and reversals are dramatized throughout the toast:

Big motherfucker from Wall Street told the sharks, 'I'm a big
motherfucker from Wall Street, you got to let me be.'

Sharks say, 'Here in the water, your ass belongs to me.'
(Jackson, 1974: 190)

Used to owning others, the capitalist is reduced to incorporation by a ravenous shark in the radical world of the toast. As Shine tells the captain in another version of the tale, 'your money's counterfeit in this big-assed ocean' (*ibid.*: 187). Away from the comforts of the capitalist world, the captain's currency, like that of his passengers, has no value. The world of the toast undermines capitalist hegemony by accentuating the working of a natural world which is no respecter of the money-god.

Despite the toast's portrayal of a neutral ocean, the actual experience of Africans in the history of the transatlantic passage belies such an optimistic reading, as the Atlantic had historically been a great respecter of money and trade, with merchants on three continents trading black bodies for money in the 'big-assed ocean'. While the toast cannot alter such past realities, in a cynical mode that brooks no sentiment, it does challenge the continued existence of racism and inequality in the so-called modern age. Its gritty realism exhibits 'a counter-culture of modernity' (Gilroy, 1993a: 1) that attempts to refigure the transatlantic passage as liberational for Africans in the diaspora as well as being the cause of their fetters. The dominance of the economic in the social world of the narrative, and hence of course in the transatlantic, is underscored by passengers offering Shine money to help them. The boot is now truly on the other foot as Shine becomes the dominant trader able to bargain for their bodies where, historically, white people had bargained for his and his ancestors'. This insistence on the economic is the legacy of a slave past where, as Houston Baker Jr contends, 'it [was] absolutely necessary for the slave to negotiate the economics of slavery if he would be free' (Baker, 1987: 39). Post-emancipation economics are just as important to the diasporan African enmeshed in a capitalist system where he is usually most disadvantaged. Shine takes advantage of his temporary freedom from the cash nexus to reject all admonishments from the drowning whites. For instance, before his encounter with the sharks, the big man from Wall Street had tried to exert his influence on Shine, only to receive an immediate rebuttal from the stoker:

> Big man from Wall Street came on the second deck.
> In his hand he held a book of checks.
> He said, 'Shine, Shine, if you save poor me,'
> 'Say I'll make you as rich as any black man can be.'
> Shine said, 'You don't like my color and you down on my race,
> get your ass overboard and give these sharks a chase.'
> (Jackson, 1974: 190)

Historically, it had been the white enslaver who had occupied the hegemonic position in his relationship with African bodies in the Atlantic. Now Shine is in a position to refuse succour to the once powerful, whose money, as he indicates in his reply, comes from a diseased culture which uses racism to promote inequality. The 99 millionaires are now merely food for the sharks in the liminal space of the Atlantic Ocean where their capitalist merchant ancestors had traded in black bodies and sometimes thrown them overboard to meet a similar fate. Through such reversals, the toasts act as 'insubordinate racial countercultures' (Gilroy, 1993a: 200), intervening in traditional narratives of Anglo-American heroism to promote a counter-narrative with resonances not only for twentieth-century politics but also for the whole history of diasporan Africans in the Atlantic. Lawrence Levine equates Shine's triumph here with other African-American heroes, both real and imagined, who 'could stand within the very centre of white society and they could stand there as black men operating victoriously on their own terms' (Levine, 1977: 438).

If money and the surplus value made on each black body was the motor that drove the triangular trade, then the pleasure derived from the abuse of such bodies was an outrageous by-product, the inevitable outcome of treating human beings as chattels. This 'pornography of empire' reached its apotheosis in the slave trade with the everyday ritual of forced sexual encounter between white slavers and female slaves shipboard. Robert Young has described how in such 'ambivalent moment[s] of attraction and repulsion, we encounter the sexual economy of desire in fantasies of race, and of race in fantasies of desire' (Young, 1995: 90). Such libidinal energies stoked (and stroked) not only the slave trade but, in its aftermath, relations between blacks and whites throughout the black Atlantic.

Shine's narrative contains its own refiguring of this libidinal economy. As he swims from the stricken ship, he is offered what within the mythology of interracial sex is meant to be his heart's desire, carnal relations with a white woman:

> Rich man's daughter came up on deck
> with her drawers round her knees and her underskirt around her
>   neck.
> Like a noonday clock Shine stopped
> and his eyes fell dead on that cock.
> She says, 'Shine, oh, Shine,' says, 'save me please,'
> say, 'I give you all the pussy that your eyes may see.'
> He said, 'I know you got some pussy and that's true,
> but there's some girls on land got good a pussy as you.'
> (Jackson, 1974: 184)

Note here the excesses offered to Shine. This Atlantic passage affords him not just the chance to break the interracial taboo but also a surplus of sexual pleasure. As earlier we saw how, in economic terms, the toast allows Shine to move to a dominant position in the financial economy of exchange in the Atlantic, so this exchange also shows his assumption of a dominant position in its sexual economy. This fantasy world reverses the actual relations that existed during the slave trade, where black men, deprived of their proper relationship with black women, were replaced by white men. Hortense Spillers details this reality succinctly: 'a dual fatherhood is set in motion, composed of the African father's banished name and body and the captor father's mocking presence' (Spillers, 1994: 480). Now it is Shine who is the mocking presence, denying not only sex but also offers of marriage with a rhetorical flourish that demeans the begging white women and displays a utopian vision of Black Power in the watery arena which had been many a black person's grave:

> She said, 'Shine, oh Shine,' say 'please save my life,'
> say, 'I'll make you a lawfully wedded wife.'
> He said, 'Your shittin' is good and your shittin' is fine,
> but first I got to save this black ass of mine.' (Jackson,
> 1974: 184)

Shine's hard-headed realism cuts across the promised rewards of the re-figured libidinal economy, a selfish perspective that is justified in this version of the toast by the countervailing example of another black man who could not deny the blandishments of the white women. Jim's return to consummate his desires with the endangered white woman leads to his inevitable demise as well. Note again how the toast glories in the excesses of the offered female body:

> Now was another fella by name of Jim
> *he* jumped in the ocean and he begin to swim.
> Another girl ran up on deck
> with her drawers round her knees and *her* underskirt around her
>   neck.
> Like a noonday clock Jim stopped
> and his eyes fell dead on that cock.
> Now she had long black hair that hang from the crown of her
>   head to the nape of her belly,
> she had a twenty-pound pussy that shook like jelly.
> Say, 'Shine, oh, Shine,' says, 'save me please,
> I'll give you everything that your eyes may see.'
> And before the last word could fall from her lip,
> Jim climbed his black ass back up on that ship. (*ibid.*: 184–5)

The repetitive phraseology in the offers made to the two black men propel the oral narrative, giving it a structure which allows the listener a static reference point from which to appreciate the different responses of the two black men. The women's excessive sexuality and oral blandishments stop both men, but Shine, though tempted, resists. He is in control of his 'black ass', which he is going to save. Meanwhile, Jim, superficially in control as he 'climbs his black ass' back on board the *Titanic*, remains beholden to white hegemony and its controlling myths and he will literally be destroyed with them. These structural parallels allow the listener to interpret more readily the moral economy of the text, whose message is a rejectionist one. In the midst of dreadful Atlantic realities there is no time for sentiment or pleasure (or indeed for pleasuring yourself); just a need to save 'your own black ass'.

Another version of the toast, however, points to an even more radical perspective. Again, the captain's daughter offers her body to the stoker, but when he refuses she threatens to 'cut out' her sexual organ 'and throw it into the sea'. Shine's answer signifies the importance of white women's sexuality as a marker of superiority in the libidinal transatlantic economy, while reiterating the pragmatic realities of survival:

> Shine say, 'Before I let that matter pass,
> I'll cut my dick off to the crack of my ass;
> I'll make my dick into an oar
> And paddle the pussy back to shore.' (Dance, 1978: 215)

Historically, the black body in passage across the Atlantic had only been important as a machine for the economic aggrandisement of Euro-Americans and their governments. Now, in a refigured transatlantic economy, Shine's body is literally turned into a floating machine for his own salvation. This reversal of middle-passage realities is heightened by the 'free ride' given to the captain's daughter's 'pussy', which demonstrates a reversal of power in favour of the hitherto excluded stoker. His body is no longer in the service of the Euro-American imperium but of his own demands and desires. The vision of Shine paddling a white 'pussy' to shore might be interpreted as a comic reversal of Stothard's *Voyage of the Sable Venus* (discussed in Chapter 3) and of other triumphant and sexualized Euro-American narratives of control over black bodies. Just as Shine paddles a female white body part across the Atlantic, so imperial Britain had transported black women across the ocean for their economic and libidinal value. Shine's pornographic imagination seeks to subvert such commonplace images of Anglo-American control of the libidinal economy.

Of course, such misogynist images, which are commonplace in most versions of the toast, call into question the radical vision of the black working-class narrators of Shine's story. However, they do not occur in a vacuum, as we can see from the images that cleave to black people in the diaspora where their dehumanization is constantly foregrounded. In promoting a counter-vision, black vernacular culture sometimes lapses into similar bad taste. For instance, the passage also signifies on a post-emancipation dismemberment of black bodies in the Southern states, where white crowds traded lynched black men's body parts as trophies in the aftermath of the brutal extra-legal executions. In this dark reversal, it is Shine who is in control of the white girl's body part as he rows to shore, rather than the traditional control of the black phallus by Southern racists. To understand the development of such troubling images, George Lipsitz's analysis of the Mardi Gras Indians is useful. He describes how 'images in negotiation with power are often ambiguous, complicated and implicated in the crimes they seek to address' (Lipsitz, 1990: 238). Shine is far from a blameless victim in these toasts, but operating in a world in which there is no fair play, he is forced to play the same Machiavellian tricks which his oppressor has employed ever since the first Africans were loaded onto the boats sailing for the New World. In a cruel world, Shine reacts not by becoming a moral leader, but by ensuring his own survival by any means necessary. His hedonism here and elsewhere in the toast illustrates how the eternally powerless diasporan African enjoys to the full his one moment of power in a cruel and unjust world.

In response to these dynamic oral narratives, critics should not become po-faced. The performers of the toasts use hyperbole not only to make polemical points but also to exhibit the verbal dexterity which makes for a dynamic and funny performance. However, the power of vernacular forms should not be underestimated either. For instance, Richard Wright, in discussing an allied form, the dozens (a ritualized exchange of verbal insults), delineates the 'affirmative power of [such] nihilistic cultural forms' which permit a Nietzschean vision that comes directly from the experience of the black Atlantic (quoted in Gilroy, 1993a: 160). These radical folktales propose a utopian counter-narrative to centuries of racial subordination and their peculiar format is a product of their genesis, as Wright explains:

> The black man's is a strange situation; it is a perspective, an angle of vision held by oppressed people; it is an outlook of people looking upward from below. It is what Nietzsche once called a 'frog's perspective'. Oppression oppresses, and this is the consciousness of black men who have been oppressed for centuries – oppressed so long that their oppression has become a tradition, in fact a kind of culture. (*ibid.*)

Looking from the bottom up gives a mordant humour to the toasts, which critique Anglo-American culture while providing social and political education for younger African Americans. For instance, in yet another version of the toast, the outrageous offers are given added piquancy by Shine's hard-headed realism, which reveals how the sexual favours of white women are only available to African Americans at moments of extremity. In dismissing the offer, he says, 'You wouldn't give me that pussy when we was on land' (Jackson, 1974: 195). Clearly a commentary on black–white relations in the post-emancipation era, it demonstrates how the toasts both look back to the Atlantic past, commenting on Atlantic racism at the time of the *Titanic* disaster, and use this familiar tale to comment on the hard-edged urban inter-racial realities of post-1945 America. This is emphasized in some versions of the toast by the elision of difference between teller and tale, so that the final lines exulting in Shine's salvation become seamlessly linked to the narrator's triumph. When Shine says in such versions, 'I just left the big swimming motherfucker forty years ago' (*ibid.*: 195), the aslant periodization confirms the narrator's wish to make the toast's survival as relevant to his place in the 1950s ghetto as it is to the north Atlantic in 1912. This mixing of periods destabilizes the linear tragic narrative of the *Titanic* and helps to ground a counter-mythology with multiple valencies.

Shine's refusal of money and sexual favours in pursuit of his own survival represents a crucial intervention as a radical narrative in the Atlantic. The death scene of the ship in mid-Atlantic, so often played out in realistic extant versions of the iconography of the middle passage, is replaced by a libidinous, comic affirmation of the will to live. As William Labov *et al.* comment on Shine's dialogues with the passangers: 'They offer all they have, but Shine rebukes them sharply by reminding them how unimportant their values are compared to life itself' (Labov *et al.*, 1973: 335). The triumphant espousal of the will to live is a reversal, too, of the vaunted death wish of many Africans in the hellish vortex of the middle passage. Like many examples of diasporic African culture, the *Titanic* toast exemplifies in its thematic interest in death at sea 'the turn towards death … [which] points to the ways in which black cultural forms have hosted and even cultivated a dynamic rapport with the presence of death and suffering' (Gilroy, 1993a: 200). Only here, instead of glorying in suicide as a release that allows him to join his ancestors in a mythically imagined homeland, Shine leaves the death ship and returns to his debauched life in the modern cityscape. Shine's narrative example posits a new liberational African diasporic reality that offers an alternative to death. It describes how, through struggling with white racist realities and in the context of an Anglo-American propensity for self-destruction, there are always fissures through which diasporic Africans can eke out a liveable (and even pleasurable) existence through struggle. In this sense, the *Titanic* toasts give the lie to depictions of such tales as mere vehicles for fantasy projection created in response to racism. Such a view freeze-frames black folk culture as merely a reactive form incapable of development or meaning beyond the narrow sub-culture. However, their function is a more dynamic one, as Lawrence Levine points out in linking Shine and other black heroes like John Henry to actual pugilist heroes like Jack Johnson and Joe Louis:

> It is evident that the folk heroes of black Americans were not merely mechanisms of escape or fantasies that brought relief from a difficult world. They were also mirrors of reality. They paralleled and reflected the changing situation of Negro Americans in the century after emancipation: their ability to publicly express attitudes which for too long had been bottled up within the individual or the group, their lessened faith in orderly progress through the American system, and their heightened dependence upon themselves and their people … [They were] moral hard men who broke the moulds that Negroes were supposed to conform to and created new roles and new possibilities. (Levine, 1977: 439–40)

The only criticism I have of Levine's discussion is the way such folk heroes and their influence are imprisoned behind the borders of the United States, when in fact the enhanced possibilities they personified had ramifications throughout the black Atlantic. Edouard Glissant points to the wider influence of such diasporan vernacular art forms when he comments on how 'folktales zero in on our absence of history' (Glissant, 1989: 85): the *Titanic* toasts are prime exemplars of such carnivalesque interventions which show how 'History is fissured by histories' (*ibid.*: 230). The absence of 'History' (or at least one that acknowledges African diasporan achievement) is filled by alternate takes which revel in remodelling the past through counter-mythology. Robert O'Meally outlines how the vernacular is a particularly apt mode for the creation of such alternate takes, emphasizing

> the treacherous unpredictability of history's flights
> .... *vernacular* art and artifacts convey this fast-changing and
> invisible history. They tell aspects of the American experience
> that do not get told in any other way and that perhaps cannot be
> told in any other way. (O'Meally, 1994: 245)

Shine's narrative is exemplary of such vernacular art, fleshing out a hidden history of the black Atlantic through a hyperbolic retelling and juxtaposition of two of its central narratives, the middle passage and the sinking of the *Titanic*. The Atlantic figured in Pierre Nora's terms as *un lieu de mémoire* is a perfect site for such admixture, while the vernacular as theorized by Robert O'Meally is the form best able to convey the new meanings that are adduced:

> vernacular expression may be described as a *lieu de mémoire*:
> that which induces a reappraisal of one's place and
> circumstances, a remaking of the official calendar, a
> reconsideration of the past, the given histories. That which
> inspires the conscious critical rethinking of attitudes toward
> history and memory. (*ibid.*)

Of course, Shine's narrative remakes not only calendars but also geographies, as distances are collapsed and changed to suit the particular ideological needs of his tale. The counter-mythology which is created by such reimaginings is based on a different version of transatlantic realities that posits Africans in the diaspora as sometimes heroic subjects rather than always tragic victims; this counter-mythology is responsible for creating, out of an Atlantic as *lieu de mémoire*, radical cultural interventions. Paul Gilroy posits a 'hermeneutics which distinguishes the grounded aesthetic of the black Atlantic ... [which] has two related dimensions – it is both a hermeneutics of suspicion and a hermeneutics of memory. Together they have nurtured a redemptive critique' (Gilroy, 1993a: 71). Gilroy's marvellous elliptical sentences point to how African diasporan suspicion of Anglo-American narratives that demean them and their past can be overwritten by the memory of, or imaginative reconstructions of, a more dynamic cultural intervention, which, if effectively remembered, can provide what Bob Marley would term a 'Redemption Song'. Shine's narratives, at their most effective, function in this way.

For instance, a version told by some adolescent boys in Philadelphia emphasizes Shine's progress from labouring for others to labouring for himself by employing the contrast between a repeated 'stokin'' in the ship and a liberational 'strokin'' in the ocean. His labour power transfigured into surplus superhuman value for himself is his salvation, as emphasized by the euphonic contrast between the two lexical terms. Shine has moved beyond stoking for others to a position of economic independence. He has rejected labouring in an insecure racialized imperial context, where he is merely servicing the engine of Anglo-American capital, to revel in a superhuman stroking to survival and freedom. He can stand as an emblem for Gilroy's critique of the limitations of a vulgar Marxist approach to the black Atlantic. As Gilroy contends, 'in the critical thought of blacks in the West, social self-creation through labour is not the centre-piece of emancipatory hopes. For the descendants of slaves, work signifies only servitude, misery and subordination' (Gilroy, 1993a: 40). Emancipation comes through flight from such work, and Shine's marathon swim is his own (solitary) escape from predatory capital. Its libidinal force might be confined to the artistic realm, but as Gilroy reminds us, within the constraining webbed network of the black Atlantic, 'artistic expression . . . becomes the means towards both individual self-fashioning and communal liberation' (*ibid.*). Laura Chrisman rightly warns against the potential such comments have for an over-aggrandizement of the artistic; but Shine's narrative is not merely about verbally jinking your way to freedom through a dynamic vernacular narrative, for it describes a revolt from below ships mid-Atlantic that succeeds in recasting class as well as race realities. While Gilroy is right that the workplace does not *generally* function as the site of emancipatory hope for a black proletariat, Shine's narrative does show how the withdrawal or recasting of labour for emancipatory purposes undermines both the capitalist and other oppressive systems. In moving from 'stoking' to 'stroking', Shine transforms his role from capitalist victim to trickster hero. In this sense, the *Titanic* toasts voice a dynamic 'working relationship between labour and play' (Chrisman, 2000: 455–6). When working-class blacks relive Shine's triumph by performing his narrative on street corners, transforming it imaginatively into their own register, they create their own autonomous space away from the workplace or ghetto that the capitalist system has confined them to. Their labour becomes the performative play which dynamically critiques the conditions of diasporan Africans in the world capitalist system.

Hence, imaginative narratives such as the *Titanic* toasts function not merely as entertainment but as pedagogical tools within a diasporan African culture. They are developed as 'popular self-generating cultural expressions [that] can challenge the hegemony of the dominant commercial culture by presenting cultural creations as having an organic "use" value rather than just a commercial "exchange" value' (José Limon, quoted in Lipsitz, 1990: 234). While confined at this level, the tales escape the commodification of much African diasporan culture, providing a cultural resource for African Americans with value far beyond the monetary. They act as a counter-narrative in a context where African diasporan culture is ignored and trivialized. Shine's 'strokin'', with its onanistic valencies, is hardly a harbinger of world revolution, but it is an appropriate and telling individual response to the centuries of silenced and deindividualized black voices in the middle passage and its aftermath. There is a dynamic transfer of labour power in the service of others to libidinal pleasure in the service of self.

The superhuman quality of this 'strokin'' is stressed by the toasts' boastful endings, where Shine is the first to bring the news of the stricken ship to land.

He is the harbinger of evil tidings to the Anglo-American polity, but, rather than broadcasting his exploits, the narrative locates him in the whorehouse or the bar in one or other (and sometimes more) of the great seaboard cities (New York, Liverpool, Los Angeles) relatively unconcerned by an event that has no bearing on him or his race:

> About four-thirty when the *Titanic* was sinkin',
> Shine done swimmed on over in Los Angeles and started drinkin'.
> But know when he heard the *Titanic* had sunk
> He was in New York damn near drunk.
> He said, 'Ladies and gentlemen,' say, 'when I die don't y'all bury
>   me at all,
> soak my balls in alcohol and lay my old rod up against my breast,
> and tell all the peoples old Shine has gone to rest.'
> (Jackson, 1974: 185)

His insouciance is calculated in the context of an Atlantic where the trade in black bodies had occasioned little comment for centuries. Shine's heroic survival is the comic narrative which will outlive (at least in African-American vernacular culture) the sentimental/tragic narrative of the unsinkable ship. For Shine is the truly unsinkable vessel in this narrative of doughty survival against the odds. This features most appositely in some versions of the tale which literally contrast the mythical unsinkable ship with the actual unsinkable Shine. In these versions, Shine widely broadcasts his version of the sinking and the joke ending is more pointed:

> Say, when the news finally got around
> that the old *Titanic* had finally gone down,
> there was Shine on Main Street, damn near drunk,
> tellin' every motherfucker how the *Titanic* sunk.
> Now a whore said, 'Shine,' say, 'darlin',' say, 'why didn't you
>   drown?'
> Said, 'I had a cork in my ass, baby, and I couldn't go down.'
> (*ibid.*: 189)

Shine's home-made technology of cork and human power is seen to prevail over the technological might of Anglo-America as he finds 'a way out of no way' and rescues himself from the deep. The *Titanic* toasts glory in black survival against the odds in the context of a transatlantic polity which has historically exploited their labour power as chattel and 'free' labourer. As Shine rises from the depths, he signifies on those sinking others in the long memory of the middle passage and projects different possibilities. In one version of the toast he does more than tame the sea monsters that harried and ate his ancestors, actually turning the tables on a man-eating whale:

> Say Shine looked over to his side and got a hell of a surprise,
> A forty-foot whale was swimming by his side.

Say, but Shine shook his head and wriggled his tail,
And did the deep-sea shuffle and fucked that whale.
(Dance, 1978: 216)

Here, his mastery over the Atlantic is emphasized by his sexual conquest of its beasts. In a reversal of the incorporation of blacks by sharks, Shine's act of bestiality tames the monster. He enters and pleasures it. His 'deep-sea shuffle' demonstrates how his survival abilities in the 'bad-assed ocean' are honed by his African-American vernacular kinaesthetic talents – his ability to dance dirty.

The use of the *Titanic* myth as a joke prop does not reach its apotheosis in these toasts but has persisted in response to Anglo-America's continued romanticism of the narrative. Hence, the success of James Cameron's epic supra-realistic telling of the tale in his 1997 film *Titanic* has occasioned a new raft of African-American responses to the legend. In Spike Lee's *The Original Kings of Comedy* (2000), for instance, one of the comedians tells a *Titanic* gag reminiscent in some of its features of the famous toasts. He asks the audience to imagine a *Titanic* peopled by blacks. Would they have stood back and gone down with the ship? Would the black band have kept playing as the ship sank? No, they'd have 'unplugged those speakers' and headed away from that doomed gig. Would the absence of lifeboats have held them back? Hell no, they'd have upturned tables, turned napkins into sails and saved their goddam black asses. As he tells the joke, the comedian mimes their life-saving actions, which is a direct contrast to the torpor depicted in Cameron's film in the immediate aftermath of the collision with the iceberg.

What this example shows is that in the twenty-first century the *Titanic* still functions as a joke about different Anglo- and African-American experiences and values. Refusing to buy into the myth of Anglo-Saxon technological invincibility, the pragmatic African Americans are intent on survival in a transatlantic crossing which has historically been their nadir. Survival is the key legacy which the *Titanic* toasts have imbued in African-American culture, and its resonances still echo even within the rampantly commercialized and popular cultural form of stand-up comedy. As Paul Gilroy attests, such vernacular forms display a tenacity which allows them to affect the wider political and intellectual culture with which they have a symbiotic relationship, and furthermore to spread far beyond their geographic localities and temporal boundaries:

> vernacular cultures and the stubborn social movements that
> were built upon their strengths and tactics have contributed
> important moral and political resources to modern struggles in
> pursuit of freedom, democracy and justice. Their powerful
> influences have left their imprint on an increasingly globalized
> popular culture. (Gilroy, 2000: 13)

Like Gilroy, I regard such vernacular cultures as in 'decline', undermined by the 'planetary commerce in blackness' (*ibid.*); however, the survival of black versions of the *Titanic* myth into the twenty-first century at least shows the continuing strength of such cultures in the face of external homogenizing commercial pressures. Folktales like these *Titanic* toasts are composed 'to dismantle the complex mechanism of frustration and the infinite forms of oppression' (Glissant, 1989: 107). Their success is testified to by their longevity, far outliving and out(Shine)ing Anglo-American oral narratives of the *Titanic*. This is mainly because the narrators take the long view: while the Atlantic has been the scene of death and rape, the humiliation and exploitation of black bodies, this arena is transfigured by Shine's narrative in a remarkably self-conscious projection of black triumph by a figure described by one of the toasts as 'so dark he changed the world's mind' (Jackson, 1974: 188). This self-description of the transfiguring nature of African-American vernacular narrative valorizes the dark skin which has traditionally been the signal for subordination in the cultural economy of the circum-Atlantic, prefiguring the later domination of black popular cultural forms in Anglo-American culture, especially music.

While the black stoker on the *Titanic* is, of course, an imaginative projection, his presence ensures that the Atlantic is overwritten with a narrative that explicates the ocean from an African-American and vernacular perspective, one that refuses to allow the majority Anglo-American and imperial narratives hegemonic sway. It is such radical narratives of the black Atlantic that begin the task of rewriting the middle passage and its aftermath through a different and more revealing lens. By doing so on the street corner in performances that are used as pedagogical tools for the building of a new counter-mythology, the narrators of the *Titanic* toasts were at the forefront of remaking their culture in their own radical image – streetwise and *hep*, and most importantly not beholden to the *Man*. In describing radical narratives of the black Atlantic, such vernacular forms should never be devalued, as they helped to frame African diasporan counter-hegemonic ideology in ways sympathetic to black working-class cultures that literary forms have only recently begun to match.

═ 3 ═
'FOOD FOR THE SHARKS'

CONSTRUCTIONS AND RECONSTRUCTIONS OF THE MIDDLE-PASSAGE IMAGINARY IN THE TRANSATLANTIC ECONOMY

The victim is a surplus taken from the mass of *useful* wealth. (Georges Bataille, quoted in Roach, 1996: 124)

we cannot truly tell ourselves a free story till we tell ourselves that we are truly the children of the Middle Passage. It is a story that brings to bear upon our daily lives the full indebtedness of our identities. When we return to the scene of our telling where whites once sought to steal the sign of ownership in African flesh we will find always before us the signs of African American artistry ineradicably embedded in the body of American thought. (Nielsen, 1994: 171)

As I fall towards the sea, my breath held
In shock until the waters quell me.
Struggle came only after death, the flush
Of betrayal, and hate hardening my body
Like cork, buoying me when I should have sunk
And come to rest on the sea's bed among
The dregs of creatures without names
Which roamed these waters before human birth ...
(Dabydeen, 1985: 21)

Despite the epic stories of travellers, travelling cultures and the insubordinate folk narratives with which I began this study, the reality of the black Atlantic is that most European narratives begin not with black voices, but with 'enlightened' white men engaged in a 'respectable' trade, exchanging finished goods for what they choose to call 'black cattle' (Irving, 1995: 113). However hard these slavers try to nullify the voices of the enslaved Africans, though, through 'significant and underscored omissions' (Morrison, 1993: 5) which deny their humanity, their journals and letters home reveal the African captives as people of active intelligence long before the boon of literacy allows them to record their own feelings for posterity. These everyday European and American documents are, in effect, in Marc Bloch's apposite phrase, 'witnesses in spite of themselves' (quoted in Mullin, 1975: x). Moreover, these slavers' relations with African traders on the coast undermine the traditional, over-simplistic narratives of wicked Europeans and exploited indigenous inhabitants, as their journals and letters reveal how 'Africa was a full partner in the development of the Atlantic world' (Thornton, 1992: 129). The willingness of the African elites and mulatto traders to trade, albeit on their own terms, is confirmed by the tortured meanderings of John Newton and James Irving, along with other slave ship captains and crew, up and down the coast in search of slaves and provisions for their transatlantic journey. Writing to his wife, when employed as a surgeon on the *Jane* in 1786, Irving laments, 'In my last I hinted that our stay would be short, but I am now sorry to say that most probably we shall be here two months hence. Trade is dull and ... exorbitant price' (Irving, 1995: 110). The desire for luxury goods was so great that these African elites would consign war captives and domestic slaves to an unknown fate across the ocean in exchange for them. However, they were usually shrewd enough to make the Europeans wait on their convenience and ensure that the slavers pay a good market price for their human cargo. As the seventeenth-century German traveller, Wilhelm Johann Muller, explains, the purchase of cloths from the Europeans showed how the African traders used canny mercantile skills to get the exact trade goods they desired:

> at one moment they like this new fashion, at another moment
> that; and whatever appeals to them at a particular time they
> must have ... This is why so many goods remain unsold and are
> sent back to Europe at great loss. (quoted in Thornton,
> 1992: 53)

This overwhelming desire for specific luxury items is of course paralleled by the insatiable need of the European and New World citizens for the plantation produce, which they believed only an efficient slave system using African chattel labour could deliver. Conspicuous consumption fuelled the slave trade at all three corners of the triangle. A flavour of the close and dynamic relationships between African traders and European merchants is evident in the correspondence which flowed between them. Ambrose Lace, a Manx merchant, had been a slave captain himself, so that when Grandy King George of Old Calabar writes to him in January 1773, it is as a commercial partner and friend, advising him on the kind of captains with whom he preferred to trade and even recommending who should be promoted from his crews to captaincy:

> So my friend marchant Lace if you send ship to my water again
> send good man all same yourself and same marchant Black. No
> send old man or man want to be grandy man, if he want to be
> grandy man let him stand home for marchant one time, no let
> him come here or all same Captain Sharp. He very good man.

> [The second mate] [a] young man and very good man. He is
> much liked by me and all my people of Calabar, so if you please
> to send him [as captain of a ship] he will make as quick a
> dispatch as any man you can send. (quoted in Wilkins, 1999: 60)

As we can see from this correspondence of equals, such African elites were, despite attempts to absolve them of blame (particularly by Afrocentric historians), 'neither passive actors nor peoples innocent of the market economy and were able to deal with Europeans on the basis of equality' (Klein, 1999: 111). As recent scholarship by Lillian Ashcraft-Eason has revealed, slave traders were not only male. She relates how the eighteenth-century merchant Fenda Lawrence was involved in the Senegambian slave trade and she was not alone as by 1749 women owned 'nine out of thirteen of the commercial properties on Goree island' (Ashcraft-Eason, 2000: 209) the notorious slave embarkation point. Slave trading was often conducted with as little general moral censure by Africans as by Europeans. The commerce of all these Africans contributed to the enforced exile of over eleven million of their fellow human beings, an aspect of the slave trade which is all too easily forgotten in the folklore and history of the black Atlantic. In the New World, while folklore developed about events in Africa and how their ancestors had been spirited away, it almost universally downplayed the active role of African merchants and elites in their enslavement. The folktales foreground the duping of naive Africans unwittingly led to their fate by their desire for cloth and trinkets. Robert Pinckney from Wilmington Island, Georgia, interviewed in the 1930s spins a typical yarn:

> Dey say duh wite mens git um tuh come on ship an dey fool um
> wid all kine uh pretty tings. Den dey lock um in duh hatch an
> wen dey git out dey way out on duh open sea. (Georgia Writers'
> Project, 1986: 105)

William D. Piersen has discussed this body of folklore in his seminal text *Black Legacy: America's Hidden Heritage* (1993), commenting incisively that such tales are allegorical and portray how 'an ill-advised greed for the imported luxuries of Atlantic commerce had lured many an African into foolishly becoming part of a monstrous trade' (Piersen, 1993: 42). This 'monstrous trade', though, has no visible African traders as the folktales airbrush them out in the same way much nineteenth- and early twentieth-century European history had elided the involvement of British, French and Dutch merchants in their side of the trade. The goods themselves are here described as worthless baubles when the actual trade often involved goods of great value to the African merchants and elites. The white men in such folktales are apparently engaged in a one-way traffic which crucially absolves Africans of all responsibility for the enslavement and subsequent middle-passage nightmare of their fellow Africans. These folktales might highlight an allegorical truth, but if taken too literally they obscure facts about the African diaspora that are crucial to our understanding of it as a function not only of European power but also of the hegemony of numerous slave-trading African cultures, mulatto traders and elites on the African-Atlantic seaboard. Basil Davidson describes how 'chiefs and henchmen generally made as good a thing out of the slave trade as their European partners: better indeed, for they had little risk in the enterprise whilst slaving captains wagered their own lives on every voyage' (Davidson, 1968: 145). Despite such qualifications, a proper reckoning of the power of such elites in their trading with the slave captains should not blind us to the voracious demand for profit of the European captains and merchants which ensured the horrendous conditions endured by the enslaved during their transatlantic transportation.

Reading against the grain of the journals and letters penned by these sea captains and ships' officers reveals much about the active involvement of the African captives in attempts to shape their own destinies, as well as the cost to the European slavers of enslaving their fellow men. It is through these half-hidden voices that a less acculturated vision of the black Atlantic in the seventeenth century and beyond can be reconstructed. In such a reading, we are able to contrast the slavers' assumption of sturdy mercantilism with the actual bloody exploitation and their apparent husbandly concern for wives thousands of miles away with a simultaneously pornographic voyeurism and sometimes literally adulterous rape. Virtually any passage of John Newton's journal, for example, illustrates the everyday mercantile nature of the trade which slavers highlighted in their writings. A portion from Wednesday, 9 January 1750 will suffice:

> This day buried a fine woman slave. No. 11, having been ailing some time, but never thought her in danger till within these 2 days; she was taken with a lethargick disorder, which they seldom recover from. Scraped the rooms, then smoked the ship with tar, tobacco and brimstone for 2 hrs, afterwards washed with vinegar. Had some more rice brought off, to which with what came yesterday, amounts to about 1600lb, and some fowls etc. Canoo brought off a lot of water. (Newton, 1962: 29)

Here the woman slave, as with all of Newton's cargo, is made anonymous by being alloted a number, and her death is merely the prelude to Newton securing his profit by making the ship more hygenic. She is almost instantly forgotten as the details of his efforts to secure enough food and water for the imminent voyage are described. His journal is the prelude to the ledger he will compose on his return to account for his voyage to the merchants who have sent him. Such a profit-and-loss account assesses the losses of the black cargo almost inextricably with the gains and losses of provisions. Hortense Spillers summarizes the trade and its denial of the humanity of the people it exchanged for goods most appositely, describing how the 'cultural subject is concealed beneath the mighty debris of the itemized account' (Spillers, 1994: 461). Spillers is correct to foreground the horrific rationality which reduces human beings to economic units; however, throughout the history of the slave trade, African captives constantly burst through the anonymous ledger figures to exhibit their individual and communal resistance to their oppression. Such rebellions against the slave power are crucial to an understanding of the agency of Africans in the middle passage, and I will discuss them at length later in this study; however, resistance was not always so active, and Newton's journal includes instances of slaves who denied their labour power through a melancholy refusal to live as slaves. Such 'fixed melancholy' is faithfully recorded in his journal when, on 13 June 1751, Newton 'buried a woman slave (No. 47). Know not what to say she died of for she has not been properly alive since she came on board' (Newton, 1962: 56). The itemized account denies the humanity of the slave, but their agency (albeit passive) often expresses itself even in the slavers' accounts.

Newton emphasizes incessantly his control over the shape and substance of his slave cargo. For instance, he relates how he often refuses to buy 'long-breasted' female slaves – for example, from 'Yellow Will' (*ibid*.: 32) – but as his gaze voyeuristically fixes on them, his mind returns to his wife left behind in Britain. Such a contrast between 'here and there, home and abroad' is typical of many a slave captain's journals and letters, which, in Cleo McNelly's apt phrase, promote a binaristic comparison between 'the white woman at home and her polar opposite the black woman abroad' (McNelly, 1975: 9–10). A letter written at the time of this trading up the west coast of Africa illuminates Newton's sense of alienation from his surroundings and reveals the workings of race and gender in mid-eighteenth-century slaving encounters:

> No one who has not experienced it like me can conceive the contrast between my present situation, distracted with the noise of slaves and traders, suffocated with heat, and almost chop-fallen with perpetual talking: and the sweet agreeable evenings I have passed in your company. (Newton, 1962: 29)

The 'sweet agreeable evenings' are, of course, purchased at the expense of his valuable human cargo. In trying to convey the intolerable conditions on board, Newton reaches for an image to describe the noise. He portrays himself as 'almost chop-fallen with perpetual talking'. This image transmutes the primary experience aboard the slaver from being oppressive to the black cargo to disturbing the senses of the white captain. He is unable to control the babble of his cargo or the traders and posits himself as lacking the accustomed power he can readily access in his own parlour – the power to control the speech of himself and others (especially his wife). His powerlessness is, however, a chimera and a figment of his overwrought imagination. In reaching for the image of being 'chop-fallen', he transmutes himself into being enslaved by his responsibilities, when the reality is that by enslaving others, his profession guarantees the comfortable and sedentary life he enjoys at home with his wife. Here, race and gender issues are seen to feed off each other: Newton guarantees his hegemony over his wife in England by his trading in black bodies abroad. His narrative is quintessentially imperial, in the sense that Carol

McNelly discussed and Richard Dyer (summarizing and extending her argument) put most appositely:

> The geographical structure of imperial narrative confirms (a)
> binarism ... the white woman as the locus of true whiteness,
> white men in struggle, yearning for home and whiteness, facing
> the dangers and allures of darkness. This naturalises white
> gender difference not so much in givens of the body but in the
> psychic structures produced in the imperial encounter with the
> world. (Dyer, 1997: 36)

Newton is empowered by his adventures abroad which entrench his position as master of his ship and human cargo, yet his locus is always towards home and a wife who is, paradoxically, made more central by his travelling. Their whiteness binds them, but crucially now in opposition to a blackness that surrounds him on the ship. This 'imperial encounter' is emphasized in Newton's journal by his use of a language of indulgence created through imperial goods. Thus, the 'sweet agreeable evenings' are purchased by the exchange of the black cargo for the sugar traded from the Caribbean. At home, this will assuage the bitterness of his tea and coffee, which makes the evenings, literally as well as metaphorically, sweetened by his participation in the triangular trade. And his wife is not absolved either, for as Robin Blackburn expresses it, by buying goods like sugar, 'her action not only expresses but makes possible a global structure of imperialist politics and labour relations which racialize consumption as well as production' (Blackburn, 1998: 16). Her privileged whiteness is confirmed by her consumption of goods traded for black bodies. Such goods have now crucially intervened as markers of her privilege in an imperial polity. The bodies traded for them are crucial too, as Dyer contends, helping to construct and nuance the intricacies of her relationship with her husband. Newton and other imperial pioneers yearn for home – a kind of nostalgia for a Britain frozen in time on the date of their departure – and their letters to wives are a testament to this; however, their trading in human bodies transforms that home into a different kind of place – one tainted by a slave system which will begin to *modernize* it beyond their wildest dreams.

In an ironic refiguring of his relationship to his wife, Newton relates in a sanctimonious and self-serving letter to her how his fellow sea captains accuse him of being 'a slave to one woman' because of his reluctance to lie with (rape) African women in his cargo (Newton, 1962: 43). Of course, it is only in the language of courtly love that he could remotely be described as enslaved, because in the reality of trading up and down the African coast he enslaves freely and is a slave to nobody.

In a letter written by James Irving over thirty years later, there is an even more specific reference to the stifling experience of being on board a slaver and how it contrasts to domestic bliss a continent away. Working as a surgeon on board the *Jane* just off Tobago, Irving closes his 2 December 1786 letter to his wife with the following: 'I'll desist as our black cattle are intolerably noisy and

I'm almost melted in the midst of five or six hundred of them' (Irving, 1995: 113). This image of being 'melted' is again an attempt to describe the unfamiliar experience to those waiting at home. But it betrays more information: Irving's description reveals his proximity to the 'black cattle' and the threat this poses to the integrity of his body, which is literally seen to be in danger of melding with his cargo. Irving is keen throughout his journals and letters to stress his distance from the Africans, who are figured as so other that they are mere 'cattle'; however, his description here betrays an anxiety that he is actually close enough to these exotic, animalistic others to become indistinguishable from them. The same–other dichotomy of the captive African portrays such racial others as a 'symbol of both what was not civilised and yet, crucially, also of what whites knew in their bones was part of their own humanity' (Dyer, 1997: 80). Irving's anxious letters home exhibit (despite himself) his vulnerability and, crucially, betray a certain lack of control in what Mary Pratt would call 'the contact zone' of the slave ship. Of course, the ship as an engine of Anglo-European commerce is a profound example of mercantile, social and racial power, but Irving's letters home exemplify a complexity in the exercise of that power that reveals its fundamental flaw – the human nature of the cargo and his close physical relationship to it.

Crucially, this 'melting' betrays a more mundane truth too: in describing the heat, Irving hopes to accentuate his own travails, but reading between his lines, we can imagine with horror the intensity of the heat endured by the 526 Africans on the *Jane* who would not land in Tobago until the end of January. There are few slave accounts of this middle-passage nightmare, but Mahommah G. Baquaqua describes the horrors from the point of view of the victim and illuminates the kind of conditions that slaves had to endure. He describes conditions when he and his fellow victims are first stowed on board:

> We were thrust into the hold of the vessel in a state of nudity, the males being crammed on one side and the females on the other; the hold was so low that we could not stand up but were obliged to crouch on the floor or sit down; day and night were the same to us, sleep being denied us from the confined position of our bodies, and we became desperate through suffering and fatigue. (Baquaqua, 1998: 27)

Baquaqua's 'suffering and fatigue' puts into perspective the travails of those above decks and make an obscenity of their letters home. While Newton's and Irving's tender letters might be free of the detail of the journals, their juxtaposition of the imagined utopian domestic space and the grim mercantile reality of the trade in human bodies make them invaluable documents for understanding the iniquities of the black Atlantic.

Irving's letters tell us more, however, as his experience in Africa was both of enslaving others and of being a slave himself. In 1789, on his first trip as a captain, his ship the *Princess Royal* is shipwrecked on the north-west coast of Africa, where he, along with his crew, is taken prisoner and enslaved by Arabs. He describes his capture in letters to his wife and those British consular officials involved in suing for his release and, in narrative form, in a journal, which has only been published in the last decade. In his letter to the Vice Consul, John Hutchison, at Mogadore in Morocco, Irving describes their capture and subsequent travails at the hands of the Mohammedans;

> O I hope you can feel for us, first suffering shipwreck, then
> seized on by a party of Arabs with outstretched arms and knives
> ready to stab us, next stripped to the skin suffering a thousand
> deaths daily, insulted, spit upon, exposed to the sun and night
> dews alternally, then travelled through parched deserts wherin
> was no water for 9 days, afterwards torn from one another and
> your poor petitioner marched to this place half dead with fatigue
> whose only hope is in God and you. (Irving, 1995: 119–20)

This description of their violent capture by those of an alien religion and culture, of continual abuse, forced marching and extreme hardship, parallels the experiences of slavery that are just becoming familiar in Britain owing to the publication of Olaudah Equiano's extremely popular *Interesting Narrative* ... (1789), which details the kidnapping of a young Ibo boy and his subsequent enslavement and transportation across the Atlantic. Equiano's remarkable narrative was published in the service of the anti-slavery movement; Irving's writing, on the other hand, emerges from his slaving experience and betrays no doubts about the peculiar institution's efficacy. His account of his capture and subsequent year-long enslavement is told without any awareness of the irony of his position: the slaver become enslaved. As a free-born Scotsman, then assimilated Englishman, Irving felt deeply about his rights to a liberty that was not appropriate to other races. Thus when, like Equiano, he is sold on by his first master, he keenly feels his status as a chattel, as an entry in his journal makes clear:

> I had been bought from Bilade at Gulimene by Sheik Brahim my
> present master, for a hundred and thirty five ducats ... Had I
> been master of the Indies I would most cheerfully have parted
> with them for liberty, a priviledge so dear to Englishmen.
> (Irving, 1995: 96)

A close reading of Irving's letters to British consular officials reveals his commitment to the conception of racial slavery. In his crew he had three Portuguese free-black sailors for whom his solicitation was not as active as for the whites. A letter of 25 June 1790 describes his difficulty in providing money to free all of his 'poor people': 'it would be dishonest in me to say I will redeem them as I have not the sum, but if your goodness extends itself towards them, *the whites particularly*, I am almost certain restitution will be quickly made (*ibid.*: 121; my emphasis). As master of the ship, Irving has just as much responsibility to the blacks in his crew as the whites, but his partiality to his ordinary white crew members betrays a commitment to a racism that under-pinned the working of the transatlantic slave system. Irving's almost constitutional racism is expressed elsewhere in his writings by his horror at the use of black 'Mahometan' slave-drivers to work his crew members (*ibid.*: 93). The harshness of this treatment resembles numerous New World accounts of cruelty on the plantations, but Irving betrays no empathy with the enslaved blacks following his own similar experience; he employs no comparisons, because he is so intent on stressing the indignity of whites being subject to blacks:

> Their master Prince Muley Abdrachman, most certainly intends to free them from their distress by being their murderer. They say that when they are struggling under their burdens and exerting their utmost strength to accomplish their tasks, that he beats them most unmercifully and stands by till his negroes beat them with sticks ... they must work if they must die under their load. They also say that they scarcely obtain provision enough to sustain life. (*ibid.*: 126)

Irving and his men's experience mirrors that of the Africans they were on their way to enslave: deprived of sufficient food – sipping on the 'same kind of mush' day after day (*ibid.*: 90) – they are forced to lie on 'the hard earth and only drink from the cistern' (*ibid.*: 97). Ironically, his own experience of slave voyages increases Irving's angst, as he recognizes that some of the treatment meted out to him is usually reserved for slaves:

> My beard was by this time very long and troublesome; the person who we met three days ago procured me a pair of scissors, although unasked for, and desired me to use them on it. That action as it so much resembled the practice followed by the slave traders gave us much trouble. (*ibid.*: 92)

As Suzanne Schwarz relates, Irving had been a surgeon on at least five slave voyages before this first captaincy and would have been closely involved in the inspection and grooming of the slaves at embarkation in Africa and before disembarkation in the New World. This would have made him keenly aware of the compromising nature of hygiene in the slave economy – cleanliness is not for the good of the slave but to ensure a good price from the buyer. Note also here the way Irving distances himself from any involvement in such practices by talking of slave traders in general, as though he had nothing to do with them. His use of the passive here betrays a discomfort with his dual position as slave and slaver which only rarely reveals itself in his narrative as a whole. Mainly, the journal and letters portray his slavery in the classic terms of a Barbary captivity narrative which describes a binary division between 'Western civilization and African barbarity', followed by a final successful redemption which illustrates the overcoming of 'barbarous circumstances' (Baepler, 1999: 33). Significantly, Irving describes himself as a 'slave to a savage race' (Irving, 1995: 94). Thus, he is able to treat others like slaves despite his own awful experiences precisely because he does not regard Africans as equal human beings but as different and savagely other. In the useful jargon of critical white studies, Irving has a 'property in his whiteness' which allows him privileges in the transatlantic economy which are denied to African captives, who are merely property. In such a schema, which seems to be reinforced by the vagaries of Irving's adventurous, if mainly impecunious, life, the institution of 'slavery provided propertyless whites with a property in their whiteness', and this 'whiteness as property was the critical core of a system that reaffirmed the hierarchical relations between white and Black' (Harris, 1998: 118).

His enslavement obviously shakes Irving's belief in his superiority, exemplified by his apology to the Consul for his first letter, which he describes as a 'shameful scrawl done with a reed' (Irving, 1995: 101). His debarring from sophisticated writing tools betokens his enslaved position, but is only ever seen as a temporary withdrawal from civilized life. As Suzanne Schwarz concludes: 'his enslavement resulted from chance circumstances, not from the sophisticated economic system of the slave trade' (Schwarz, 1995: 68).

That system was one he would return to only a little over a month after his return home to his wife in Liverpool. He had written to his wife at the end of his ordeal 'that my life through sickness during my slavey had well nigh fallen a prey to it' (Irving, 1995: 137), but it was not his slavery which was to kill him but his slaving. He died aged 32 in 1791 during his very first voyage back in the slave trade on the *Ellen*. His captivity and the costs he had incurred to secure his redemption meant he felt he had no choice but to continue in the trade. Far from opening his eyes to the inappropriateness of trading in 'black cattle', his experiences as a slave merely buttressed a belief in his superiority over the heathen other. Again, it is only by reading between the lines that we sense any anxiety in his position. For his letters and journal usually emphasize what Winthrop Jordan has called European conceptions of the *'savagery'* of the African which 'were major components in that sense of *difference* which provided the mental margin absolutely requisite for placing the European on the deck of the slave ship and the Negro in the hold' (Jordan, 1969: 97; emphasis in original). Like many other Europeans, Irving could only recognize 'the humanity of those who had something to sell – of the African merchant or monarch, not of the African captive' (Blackburn, 1998: 16). Irving's explicit and implicit espousal of these hegemonic beliefs makes his writings crucial to a nuanced understanding of the slave trade and the racial beliefs which underpinned it. Intriguingly, too, Irving's unusual and atypical nautical career gives us a unique insight into the motives and justifications for slaving at the height of the transatlantic trade, highlighting the primacy of racial difference without abrogating the important role played by Africans as both slavers and traders. That Irving's own white body is traded is shocking to Irving and his contemporaries; his own trade in black bodies, by contrast, is so commonplace and unexceptional as to be hardly worthy of critical commentary.

Another valuable source for perspectives on the black Atlantic can be found in documents prepared to aid slavery's abolition. James Arnold, a surgeon on the brig *Ruby*, gave testimony to the Parliamentary Committee on the Abolition of the Trade in 1789, detailing the abuse regularly dispensed by the captains and crew of the slavers. Arnold relates how the captain took advantage of his omnipotent position: 'It was his general practice on receipt of a woman slave – especially a young one – to send for her to come to his cabin so that he might lie with her. Sometimes they would refuse to comply with his desires and would be severely beaten by him and sent below' (quoted in Dow, 1927: 191).

Within this horrific world of rape, physical abuse, sickness and death, characterized by those engaged in the trade as commonplace (if rather dirty) trading, Africans are revealed not just as victims but as engaged in attempts to frame their own destiny. Arnold relates how a conspiracy of slaves on the *Ruby* nearly succeeds because of an impressive show of solidarity, which the final slave to be captured revealed: 'The third man told the trader that he would sooner die than surrender as he had entered into an oath which they call *sangaree* (an oath to stick to each other and made by sucking a few drops of another's blood)' (*ibid.*: 193).

Such solidarity shows the workings of an active community shipboard despite the oppressive conditions of their transportation. This community does not only reveal itself in the extreme condition of violent revolt but most especially in cultural acts such as singing and dancing. Slave captains would encourage dancing to ensure exercise was taken and would put up with singing if the words to the songs were not seditious. The active and communal nature of such African–American musical performance is best described through the term 'musicking' (Small, 1987: 69). An example of such musicking is related by Thomas Philips, who describes how the crew of the *Hannibal*, on its 1693 voyage, provided an apparently Celtic accompaniment to the Africans' dancing:

> We often at sea, in the evenings, would let the slaves come up
> into the sun to air themselves, and make them jump and dance
> for an hour or two to our bagpipes, harp and fiddle, by which
> endeavours to preserve them in health; but notwithstanding all
> our endeavours, 'twas my hard fortune to have great sickness
> and mortality among them. (*ibid.*: 77)

Dena Epstein uses this account to demonstrate have how Africans did not have to wait until they landed in the New World to be exposed to European musical forms but were involved in syncretic musicking mid-Atlantic. Hybrid Afro-European forms were a feature of the middle passage as well as of later enslaved communities, exemplifying how Afro-Celtic developments in a culturally liberal world music scene of the late twentieth century have a far from innocent genesis. Forced acculturation would reach its apotheosis once the Africans arrived in the New World, where they would be 'seasoned' (forcibly acclimatized to slave conditions); but even shipboard slaves were being prepared for a different sound world. Back on the *Ruby*, Arnold reports on resistance to such acculturation:

> the women were driven in one among another all the while

singing or saying words that had been taught them: – 'Messe, messe, mackarinda,' that is: – 'Good living or messing well among white men,' thereby praising us for letting them live so well. But there was another time when the women were sitting by themselves, below, when I heard them singing other words and then always in tears. Their songs then always told the story of their lives and grief at leaving their friends and country. (*ibid.*: 195)

Here is an early instance of masking in black Atlantic culture, as the women sing the song in praise of the white men to gain a space later, when they think they are unobserved, to sing songs that help them to cope with their losses and survive the middle passage. Memories of their former home provide a means of surviving an inexplicable and horrendous present and communal singing helps to assuage their individual sorrows. On 16 June 1751 Newton's journal reveals a retention from the slaves' African home with potentially even more power:

In the afternoon we were alarmed with a report that some of the men slaves had found means to poyson the water in the scuttle casks on deck, but upon enquiry found they had only conveyed some of their country fetishes, as they call them or talismans into one of them which they had the credulity to suppose must inevitably kill all who drank of it. But if it please God they make no worse attempts than to charm us to death, they will not much harm us, but it shews their intentions are not wanting ...
(Newton, 1962: 56)

The fetish, like the oath of *sangaree* mentioned earlier, acts as a significant intervention of African cosmology within the Anglo-European frame of Newton's journal. In Gilroy's terms this attempt to forestall Western rationality could be interpreted as part of a 'counter-culture of modernity'. The Africans attempt to overcome technological superiority (the Europeans have guns and navigational control of the ship) by the use of resources from their African past. Ironically, Newton ascribes its failure to God's providence (so much for rational Western man). Hardly passive victims, then, the African slaves are using all means possible to subvert the power of their European enslavers.

The regime on board most slave ships was designed to prevent such revolutionary actions, prioritizing routine to such an extent that the descriptions of its application often seem to prefigure a fully industrialized environment. Theophilus Conneau's description of the 1827 voyage on the *Fortuna*, twenty years after the abolition of slavery in Britain and America, includes a description of the organization of a mealtime which was conducted with military precision: 'At a signal given they all dip their hands and in rotation take out a handful, a sailor watching their movements and the punctuality of their regular turns' (Conneau, 1976: 82). The mealtime is followed by a communal washing under the supervision of crew members armed with whips, again organized to minimize the slaves' autonomy. This dehumanizing and deindividualizing process is prefigured in the very stowing of slaves aboard ship. Their positioning in the hold is designed to accommodate maximum numbers. Conneau again gives us the most precise description of this process of stowage:

> Those on the starboard side face forward and in one another's lap, vulgarly called spoon fashion. On the port side they are stowed with face aft; this position is considered preferable for the full pulsation of the heart. The tallest are selected for the greatest breadth of the vessel, while the short size and youngsters are stowed in the fore part of the ship ... This discipline of stowing them is of the greatest importance on board slavers; otherwise every Negro would accommodate himself with all the comfortability of a cabin passenger. (*ibid*.: 84)

Like Newton and Irving before him, Conneau's apparently straightforward description reveals much by his choice of language. His hyperbolic and laughably ironic assertion that Africans chained on board a slaver might arrange themselves as though free men and women if not forced into their cramped position highlights, by its juxtaposition of slave and free travel, the horrors of the trade. His narrative as a whole does more than this, though. With its descriptions of African savagery and paganism, it recalls a whole history of pro-slave thought and imagery which sought to justify slavery and occlude the horrors of the middle passage by imagining a trade that was beneficient to the benighted African transported from the 'Dark Continent' to the enlightened Christian New World. In 1592, in a written disposition, the Spanish official Francisco de Auncibay states:

> The negroes are not harmed because it is very helpful to these wretches to save them from Guinea's fire and tyranny and barbarism and brutality, where without law or God, they live like savage beasts. Brought to a healthier land they should be very content, the more so as they will be kept and live in good order and religion from which they will derive many temporal and, which I value most, spiritual advantages. (Quoted in Blackburn, 1998: 152)

Apart from spiritual advantages, slaves in this narrative were also saved from a far worse African slavery. As a report on the Antigua slave conspiracy of 1736 elucidated: 'their condition in our Colonies, is a State of perfect Freedom, compared to the native Slavery of their own Country' (quoted in Gaspar, 1993: 316). Probably the most pernicious of the images associated with this view of the benign nature of the slave trade was Thomas Stothard's 1793 engraving of *The Voyage of the Sable Venus from Angola to the West*

Figure 2   Thomas Stothard, *The Voyage of the Sable Venus from Angola to the West Indies* (1793).

Indies (Figure 2), which appeared in Bryan Edwards's *History Civil and Commercial of the British Colonies in the West Indies*. This engraving depicted the middle passage as a glorious procession across the Atlantic of a near-naked black figure surrounded by white cherubs and cavorting sea monsters. Venus steers two dolphins, who propel her scallop-shell vessel over a placid ocean, her bound feet and collared neck the only manifestations of her enslaved status. The sea god Triton accompanies her carrying a British ensign, revealing the imperial manifestations of this image. Overall, the engraving exudes luxury and ease, emphasizing what Marcus Wood calls a 'late Baroque extravaganza' (Wood, 2000: 21) which is emblematic of pro-slave discourse in the late eighteenth century.

Twenty-first-century consumers of the piece should not be too shocked by such wilful distortion, however, as the image of the Sable Venus is more representative of the consequences of the slave trade than of its reality. Its portrayal of luxurious ease is a projection of the surplus value attendant on this black body. This will ensure a more comfortable life in Europe and America, with the guarantee of an endless supply of free labour which will eventually reproduce itself at no extra cost. As Robin Blackburn asserts, 'captive Africans and their descendants paid with their blood and sweat for the phenomenal expansion of human possibilities in the Atlantic world' (Blackburn, 1998: 23). There is, of course, none of the blood and sweat in this image, only the enhanced possibilities that slavery opened up for Europeans. The solicitous care afforded the Sable Venus is not for who she is but for what she represents: the African labour, 'the strength and sinews of this Western World' (Fryer, 1984: 16) which will produce consumer plantation products in the New World that are the motor for capitalist development in the metropolis; for, as merchants like Joshua Gee, writing in 1729, understood, 'all this great increase of our Treasure proceeds chiefly from the labour of Negroes in the Plantations' (quoted in *ibid.*: 17). Cedric Robinson has asserted that 'the development of the capitalist world system depended on labour its metropolis could not reproduce' (Robinson, 1983: 162); its replacement by slave labour allowed the phenomenal expansion of trade that gives images such as this their potency. The preponderance of white cherubs cosseting the Sable Venus betrays the importance of her labour (and procreative) power to the development of Western capitalism, a system within which she is as disposable as the products her labour power will produce. Robert Young describes this crucial conjunction of goods and bodies:

> For it is clear that the forms of sexual exchange brought about
> by colonialism were themselves both mirrors and consequences
> of the modes of economic exchange that constituted the basis of
> colonial relations; the extended exchange of property which
> began with small trading posts and the visiting slave ships
> originated indeed as much as an exchange of bodies as of goods,
> or rather of bodies as goods. (Young, 1995: 181)

While the image of the *Sable Venus* contains no goods as such, its opulence points to the consequences of a conspicuous consumption developed directly from the riches of stolen labour. Of course, the Venus herself is the paradigmatic 'body as goods', furnishing both surplus labour value and surplus libidinal value. Marcus Wood emphasizes the importance of the latter signifier, describing the engraving 'as a version of the Birth of Venus', where 'slave owners and traders ... are ironically portrayed as her powerless victims' (Wood, 2000: 20). This hyperbolic distortion that seeks to erase the actual rape of slave women on the ships and in plantation society and portray relations between black and white as typically consensual illustrates an

Achilles' heel in pro-slavery propaganda: sex. If the slaves are mere 'black cattle', then why are the women so wantonly desired by white captains and crew? In the engraving, the Sable Venus wears a covering undergarment, yet the framing shell acts as simulacrum of her opened sex, while the whale blowing water in the background stands in for the exploding phallus of the viewer. The gaudy excess of exposed flesh in a joyful libidinous scene is, of course, in stark contrast to the actual middle-passage reality of black flesh exposed to rape and excessive cruelty, where 'flesh [is the] primary narrative ... we mean its seared, divided reality, riveted to the ships hold, fallen or escaped overboard' (Spillers, 1994: 452). In Stothard's image, flesh is the 'primary narrative' too, a fantastic cornucopia of utopian sexual possibility which, as Edwards himself in his accompanying text outlines, is exhibited through a system of concubinage in plantation society.

Pro-slavery propaganda can only hint at the libidinal possibilities of miscegenation, but there is no doubt about the potency of such images to consumers during this period as well as to a variety of Enlightenment thinkers. For instance, the slave-owner, founding father and eventual President of the United States, Thomas Jefferson, illuminates the sexual potency of the image of the dark Venus figure in a reverie contained in his 'Notes on a Tour of English Gardens', in which he describes 'a small, dark, deep hollow with recesses of stone in the banks on every side. In one of these is a Venus *pudique* turned half round as if inviting you into her recess' (quoted in Jordan, 1969: 463). As Winthrop Jordan points out, this meditation appears 'in an otherwise matter-of-fact account' of a visit to Lord Westcot's Hagley estate in 1786 (*ibid.*: 463). These racialized Venus figures are both inviting and threatening to such pro-slavery white men, combining the allure of illicit sexual intrigue with their fear of the racial other. Describing the attraction of certain desirable, stereotypically black qualities, Richard Dyer sheds light on the power of such figures which 'are by no means intensely despised, they were intensely desired as well' (Dyer, 1997: 80). In the Stothard engraving, the fear is neutralized almost entirely through the foregrounding of white desire, exemplified by the white entourage which intentionally undermines her threat (even domesticates it – the image is consciously reminiscent of a lady's dressing room where servants pander to her every whim). Jefferson's Venus, however, inviting him into her 'dark, deep hollow' more appositely encapsulates the fear of being swallowed by black womanhood, while retaining, in his sensual description of her 'turned half round' invitation, the intensity of the desire.

Such a complex interracial libidinal economy illustrates the ambivalence of white desire under the controlling power of a masculinist white gaze. Richard Dyer, following Sander Gilman, describes how the 'projection of sexuality on to dark races was a means for whites to represent yet dissociate themselves from their own desires' (*ibid.*: 28). The representation and denial of desire makes such encounters fraught with an anxiety, which seems simultaneously to undermine and intensify the erotic charge they engender for the imperial male subject. Of course, such a distorted representation of black bodies makes it increasingly difficult for those bombarded with these images to acknowledge the humanity underneath the stereotypes. Such representation, then, engenders a denial of status to those subjected to it and means the majority culture too often encounters the world blinded to its own misrepresentation. Or, as Susan Gubar succinctly puts it, 'one of the predicaments of white culture has resided in its blindness about its dependency on represented (and thus effaced) black bodies' (Gubar, 1997: 40). Both Jefferson's and Stothard's version of Venus is representative of their anxiety about the centrality of black women in a transatlantic economy (both monetary and libidinal) where this reality is constantly elided.

Robert Young describes the ode that accompanies Stothard's image as an 'early articulation of the sexual economy of desire in the fantasies of race' (Young, 1995: 153), a description which holds for the engraving too. I would, however, emphasize the economic as the most crucial element for understanding the Stothard engraving. While the Sable Venus is portrayed as an extreme object of desire, her transatlantic birth was as much to do with the mundane production of extreme surplus value as it was with the development of a new sexual economy. Young foregrounds this by describing how, in Bryan Edwards' text, the description of the Sable Venus is followed by an inventory of the number of Africans transported across the Atlantic, showing how 'the cultural construction of race has always been fuelled by the corrupt conjunction of such hybridized sexual and economic discourses' (*ibid.*: 158). Joseph Roach also speaks to this reality, describing how images of Africans mediate between sexual and cultural capital for a European public engaged in a kind of cannibalistic conspicuous consumption:

> Africans often appear in representation as infantilized,
> feminized objects of domestic luxury and consumption. Here,
> like [white] women their labor is effaced even as their value as
> possessions is performed ... the European incorporation of
> Africa and Africans may be at once acknowledged as
> conspicuous consumption and disavowed as the vital business of
> the nation. Involuntary servitude is domesticated, privatized,
> trivialized. (Roach, 1996: 127–8)

These constructions are not just created by heterosexual encounters but also by the homoerotic. For instance, one of the earliest non-stereotypical images of a black figure in the Anglo-American fine art tradition appears in John Singleton Copley's 1778 history picture *Watson and the Shark* (Figure 3), where the naked white body of Brook Watson is depicted being attacked by sharks in Havana harbour while a black man is shown in the rescuing party: their proximity and the parallels between them betoken an intimate attachment, as does the pink flesh-coloured, flowing neckchief around the black man's neck, a vibrant, horizontal phallic signifier that links him to the naked pink-tinged white figure in the water. Watson's whitish body is emphasized by his flowing blond hair, which sutures into the sperm-like foam of the sea and is contrasted to the black face of the anonymous white-gowned black man whose race is accentuated by the light sky in the background. Their contrastive appearances – naked and clothed, black and white – and yet similar body

Figure 3 John Singleton Copley, *Watson and the Shark* (1778). Ferdinand Lammot Belin Fund, Photograph © 2001 Board of Trustees, National Gallery of Art, Washington.

positions, wherein they each hold out their right hands to one another inexorably draw the two men together as central characters in the composition. In describing the use of black characters in Anglo-American fiction, Toni Morrison talks of 'the strategic use of black characters to define the goals and enhance the qualities of the white characters' (Morrison, 1993: 52–3). This finds a parallel in the Anglo-American fine art tradition, of which *Watson and the Shark* is exemplary in its strategic positioning of the African figure to enhance Adams's whiteness. In some ways, the white naked figure depends on the black figure to flesh out fully its essence, psyche and meaning. Richard Dyer describes the crucial nature of such blackness within Anglo-European representation in his seminal study *White* (1997):

> At the level of representation whites remain, for all their
> transcending superiority, dependent on non-whites for their
> sense of self, just as they are materially in so many imperial and
> post-imperial, physical and domestic labour circumstances.
> (Dyer, 1997: 24)

This material dependence on non-whites is, of course, the reason for the constant slippage which enables their presence, which, in fact, makes it crucial. Just as the Anglo-European economy is crucially dependent on African labour, so their images obtrude into representations that seek to portray or explicate that economy. Thus, whatever kind of black representation is created in the Anglo-American visual economy, it cannot escape into the realm of the ordinary and the merely *represented*. It is always, already *representative*. Kobena Mercer describes the working of such images in a comment which applies in some ways to the visual economy of late eighteenth-century Anglo-America (and indeed to many other earlier and later periods in the tradition):

> Whether it is devalorized in the signifying chain of negrophobia, or hypervalorized as a desirable attitude in negrophilia, the fetish of skin colour in the codes of racial discourse constitutes the most visible element in the articulation of what Stuart Hall calls 'the ethnic signifier'. (Mercer, 1994: 183)

The black figure in *Watson and the Shark* encapsulates neither a negrophiliac nor a negrophobic representation, but its neutrality should not blind us to the force of its representation and the importance of the figure's blackness to the ideology of the painting. Skin colour here is crucial to the way we and earlier contemporaries of Copley read his epic work. However, not all the critics agree. Despite a finely nuanced reading of this complex painting, Albert Boime disputes the centrality of the black figure, describing him as 'an exotic servant who awaits his master's next move' (Boime, 1990: 32) and 'as a decorative adjunct to the composition' (*ibid.*: 36). His importance is surely greater than such comments imply (and indeed much of Boime's critique works against such bald statements). This is especially evident in the black figure's linkage through historical circumstance to the dark beast, the shark, who, having mangled Watson's leg, is returning for the kill. The shark, as Boime reminds us, is a crucial player in the bodily economics of the black Atlantic, consuming the 'refuse' of the slave trade, the black bodies thrown overboard, both dead and alive, from slave ships. Numerous accounts relate how sharks were constant companions of the stinking ships. One nineteenth-century narrative relates how in times of fever aboard, 'the sharks followed us as if they smelt sickness' and '[we] soon began to feed corpses to the following sharks and one day hauled sixty bodies out of the hold' (Dow, 1927: 262). Surgeon Alexander Falconbridge's narrative of 1788 describes how slave suicide could also provide meat for the sharks: while he was sailing down the Bonny River one Negro 'jumped overboard and was devoured by sharks', and a Liverpool vessel lost another fifteen, who 'found means to throw themselves in the river and very few were saved; the rest fell a sacrifice to the sharks' (*ibid.*: 164).

Unusually, in *Watson and the Shark* the body under threat is not black but luminously white. Watson will be saved, because his white body, unlike so many of the black bodies consigned to the deep, is unconditionally cared for in the dangerous waters (his right to life is not compromised by his race; Watson is a resurrecting figure), emphasized by his taut nakedness – for whom the water is a savage world overcome, as the 'spectacle of the white male body suffering conveys dignity and transcendence in pain' (Dyer, 1997: 28). Like Christ, in fact. Contrapuntally, the black figure is present as a reminder of the black slaves continually sacrificed on the altar of profit in the trade for whom there is no salvation (at least not in this world). In Havana the black figure could of course be a 'free Negro'; however, the pictorial representation employs him as a symbolic stand-in for the African slaves transported across the Atlantic. This is emphasized by the rigged and semi-rigged ocean-going ships in the background, which are the machines that facilitate the massive transfer of slave labour from Old to New World; while the wooden planks on the deck are the focus of adventure for the likes of Brook Watson, all too often, the holds below represented a death scene for African captives.

The painting seeks to enhance Watson's standing by showing him overcoming dangers in foreign climes, but it cannot obscure (whether or not that is its intention) the savage trade which underpins mercantilism in the Atlantic that is highlighted by the presence of the shark and the black man in the rescuing boat. While the homoerotic charge between the naked Watson and the anonymous black man betokens the social intersections that exist between white man and black as master and slave, the presence of the shark shows the inevitable violence which supports the mercantile and libidinal economy of the black Atlantic. The black presence here crucially transforms the painting from a discourse on Watson and heroism to a meditation on the transnational ramifications of race in the second half of the eighteenth century. Toni Morrison has said:

> Explicit or implicit, the Africanist presence informs in compelling and inescapable ways the texture of American literature. It is a dark abiding presence, there for the literary imagination as both a visible and an invisible mediating force. Even, and especially, when American texts are not about Africanist presences or characters or narrative or idiom, the shadow hovers in implication, in sign, in line of demarcation. (Morrison, 1993: 46)

As we have seen in the narrative of *Watson and the Shark*, the Africanist presence is a similar 'dark abiding presence'. The painting foregrounds middle-passage meanings in a sheltered Caribbean harbour. John Singleton Copley honours his friend Brook Adams's heroism, but a shadow hovers to put this dismemberment into perspective, a black Atlantic perspective. As Joseph Roach has explained, Europeans, in order 'to perform as protagonists of gendered whiteness ... must rely on an unnamed black antagonist, who, like millions of indispensable actors in the drama of the circum-Atlantic world, remains forgotten but not gone' (Roach, 1996: 31).

There is more to this image, though: Watson's vulnerability also demonstrates the essential paradox of white power in action, for it is exposed by human frailty. Dyer illustrates this by describing how 'the exposed white male body is liable to pose the legitimacy of white male power. Why should people who look like that – so unimpressive, so like others – have so much power?' (Dyer, 1997: 146). Watson's vulnerability, emphasized by his luminescent, naked white body reminiscent of Christ at crucifixion, poses the question as to the legitimacy of his (and other white men's) power in the transatlantic economy. Based merely on pigmentation, it is a chimera, an accident of the power-play of historical forces, but one that is defended to the death (as here) against the shark's unwelcome and unusual predilection for white flesh. Furthermore, by its emphasis on white dismemberment, the painting suggests how the systematic enslavement of African peoples endangers the bodily integrity of the white enslavers and their countrymen as well as the slaves: in such a counterfactual allegorical reading, the shark could stand as well for that voracious and peculiar institution, slavery, which indiscriminately eats away at the body politic of Anglo-America. Brook Watson, Anglo-America's ambivalent mercantile representative, lives to have his 'heroism' mythologized by Copley, but *Watson and the Shark* (maybe even despite its own best endeavours) illustrates a dark counter-narrative in which Anglo-American heroism is compromised by a triangular trade that enmeshes both loyalists and patriots, Englishmen and Americans. While the black figure as 'ethnic signifier' is pivotal in unlocking the troubling transatlantic discourse at the core of the painting, so too is the shark, which underlines the middle-passage violence so many Anglo-American apologists, such as Thomas Stothard and Bryan Edwards, would later seek to hide.

Figure 4   J. M. W. Turner, *Slave Ship* (*Slavers Throwing Overboard the Dead, Dying, Typhoon Coming On*), 1840; Oil on canvas; 90.8 × 122.6 cm (35¾ × 48¼ in.) Henry Lillie Pierce Fund, 99.22. Courtesy Museum of Fine Arts, Boston. Reproduced with permission. © 2000 Museum of Fine Arts, Boston. All Rights Reserved.

If the shark emphasizes middle-passage realities in Copley's picture, J. M. W. Turner's epic *Slavers Throwing Overboard the Dead and Dying, Typhoon Coming On* (1840) (Figure 4) needs no clues to its subject matter. As Marcus Wood brilliantly describes in his *Blind Memory: Visual Representations of Slavery in England and America 1780–1865* (2000), the painting is an emotional meditation on the meaning of slavery, painted just seven years after its abolition in the British Empire and only two years after its abandonment there. Set against a blazing sunset, the painting depicts a slaver throwing overboard its dead and dying in a stormy sea. In the foreground, a chained black leg floats in the sea, while other chains and limbs, 'the flotsam and jetsam of humanity' (Honour, 1989: 162), are scattered about the wide ocean. Edouard Glissant would envisage such a scene years later, but from the perspective of the African captives: 'Then the sea, never seen from the depths of ship's hold, punctuated by drowned bodies that sowed in its depths explosive seeds of absence' (Glissant, 1989: 9). Turner painted these 'drowned bodies' in an attempt to memorialize what Glissant elsewhere describes as their 'invisible presence' (*ibid.*: 67). Positing 'Slavery as a struggle with no witness' (*ibid.*: 231), Wood describes how the painting is, in part, a response to Stothard's engraving of the *Sable Venus* (a wilful attempt at forgetting and mythologizing), showing how its benign seascape with placid dolphins is reinterpreted by Turner (who is literally *bearing* witness). For, in Turner's phantasmagorical allegory, these sea monsters feed on black flesh in the malignant ocean. Many commentators have identified the incident depicted in the work as the infamous murder of 132 slaves, thrown overboard from the *Zong* in 1781 under the captaincy of Luke Collingwood. Fearing that the shipowners would have to bear the loss if the slaves died of natural causes, Collingwood calculated that the insurers would have to foot the bill if they died in the sea. There is no doubt that Turner was influenced by this incident and its use as a heinous case study in the run-up to the World Anti-Slavery Convention in London in 1840 (Boime, 1990: 69).

The use of this incident as a leitmotif for the evils of slavery was so widespread that five years earlier a performance had been staged at the Surrey Theatre, London, of John Thomas Haines's melodrama, *My Poll and My Partner Jo*, which told of the pursuit of an illegal slaver and the captain's jettisoning of a female slave, Zanga, as a decoy to slow down his pursuers (Lhamon, 1998: 261). Though set after the abolition of legal slave trade, the events and the names of the principal Africans, Zinga and Zanga, clearly carry echoes of the infamous *Zong* case. At the same time, though, the play critiques the contemporary illegal trade. Turner's work exhibits a similar duality, which mitigates against oversimplified explanations of his work. For instance, Boime's contention that the *Zong* is the primary source for the painting had led him to conclude that

> Turner focused on an incident that had occurred in the previous century and was familiar to all. As a result his image reduced to melodrama the tragic circumstances of the *Zong* and allowed

the theme to be almost totally lost amid the artifices of pigment.
(Boime, 1990: 70)

However, the *Zong* was not the only slaver to jettison its cargo, and in the
illegal trade of the nineteenth century such incidents increased as slavers dis-
posed of the evidence of their trade when they felt endangered by British
patrols. Thus, Turner's painting, like Haines's melodrama, points not just to
eighteenth-century realities in a nostalgic gesture of rebellion against a trade
already consigned to history but also to an illegal trade which even twenty
years after the painting was first exhibited was still throwing black bodies
overboard, and requiring the full force of radical sentiment to rail against it.
Edward Manning relates how in a later 1860 voyage:

> We found five or six dead bodies which were at once hoisted to
> the deck and consigned to the deep. There was no pretence of
> religious ceremony. Just as they were naked and forlorn, they
> were tossed overboard and for a long time we could see the
> bodies floating in the wake of the ship. (quoted in Dow,
> 1927: 324)

Turner, then, cannot be accused of 'reducing to melodrama' an incident
which is only one of the sources for the painting; he is also describing the
horrors of a still extant slave trade, memorializing 'all those Africans weighted
down with ball and chain and thrown overboard whenever a slave ship was
pursued by enemy vessels and felt too weak to put up a fight' (Glissant, 1989:
66–7). It represents Turner's contribution to a general railing against slavery, a
cultural critique, just one part of a mass transatlantic movement bent on
forestalling the illegal trade and ending slavery in the Americas. The symbolic
dimensions to the work reveal that it is far from mere melodrama, and crucially it is 'the artifice of pigment' that Boime finds so distracting which is
finally revelatory. Marcus Wood describes how the waters perform 'a memorial function' (Wood, 2000: 45) as the sea becomes 'witness, executioner,
victim and tomb' (*ibid.*: 63). He then proceeds to a closely contextualized
reading of the work's multiplicities, using Ruskin's famous discussion of the
painting to reveal how it is 'an act of artistic salvage', as

> the deaths of the slaves thrown overboard are to be saved from
> their debased historico-economic context . . . Turner makes these
> deaths mean something, by bathing them in one of his most
> terrific seascapes and one of his most sublime sunsets. The gold
> of the slave trade is shifted into an ironically gorgeous light.
> (*ibid.*)

Wood's final sentence describes how the primary valency of the economic in
depictions of the slave trade is here transmuted into a symbolic light which
gilds the sky surrounding the ship. He describes how 'Turner paints guilt in the
Slave Ship', projecting 'British crime on a vast scale'. Meanwhile, the red in the

painting signifies 'blood diffused in water and in light, resurfac[ing] as a signification of the guilt, the fury and the enormous sadness of slavery' (*ibid.*: 67).
While Wood's reading of the work is exemplary and multi-layered, the
painting is, I believe, even more specific, if crude, in its economic symbolism.
The accentuated chained black bodies represent the labour power that is
exploited by the bloody slave trade, depicted here by the red colouring around
the ship which alchemizes the base metal of the chains into the gold of the
sunset. Unfree labour is the key to British prosperity, and Turner memorializes
the sacrifices made by these slaves, their contribution to British wealth and
influence and the continuing deaths of African slaves mid-Atlantic with his
explosion of red and gold. A 1788 poem on the slave trade by the American
Thomas George Street concludes with the lines, 'These *Britons* barter human
blood for gold' (quoted in Jordan, 1969: 372); Turner's painting exemplifies
this barbaric exchange of flesh and chains for currency, illuminating the
horrific realities of the mid-Atlantic. The painting reminds its British audience,
at a time of smug superiority, that though they might have abolished the trade
and the institution, they are still guilty of a crime against humanity. Paul
Gilroy illustrates the contemporary political valencies of the picture,
describing how 'The picture deploys the imagery of wrathful nature and of
dying slaves as powerful means to highlight the degenerate and irrational
nature of English civil society as it entered the 1840s (Gilroy, 1993b: 81).

Only a few years after this emotionally charged explosion of colour, Karl
Marx described the workings of an increasingly voracious capitalist machine:
'Capital is dead labour which, vampire-like, lives only by sucking living labour
and lives the more, the more it sucks' (Marx, 1990: 342). Such language
accurately describes a painting in which black bodies bought as labouring
machines are consumed by fantastical sea monsters symbolically enacting the
cannibalistic consumption that feeds the whole exploitative stystem. As
Marina Warner comments, Turner 'gives so many different strokes and colours to the single metaphor of consuming, being consumed, devouring and
being devoured' that the whole painting is a cannibalistic phantasmagoria. As
she goes on to say, though, foregrounding the economic: 'consuming retains its
mercantile meaning too' (Warner, 1994: 67). For the economic system of
chattel slavery was industrial capitalism's precursor and, according to many
commentators (especially Marxist historians such as Eric Williams and C. L.
R. James), the engine which helped to create it. The biographies of slave
captains and traders in the north-west of England attest to the link between
wealth earned from the slave trade and a push toward industrialization. The
slave captain and later partner in voyages from Lancaster and Liverpool,
Thomas Hinde, used the surplus capital amassed from his and his sons' successes in the African trade to develop a worsted mill in the village of Dol-
phinholme in 1795, while Thomas Hodgson had earlier invested the profits
from his Liverpool slave trading in the Low Mill at Caton in 1784 (Elder,
1992: 188). Such individual successes were repeated throughout the country
by those directly and indirectly involved in slavery's ill-gotten gains. As Robin
Blackburn succinctly puts it: 'the pace of capitalist advance in Britain was
decisively advanced by its success in creating a regime of extended private

accumulation battening upon the super-exploitation of slaves in the Americas' (Blackburn, 1998: 572).

Thus, Boime is right to detail the close temporal links between Turner's painting and the industrial landscapes he is just beginning to paint. While *The Slave Ship* does 'symbolize the passing of an outmoded institution' (Boime, 1990: 69), it is also much more embroiled in Britain's progress to industrialization than Boime's reading of it as antediluvian and sentimental gives it credit for. The steam of *Rain, Steam and Speed* is created in part by the fiery maelstrom of his earlier *Slave Ship*.

Turner's allegorical depiction of the creation of modern industrial life from the fruits of transported African labour had had a significant influence on some of the most dynamic imaginary work on the middle passage of the late twentieth century, which continues to use tropes and images he helped to inscribe as quintessential elements of the depiction of the slave body mid-Atlantic. These artists from the African diaspora, however, inhabit these images with their own signification which dynamically intervenes in the discourse on the black Atlantic. The African-born British resident Lubaina Himid is probably the most arresting of these artists, who, in a series of studies and large canvases through the early 1990s, developed a body of work that crucially intervened to create an African diasporan take on the middle passage. As she says, 'I have taken when and what and where it has seemed appropriate, from whom I wished to borrow and reinterpret. There are references to Turner and Tissot, Hockney and Hodgkins, Riley and Bell, Sulter and Laurencin' (Sulter, 1992: 31). Her sequence entitled *Revenge*, and its revelatory catalogue, exhibited at the Rochdale Art Gallery in 1992 included sketches, finished works, installations and text that built into a commentary on the transatlantic slave trade. Her 'Study for a Memorial to Zong' (Himid, 1992: 10) shows a hand groping out of the blue ocean in a conscious invocation of Turner's monumental painting. The hand replaces the foregrounded chained leg in a kind of minimalist reinterpretation of Turner's cluttered canvas. This accentuates a memorial function, as the hand stands in for all the Africans lost in the transatlantic trade and comments adroitly on the insufficiency and limitations of Turner's chained leg with the signifying rows of helpless Africans it conjures up. Africans are reimagined as more than merely the flotsam and jetsam of the ocean, more than just ciphers for British guilt. The accompanying text poetically invokes the *Zong* incident and its ability to stand as a leitmotif for the economics of the middle passage:

> Water, deep water salty. Wooden boats. Cloth wrapped around
> wounds, blood soaked. Water fresh the key to life. Sails flags
> english flags spanish flags portugese flags flapping. Sails
> straining. Splashing, body after body thrown overboard. Too ill
> to ever work. Dead. From shock from beating from wounding.
> Splashing body after body thrown overboard. £30 can be
> claimed for each body. Insurance. Ill people are not worth
> wasting water on. Fresh water. Thrown overboard into the sea.
> Water salty. (*ibid.*: 11)

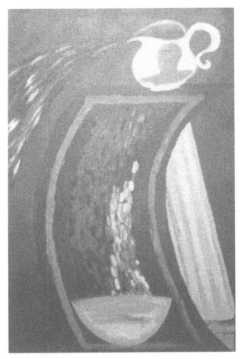

Figure 5   Lubaina Himid, *Memorial to Zong* (1991). *Revenge* series. Reproduced by permission of the artist.

Himid's more elaborate 'Memorial to Zong' (1991) (Figure 5) signifies on the imperial tradition of memorialization through its central feature, a marble plinth. Instead of a doughty hero of empire, Himid places a white jug with an African head and shoulder portrait on top of the plinth. This exemplifies the crucial white–black dichotomy in the middle passage, highlighted by the *Zong* incident's disavowal of the importance of black lives. The jug leaks water from its spout, which symbolizes the dispersal of African lives in this incident and numerous others. As Himid herself attests, 'The fountain is a memorial to the slave trade and those who died in it.' She wanted to commemorate the 'throwaway people' of the middle passage (Himid, 2001). The picture is completed by a dark cloth shaped like a sail with a bowl that collects water composed of numerous closely packed human figures. The former stands in for the countless voyages that have created the forced African diaspora, while the water flowing into the bowl represents the human cargo and its survival despite the horrors of the voyage. Himid wants to emphasize the 'waste' of lives while also celebrating the 'contribution' made by the survivors to diasporan African culture. The fountain represents the 'rejuvenating' power of water and comments ironically on its centrality in the narratives of the *Zong* voyage, where a scarcity of water supposedly led to over 100 slaves being thrown overboard. Again, the accompanying text explains the image:

Water cascading falling spouting sparkling frothing whooshing

Figure 6 Lubaina Himid, *Between the Two My Heart Is Balanced* (1991). *Revenge* series. Reproduced by permission of the artist.

> trickling spurting foaming running pouring falling pooling puddling raining filling overflowing. A fountain a monument a memorial to people for water. For water to people wasted in water. A memorial to Zong. Singing buried treasure. After the mourning comes revenge. (Himid, 1992: 13)

Thus, the memorial is not just a mourning but a call to action. Himid's work seeks to put back together the dismembered bodies of Turner's ultra-realistic portrayal of the black Atlantic and to show an African culture surviving the middle-passage nightmare. Nowhere is this more evident than in her stunning refiguring of an ocean's journeying in 'Between the Two My Heart Is Balanced' (1991) (Figure 6), which is currently on permanent display at Tate Britain. There is an irony here, as Himid had commented acerbically on how her curated exhibition of black British art (*The Thin Black Line*) at the Institute of Contemporary Arts in 1985 had been exhibited 'in the margins of the corridor and stairwell, not in its main gallery' (Mercer, 1994: 26). Now, a mere decade later, her work is prominently displayed in the most prestigious gallery space in Britain. However, it would be wrong to read into this a radical change in the traditional marginalization of black British art. Himid, herself, refuses to get carried away by her success, looking back to the 1980s as a decade marked at least by movement and interest in the issues black artists raised, in contrast to the ossification in the 1990s that has not seen a move from the margins. She asks the question: 'How is it that black artists making work about our history and the real danger of our everyday became so old fashioned, so eighties, so swept under the carpet? Why did we allow it to happen?' (Himid, 1999a: n.p.).

While her painting might be displayed in prestigious surroundings, I would contend that its setting rather decontextualizes it from its radical roots. It would be better placed in direct juxtaposition with other paintings in the collection like Francis Wheatley's 1775 *Family Group in a Landscape*, where a traditional portrait of an English elite family is given added prestige by the presence of a black slave boy, an exotic servant to the family. Himid's painting is a direct reply to such tragic events of diasporan exploitation, and it would more readily reveal its political significance in such a context. In Stephen Deuchar's opening hang of Tate Britain in 2000 the painting was situated in 'Home and Abroad', where, as Margaret Garlake contends, it dominated the other pieces in the room by its brilliance at 'interrogat[ing] the fluid and unpredictable nature of a journey ... whereas the rest are firmly fixated, like most travellers, on their destinations, real or imagined' (Garlake, 2000: 8). This fluidity and emphasis on the routedness of certain British experience which the picture so brilliantly emphasizes is only hinted at in this description; but then this is hardly surprising, as its hanging effectively depoliticizes it, making it just one more story of the British abroad rather than a particular story of enslavement, colonialism and exploitation that has been dramatically challenged and refigured. Deuchar's new hang seeks to deliver 'bold but nuanced juxtapositions that are only made possible by abandoning the straitjacket of the chronological imperative for a thematic cross-period approach' (*ibid.*: 7). Its failure to juxtapose Himid's painting with the middle-passage history it addresses reveals the timidity of curators when it comes to narrating black British history. Himid, true to her twenty-year espousal of the centrality of politics in black women's art, had not been reluctant to empha-size the context of her piece. A decade after its first unveiling, she insists the painting is a 'call to arms and is not designed to make people guilty or mis-erable' (Himid, 2001). However, the painting does not need explication, as it wears its politics on its (native African cloth) sleeve.

In her dramatic portrayal, two African women in native dress sit in an open boat mid-ocean, an African cloth design between them, which in fact consists of a pile of maps and charts. They proceed to tear up the navigation charts and throw them overboard (Himid, 1992: 14). This utopic, calm scene depicts the survival of African culture despite the intervention of slavery and coloni-alism. The women take control mid-ocean consigning Western charts, which have been the bane of the enslaved blacks – crucially allowing Europeans to steer more accurately between African and American slave ports – to the depths of the sea. As Himid explained, 'the painting is a musing on what would happen if black women got together and started to try and destroy maps and charts – to undo what has been done' (Himid, 2001). Their counter-cultural chart seems to be the cloth which one woman holds up between them, invoking the African culture that links blacks across the ocean. As Maud Sulter contends:

> [the paintings] weave around the concept of fabric. The making
> of cloth, the creation of patterns, women's clothing and fabric,
> the existence of fabric as a form of Black women's creativity.

> Lubaina has chosen fabric to be the ground, the arena for the
> battle with imperialism. (Sulter, 1992: 24)

The work is given added poignancy by its reference to a James Tissot
etching of the same title. This sentimental Victorian work depicted a British
soldier seated in an open boat between two women (one fair and one dark),
occupying a position of patriarchal power as he decides where his romantic
interest lay. Himid mocks Tissot's vainglorious hubris and aligns its male
chauvinism with an imperial chauvinism which typified relations with Africa
both during slavery and afterwards. Her painting replaces the soldier with the
cloth, symbolically readdressing the ocean crossing in terms not of white male
power and female impotence but of the doughty survival of African women's
mores, despite forced removal. The title, then, updated by Himid, becomes
multidimensional, referring to the artist and viewer's choice between the two
stellar African women and the choice these women make between different
worlds separated by an ocean. Here, imperialism is being neutralized by a
womanist, African, oceanic alliance. Her practice is exemplary of African
diasporan artists in her use and radical reinterpretation of motifs from the
dominating white culture. As Kobena Mercer describes it, there is

> Across a whole range of cultural forms ... a powerful syncretic
> dynamic which critically appropriates elements from the master
> codes of the dominant culture and creolizes them, disarticulating
> given signs and rearticulating their symbolic meanings
> otherwise. (Mercer, 1994: 63)

As in the use of an imperial trope in 'Memorial to Zong', Himid is not
afraid to use imperial imagery against itself, to destabilize its seemingly
hegemonic meanings. This she had done earlier in the sequence in her 'Mansa
of Mali' (actually completed later, in 1992), which shows two juxtaposed
African cloths in the shape of flags, one sporting a Portuguese man of war in
its top corner picked out against a vivid blue background. The ship's 'jutting
into the canvas ... depicts invasion formally through the picture structure'
(Sulter, 1992: 24). As Sulter explains, the patterns of the African cloths 'signify
the rich culture of Africa' and its brutal dispersal by the ravaging forces of
imperialism. Again, the accompanying text highlights the message of the
painting:

> Sails straining in the wind. Flags flapping at the bow. Sea
> voyages wind currents maps navigation charts water ships gold
> tobacco sugar slaves. Invasion. Division of land. Murder. Theft.
> Guns greed gold. Sails straining in the wind. (Himid, 1992: 8)

Imperialism has its triumph over the Africans, but the cloths, representative
of a dynamic living culture, outlast its ravages. African survival throughout the
diaspora is the dynamic message of Himid's whole sequence of works from
this period. Crucially, it is not survival in a separated Afrocentric space but

one fought for in the belly of the beast of the Western fine art tradition: 'Lubaina Himid's work has developed an aesthetic vocabulary for challenging the pigeonholing that is so much part of maintaining the exclusivity of the Western canon' (Pollock, 1999: 171). Knowledge of the majority culture's praxis leads to the creation of works which can intervene and recapture space for black women's expression. In talking about her novel *Liliane*, Ntozake Shange had said its major character was 'trying to create ... a world in which the centre of the vortex is not in fact embedded in whiteness or maleness' (quoted in Read, 1996: 150). Similarly, Himid's counter-hegemonic intervention in the tradition of paintings about the middle passage emphasizes the agency of Africans and women, centralizing their role, in contradistinction to their traditional marginalization. Himid, herself, articulates this praxis best:

> With these works I want to say I know your game I know what I want to say with my medium and my tools. I want to show my truth my illusion and my prophecies and legends ... I am interested in the power that a painting, however small and seemingly domestic, can have. I engage with location; public space private space the obsession with the control of space, of land of the sea and of people. (Himid, 1992: 31)

In these paintings, Himid is engaged in the task of refiguring the way Africans are depicted in the art of the Atlantic. She moves from the salacious and everyday to the reverential and magical. Ntozake Shange had described how blacks are typically represented as 'part of the landscape' (quoted in Read, 1996: 150), and to an extent, despite its marvels, Turner's magnificent canvas consigns its black bodies to that space; Himid moves these formerly effaced black bodies centre-stage, making them crucial players in their own drama, in paintings which begin to tell a very old story in radically new ways.

Of course, Himid is not alone in reinterpreting the visual imaginary of the middle passage from a black perspective. Tom Feelings, an American artist and book illustrator, also creates arresting images that rework earlier depictions of the slave trade in his monumental sequence *The Middle Passage: White Ships, Black Cargo* (Figure 7), which appeared as a book in 1995. It narrates the human cost of the trade in a series of images which tell of the journey from Africa through a middle-passage hell to exile in the Americas. Central to his gothic imagery in his wonderful chiaroscuro drawings are the 'pale white sailing ships like huge birds of prey' (Feelings, 1995: n.p.) that are the predators of African humanity. He does not undermine African complicity in the trade, showing how African elites made money and gained hegemony through the power of the gun at the point of sale. However, it is the ghostly white apparitions that man the ships who are portrayed as literally preying on African humanity. Like Copley and Turner before him, sea scavengers are a feature of the middle passage, as the sharks circling the ships awaiting their inevitable meal are aligned with the Europeans as greedy predators. Repeatedly, though, Feelings returns to images of ships as the defining symbolic of the middle passage. This reaches its apotheosis in images where ships are literally

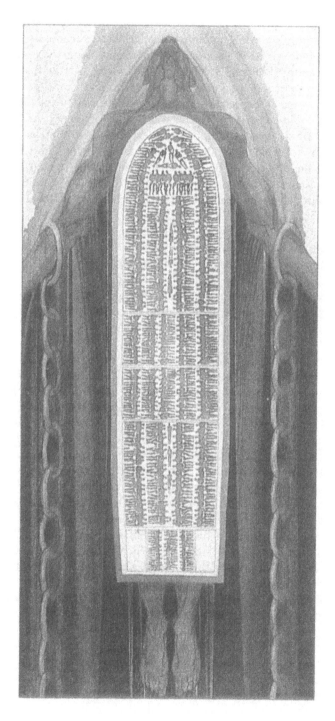

Figure 7 Tom Feelings, image from *The Middle Passage: White Ships, Black Cargo* (1995). Dial Press, NYC. Reproduced by permission of the artist.

inscribed on African bodies to symbolize the forced transportation of millions across the Atlantic. European technological advantages are stressed in such drawings, where speeding, fully rigged, multi-masted vessels are etched into the faces of screaming Africans transported across the ocean. Such drawings reflect Anglo-American pride in technological progress and the important role wealth from the slave trade played in its advance. Feelings's emphasis on African faces as literally scarred by this development of Western civilization highlights the enormous human cost of the expansion of Western capitalism and is reminiscent of the African-American poet Robert Hayden's litany of beautiful slave-ship names in his poem *Middle Passage*:

> *Jesus, Esterella, Esperanza, Mercy* ...
> Middle Passage:
> > voyage through death
> > > to life upon these shores ...
> *Desire, Adventure, Tartar, Ann* ... (Hayden, 1962a: 1501)

These multi-masted ships are traditionally portrayed as machines of awesome beauty, well suited to their beautiful nomenclature. Feelings, like Hayden before him, exposes the reality beneath their lily-white image, choosing not to depict an 'overly calm picture' but the 'anxious, diabolical nature of such an experience *where no individual remains himself*' (Glissant 1989: 108; emphasis in original). This is portrayed in part by the literal inscribing of middle-passage realities on the black bodies Feelings depicts. The ships' riggings come to inhabit the faces of those who endured the nightmare journey, haunting them, as their scarred faces reveal.

In another image, Feelings transposes a slave-ship diagram onto the naked body of a chained black man. This acts like a cross-section of the African man, whose inner workings are portrayed not as functioning organs but as the diagrammatic portrayal of the slave ship. Feelings again highlights the deeply scarred reality of the middle-passage nightmare for those in the diaspora. It infects their very bodies, is seared into their flesh. This is made more potent because the ship diagram is instantly recognizable to any historian of slavery as the Liverpool slave ship *Brooks*, which was used by abolitionists in the late eighteenth and early nineteenth centuries to dramatically render pictorially the packing of slaves on a ship. Its chronology and multiple meanings are usefully delineated in Marcus Wood's study (Wood, 2000: 16–40). He describes how it became a most effective abolitionist image, as 'the conjunction of a technical engraving with the depiction of a mass of black human flesh is a superb semiotic shock tactic' (*ibid.*: 27). Curiously, despite tracing its modern manifestations to record covers and book jackets, Wood omits Feelings's dynamic reworking of the image which renders the 'semiotic shock tactic' as a refigured image of African pain and survival in the diaspora. As Wood contends, the *Description* (1789) was such a potent image, because it seemed so accurately to reflect an imagined Enlightenment rationality about the trade which many of the participants described, even (as in the case of John Newton) after their conversion to abolitionism. Newton's description of a methodical orderliness in the packing of the slaves is described aptly by Wood as 'a display obscene in its seemliness' (*ibid.*: 23). The *Brooks* diagram is faithful to such descriptions, evading the actual jumbled reality of life below deck for a diagrammatic lie of perfect order. Joseph Roach describes how the Enlightenment had worked towards such a 'radical rationalization of space' (Roach, 1996: 54), in which death had been ordered and marginalized to the outskirts of the towns and cities. He sees the slave ship as an exemplar of such rationality, 'the triangular trade's simulacrum of hell, where each of the living dead occupied no more space than a coffin, and the daily wastage disappeared over the side to a grave unmarked except by the sea' (*ibid.*: 55).

Feelings reworks this pivotal image by comparing its ordered rationality with the chained figure on which it is imprinted. As he raises his head in a scream, this figure becomes representative of those silenced in (and by) the diagram – Feelings literally gives them a voice. The man's chains are accentuated (if anything enlarged) in juxtaposition with those Africans in the *Description*, whose chains are only hinted at. The size of the imprinted *Description* is important in Feelings's image, as its grown-man size shapes it as a coffin. This coffin does not contain the screaming man, however, showing as in Himid's work that the middle-passage horror is not wholly defining to Africans in the diaspora. Despite its potency as an abolitionist motif, the *Description* was an image that froze Africans as passive victims, beholden to white abolitionists for their freedom. Feelings's reworking of the image gives the African agency and voice, despite the chains. The image is overtly masculinist, portraying a muscled black man raging against the iniquity and inhumanity of slavery. As such, it foregrounds the losses suffered by African men and more particularly the image of 'the painful figure of the father', which 'reinvokes those memories around slavery and what slavery mean[t] in terms of the construction, deconstruction and destruction of the black family' (Young, 1995: 112). The howl of masculine rage can be compared to Himid's more studied feminist revenge, exemplifying a range of African diasporan responses to the legacy of slavery and colonialism.

Both Himid and Feelings rework the Anglo-American depiction of the Atlantic, infusing it with meaning for Africans in the diaspora. They take the stock images and remould them so that they have redolence for their communities. Their work is a literal *Revenge* on an Anglo-American culture that traditionally downplays African contributions and seeks to elide the tortured history of slavery and racism. Such cultural resistance is characterized by successful reimaginings using images, symbols and metaphors from the majority culture's tradition. As Coco Fusco explains:

> Resistance within a colonial context is rarely direct, overt or literal; rather it articulates itself through semantic reversals and through the process of infusing icons, objects and symbols with different meanings ... They are among the many ways oppressed people have developed to take their identity back. (quoted in Ugwu, 1995: 64)

Himid's and Feelings's works succeed because they conduct a dialogue with the whole tradition of the transatlantic imaginary. By questioning and reworking this Anglocentric imaginary, they successfully reimagine it. For both of them, 'opening the grave, freeing the ghosts, mourning the dead ... [is] a start in the process of anamnesis' (Verges, 1996: 64). Their painful explorations achieve for more than merely jogging their own individual and racial memories. For, crucially, they are involved in the creation of a more inclusive collective memory in which the African experience of the middle passage becomes central and determining, humanized and, most importantly, effectively remembered.

= 4 =

'UP TO THE HIGHEST POINT'

LIBERATION AND THE FLYING SYMBOLIC IN BLACK ATLANTIC CULTURE

As Caribbean people we are obsessed with Roots, when maybe we should be signifying ourselves by Wings. (John Figueroa, quoted in Nichols, 1996: 77)

Being a dancer for me was like the ultimate activity in life because to reach people with simply the force of one's body is such a grand and lovely idea. Black people were valued for our physical labor – our bodies' labor during slavery – we were valued for our bodies when they were having the infant syndrome during the '20s. We were valued for our labor during the '30s when they were breaking unions with Black labor. Our bodies, our physical presence, has been a political ploy for the last four hundred years, if you include slavery. (Ntozake Shange, quoted in Splawn, 1998: 192)

If you will have me Dance upon my Head or Caper on the top of the House, I must do it, though I break my Neck: for you are become Lord both of my feet and every part of me. (Epstein, 1977: 29)

This response from a slave to his master, reported by Thomas Tryon in 1684, reflects the extent of the control exerted by the dominant exploiting figures in transatlantic slave relations, the white overlords. The slave body here is beholden to the master's every whim, even if it leads to destruction. However, the very framing of the slave's rejoinder using the material reality and symbolic power of dance contains within it the seeds of rebellion, as the quotation from Shange demonstrates. As Jacqui Malone states, dance 'provides rich opportunities to symbolically challenge societal hierarchies by offering powers and freedoms that are impossible in ordinary life' (Malone, 1996: 1). For, the dancing slave body often exists beyond the controlling gaze of white overseers and masters, exhibiting acrobatic feats that, far from threatening bodily integrity, are intimately linked to bodily and mental health despite the rigours of forced labour. Hence, the very acrobatics figured here as enmeshed in the power politics of the racialized slave relationship are transformed in communal dancing among plantation blacks into symbolically liberational moves which invoke and glorify an African reality that gives them a toehold in a culture an ocean away. In an insightful essay, Genevieve Fabre discusses how even dances on the slave-ship voyages themselves, organized by the slave captains to exercise the 'cargo' and keep the slaves in good condition for eventual sale, could be transformed by the Africans into proto-liberational acts that helped to preserve African cultural forms despite the slavers' attempts to obliterate them (Fabre, 1999: 33–46). As Wilson Harris has discussed, such tortured forms are recalled in the contemporary limbo-dance tradition of the Caribbean (Harris, 1999: 152–66). Such a 'limbo imagination points to new horizons' (*ibid*.: 159) beyond the slave ship. Fabre summarizes the meaning of historical slave-ship performance thus:

> The slave ship performance was not simply an atavistic spectacle or a meaningless grotesque dance 'under the whip' but a creative phenomenon of importance for the newly enslaved. Haunted by memories of Africa, beset by the slave trade whose laws and economic proscriptions violate their inner beings, the dancers perform an epic drama that announces the emergence of the New World Negro. (Fabre, 1999: 42)

While this 'New World Negro' is created from the conjunction of European and African musicking, African forms are not obliterated by such syncretism, merely adapted to it. As Melville Herskovits asserts, 'dance has carried over to the New World to a greater degree than almost any other trait of African culture' (quoted in White and White, 1999: 285), and communal dancing with other Africans was vital for the retention of human dignity despite oppression and for communicating meaning between captives whose voices were muted by that very oppression.

Africans in the middle passage and in the Americas would engage particularly in dancing and musicking to use Christopher Small's apposite expression which emphasizes the dynamic quality of *making music*, which invoked what Pierre Nora might have called '*milieux de mémoire*': that is, 'real environments of memory' (Nora, 1994: 284) that enabled them to display very strong links to the African cultures from which they had only recently been snatched. Such ceremonials would conjure up ideas and ideals which predated their enslavement. Through musicking and dancing they could remember a past which the slave system, through acculturation, attempted to obliterate. Sometimes slaves went further and physically moved to reinstate the past. As Michael Mullin, following the Brazilian scholar Roger Bastide, contends:

> slave resistance was often cultural as well as political: the resistance of a people to being swallowed up by a foreign way of

life. In this case resistance may be understood as a refusal to abandon one's values and traditions as well as – at another more familiar level – singular acts ranging from quiet sabotage to organizing and fighting back. (Mullin, 1992: 2)

The combination of the cultural and political suffuses the history of revolt in the Americas, and is particularly evident in slave uprisings and conspiracies like that of 1736 in Antigua, where Coromantee rebels (from the Gold Coast) would perform remembered dances in the Akan tradition. In one example that took an especially radical turn, the leader of the putative rebellion, Court, 'staged a military "ikem" (in Akan *ekem* or *aykem* meaning "shield") dance, or "one grand Test" to ascertain how many followers he could count on' (Gaspar, 1993: 250). This elaborate ceremonial dance followed closely the pattern of the ikem dance from the Gold Coast and was performed publicly by around 2000 slaves. It proved particularly heartening for the slaves, as although it was viewed by whites, none of their masters at the time realized the ceremonial's deadly significance. We can get a flavour of the dance from an eyewitness account which describes Court's (the Prince's) duet with his Chief General:

> Then the Prince Stepping into the Area of the Semicircle, with his Chief General and taking a Cutlass in his hand moves with a Whirling motion of his Body round a Bout, but dancing and leaping up at the same time from one Horn or point of the Semicircle, quite to the other, so as distinctly to be viewed by all; and then returning to the Center of the Semicircle, with his General, makes several flourishes with the Cutlass, gently touching with it the General's Forehead; and having at the same time the Ikems (the number of which is uncertain) held between his own and the others Body. (quoted in *ibid.*: 250–1)

This energetic dance of leaps and twists, accompanied by boisterous music and witnessed by an engaged African and Creole (that is Caribbean-born slaves of African descent) audience of thousands, shows how dance provided an important radical counter-culture for the slaves that undermined the owners' lordship of their feet and other parts. These communal acts of resistance were not only performed by Africans but also by Creoles, who adapted to these African ceremonials because of their functioning as a counter-hegemonic force in the slave economy. As David Gaspar asserts, leaders of revolts 'drew heavily upon functioning resources of African tradition, which is clear evidence of the cultural resistance that was possible under slavery, under certain conditions' (*ibid.*: 256). Such challenges to the slave-owner's hegemony were a noteworthy feature of many slave cultures. For instance, the Stono rebellion of 1731 in South Carolina featured dancing displays which Mullin rightly describes as resembling 'a Caribbean rebellion of the spear' (Mullin, 1992: 43). Again, extant contemporary accounts give the flavour of a spontaneous, engaged crowd fully conversant with ceremonials and musicking that promoted autonomy from their masters and links to their African past:

> Several Negroes joyned them, they calling out Liberty marched
> on with Colours displayed, and two Drums beating, pursuing all
> the white people they met with ... They halted in a field and set
> to dancing ... thinking they were now victorious over the whole
> Province, having marched ten miles & burnt all before them.
> (quoted in *ibid*.: 43)

While their victory dance was premature, the ceremonial nature of their progress, with unfurled 'Colours' and beating martial drums, displays links to Angolan ritual and provided the rebels with a cultural context to their rebellion which united them through their shared African past.

Central to many of the slave rebellions were oath-taking rituals, which developed directly from African cultures. For instance, during Court's 1736 conspiracy, putative rebels drank liquor containing earth to demonstrate their commitment to the cause. Such oaths would often be taken with their own blood and a 'grave dram' where the earth came from 'the graves of deceased slaves' (Gaspar, 1993: 244). As Gaspar explains, such draughts were part of the Akan ceremonials of ancestor worship that enlisted the power of the dead by imbibing their grave dust. The enhanced power bequeathed to the living by the ancestors would then be an additional weapon in destroying the hated slave regime. Such practices occurred throughout the diaspora: Esteban Montejo describes their manifestation in nineteenth-century Cuba (Montejo, 1968: 26), while the ubiquity of such practices throughout the Caribbean over an extended period is confirmed by examples of oath-taking recorded in Jamaica at about the same time as Court's conspiracy. Charles Leslie observed one such ceremonial:

> They range themselves in that Spot of Ground which is
> appropriate for the Negro's Burying-place and one of them
> opens a Grave. He who acts the Priest takes a little of the Earth,
> and puts [it] into every one of their Mouths; they tell, that is any
> has been guilty [of breaking the oath], the Belly swells and
> occasions their Death. (Mullin, 1992: 67)

If the presence of the ancestors was a potent symbol of autonomy for the African slaves which enabled them to contemplate rebellion, other related beliefs also allowed the enslaved blacks to construct a utopian cosmology despite their captivity. The belief that when they died they would return to their homeland was very strong and gave friends of the deceased a potent link to Africa. In Barbados later in the eighteenth century, for instance, the burial of a first-generation African, Jenny, represented a potent symbol for the mourners of links across the ocean to their African ancestors. As the women mourners threw handfuls of earth into the graves, they chanted out

> God Bless you, Jenny, goodbye! Remember me to all friends
> t'other side of the sea, Jenny! Tell 'em me come home soon!
> Goodby, Jenny, goodby! See for send me good-tonight, Jenny!
> goodby, goodnight, Jenny, goodby! (*ibid.*: 65)

Here, there is a more assimilated, Christian feel to the ceremonial, but the women's insistence on the transmigration of their dead friend's soul back to her home in Africa is redolent of a more animist belief in the fluid relations between the living and the dead which informs many African belief systems. Again, such beliefs are displayed throughout the diaspora. For instance, in Virginia in 1816, a funeral once again occasions a ceremonial which looks to Africa, as the mourners reportedly 'sing and dance and drink the dead to his new home in Old Guinea' (quoted in Epstein, 1977: 66). In such ceremonials, death is figured as a release from slavery and prefigures a return across the Atlantic to Africa. With such a belief system underpinning African spiritual praxis in the New World, it is little wonder that suicide was seen by many Africans as a perfectly legitimate response which might hasten their passage 'over grandywater' and back home (Mullin, 1992: 40). Colin Palmer describes the importance of such a 'death wish [which] was one way, however tragic, of regaining control of one's personal destiny' (Palmer, 1997: 34). For instance, in his 1671 *A True and Exact History of the Island of Barbadoes*, Richard Ligon records the African captives' belief in the efficacy of suicide as a means of return to their homeland:

> they are not altogether of the sect of the *Sadduces*: For they
> believe a Resurrection, and that they shall go into their own
> Countrey again, and have their youth renewed. And lodging this
> opinion in their hearts, they make it an ordinary practice, upon
> any great fright, or threatening of their Masters, to hang
> themselves. (quoted in Abrahams and Szwed, 1983: 60)

It hardly needs to be said that suicide in itself struck a blow against the very institution of slavery, removing the productive body from its abuse in the system of chattel slavery. As Moira Ferguson succinctly asserts: 'suicide [was the] final autonomous act for labouring, remembering, myth denouncing, suffering individuals, [it] affirm[s] orthodox African belief, destroys the plantocratic economic base in capital, goods and machinery' (Ferguson, 1992: 244).

Africans themselves saw suicide as a utopian act of homecoming. Their bodies, beholden to slaveholders in life, become autonomous transmigrating souls after death, heading for Africa and freedom. Their cosmology often promoted the efficacy of moving beyond this world's inequities to a post-death utopia back home. Ceremonials were crucial to this, and would often be arranged away from the gaze of their white masters. During these dynamic events, some of them uncannily mimicked their souls' watery transmigration, as one particular incident in North Carolina in 1800 demonstrated: a group of African–Americans were espied:

> At night they would begin to sing their native songs, and in a short while would become so wrought up ... they would grasp their bundles of personal effects and setting their faces to Africa would march down into the water singing. (Epstein, 1977: 73)

Such acts of jubilee show how strong was the desire for reinstatement in the homeland despite years of acculturation in the New World, and they continued to be a feature of slave culture until its abolition. One of the most famous instances of a wished-for suicide (following successful infanticide) in the history of slavery was the Margaret Garner incident of 1856, which Toni Morrison would use as the primary source for her novel *Beloved*. Garner escaped enslavement across the frozen Ohio River with a group that included her husband and four children. In danger of recapture, she murdered her three-year-old daughter and was intent on murdering the others when she was taken by slave-catchers. Paul Gilroy uses this incident to illustrate the way that African-American culture, constructed in large part by the experience of enslavement, regards death in a fundamentally different way to the majority culture. Enlightenment rationality, with its disavowal of suicide and acceptance of the inevitability of slave status, 'expressed in the Hegelian slave's preference for bondage rather than death' (Gilroy, 1993a: 68) is deprivileged in favour of a welcome for death. As Gilroy explains, such instances reveal

> a positive preference for death rather than continued servitude [which] can be read as a contribution towards slave discourse on the nature of freedom itself. It supplies a valuable clue towards answering the question of how the realm of freedom is conceptualised by those who have never been free. This inclination towards death and away from bondage is fundamental. It reminds us that in the revolutionary eschatology which helps to define this primal history of modernity, whether apocalyptic or redemptive, it is the moment of jubilee that has the upper hand over the pursuit of utopia by rational means. (*ibid.*)

In the maelstrom of the slave system, Garner and other African-Americans see death not as a defeat but as a kind of victory over the slave power. This is emphasized by her and her fellow captives' stated desire to 'all go singing to the gallows' rather than be returned into slavery (quoted in *ibid.*: 68). This phrase, inviting death as preferable to unfreedom in life, links Garner's actions to those of her forebears as they sang their way to a drowning in the river, and exhibits a continuity in African-American responses to death and a positive reaction to suicide that will continue even after the abolition of slavery, as Gilroy delineates in his study. Through such radical perspectives, enslaved Africans in the diaspora were, in David Gaspar's words, 'able to exploit available social and psychological space that allowed them to develop a world of their own that whites did not penetrate and whose resources could be used to challenge the power of the master class' (Gaspar, 1993: 256). Gaspar is referring to the specific outcomes of the Antigua slave conspiracy, but its ceremonials were only the most visible of a core of folk beliefs throughout the diaspora which enabled slaves to develop what Gilroy has called a 'counter-culture of modernity'.

Such radical counter-hegemonic ideas found their way into folk beliefs. The potency of these in African-American culture can be gauged by their modulation into oral tales and legends which suffuse the folklore of the diaspora. In a veritable orgy of wish-fulfilment, a widespread group of these tales describe African-Americans refusing to endure the harsh conditions in the slave quarters and transmigrating to Africa. Many of them feature flying heroes and heroines, who by magical means alter their status and through sheer force of will, wing their way home to a reinstated pre-slave past in a utopian Africa. These tales describe how the living can return home as well as the dead: as in the Cuban ex-slave Esteban Montejo's description of how his fellow captives 'escaped by flying. They flew through the sky and returned to their own lands. The Musundi Congolese were the ones who flew the most; they disappeared by witchcraft' (Montejo, 1968: 43–4). These tales have been preserved most fully in the Gullah regions of South Carolina and Georgia and continued to be told into the twentieth century. The flying Africans in the folklore are thus transmogrified from labouring slaves, beholden to others, into heroes riding free on the air:

> My gran use tuh tell me bout folks flyin back tuh Africa. A man
> an his wife wuz brung frum Africa. Wen dey fine out dey wuz
> slabes an got treat so hahd, dey jis fret and fret. One day dey
> wuz standin wid some udduh slaves an all ub a sudden dey say,
> 'We gwine back tuh Africa. So goodie bye, goodie bye.' Den dey
> flied right out of sight. (Georgia Writers' Project, 1986: 18)

The slaves who possess the magical ability to transmigrate are usually first-generation Africans new to plantation life. Unable to acclimatize to the harsh conditions on a new continent, they disappear, and legends develop about their return to the homeland. As in many of the narratives about flying collected here and elsewhere, the action is described in commonplace terms that exhibit little wonderment at the magical transfiguration. Flying back to Africa is akin to popping out for a while on an errand. Even more laid back are what I will term 'commuting tales', in which Africans use their conjuring power to slip back and forth between America and Africa. Serina Hill describes a couple's commuting thus:

> Muh ma tell me many times bout a man an his wife wut could
> wuk conjuh. Anytime dey want tuh dey would fly back to Africa
> an den come back agen tuh duh plantation. Dey come back cuz
> dey hab some chillun wut didn hab duh power tuh fly an hab tuh
> stay on duh plantation. One uh duh daughter wanted tuh lun
> tuh fly an wuk conjuh. Duh faduh tell uh she hab tuh lun duh
> password, den she hab tuh kill a man by cunjuh. (*ibid*.: 81)

This tale exemplifies how autonomy within slavery is possible if you have the mind and magical power to pursue it. Despite the privations, skilled slaves can fly away and slip into an African reverie and yet still remain connected to kinfolk in America. Allegorically, the narrative reveals slaves functioning autonomously from the plantation economy: literally free in their minds. However, while flying back to Africa might appear commonplace, it is based on a system of conjuring which is open only to the extremely dedicated and skilled.

These flying tales have a pedagogical function, demonstrating to African-Americans the closeness of their African roots despite the ocean in between, and allowing them to imagine the Atlantic as 'more than a one way trip between the decks of a dirty slaveship' (Cohn and Platzer, 1978: xiii–xiv). Their emphasis on routes rather than roots exemplifies Paul Gilroy's insistence on the dynamic restlessness of African diasporic cultures, even when enmeshed within rigid and repressive plantocracies. The tales of flying Africans are powerful symbolic markers of African-American and African-Caribbean counter-culture at a time when plantocracies repressed African ceremonials and banned drums. Physical repression is highlighted in many of the tales by the context surrounding the flight, where punishment or its threat is the immediate spur to flight. Shad Hall tells such a tale:

> Doze folks could fly too. Dey tell me deah's a lot ub um wut wuz bring heah and dey ain much gud. Duh massuh wuz fixin tuh tie um up tuh whip um. Dey say, 'Massuh, yuh gwine lick me,' an wid dat dey runs down tuh duh ribbuh. Duh obuhseeuh he sho tought he ketch um wen dey git tuh duh ribbuh. But fo he could git tuh um, dey riz up in duh eah an fly away. Dey fly right back tuh Africa. (Georgia Writers' Project, 1986: 169)

The allegorical message here is clear – remain true to your African ancestry and you can undermine the power of slavery. Clearly, airborne flight becomes symbolic of a need to escape from repression, which some slaves would pursue as runaways. Such tales provided both a necessary allegorical explanation for actions which often led to the break-up of families on the plantation, and described a diasporic African cosmology within which such seemingly selfish actions could be justified. Reinstating home in Africa through such mythology means the sacrificing of domestic life on the plantation, a sacrifice that is validated by emphasizing the degrading abuse which is the cause of flight. Bodily integrity can only be reinstated by flight, both metaphorically to an African homeland of the mind and spirit and literally away from the scene of degradation, the plantation itself. Whippings from harsh overseers and masters provide the backdrop to many of these tales. Wallace Quarterman describes how Mr Blue, an overseer, is unable to make some new African slaves work:

> Dey gabble, gabble, gabble, an nobody couldn unduhstan um an dey didn know how tuh wuk right ... He got tuh whip um, Mr

> Blue, he ain hab no choice. Anyways, he whip um good an dey
> gits tuhgedduh an stick duh hoe in duh fiel an den say 'quack,
> quack, quack,' an dey riz up in duh sky an tun heself intuh
> buzzards an fly right back to Africa. (*ibid.*: 150–1)

Their strike action is an exemplary response to the harsh regime which held mastery over them. By flying away, they deny their labour power to the plantation owners. Through conjure, their transmogrification into buzzards and consequent escape to Africa transfers their labour power, once beholden to white masters, to its use in reinstating their African autonomy. Such folklore conjures up utopian possibilities in a world of drudgery, signifying an extant diasporic culture despite Anglo-American attempts at forceful acculturation. The most realistic of the tales, though, exemplifies the dangers of such profound wishing, as Charles Singleton relates:

> Ise heahd lots uh stories bout folks wut could fly. Some time
> back I wuz libin in Woodville wen a man came tru deah. He wuz
> from Liberty County. Dis man talk lot boutduh story uh duh
> Africans wut could fly. He say all dis wuz true. He say he wuz
> takin awduhs fuh wings an dey wuz all yuh need tuh fly. A peah
> uh wings coss twenty-five dolluhs. Duh man take yuh measure
> an a five dolluh deposit an say he collec duh balance wen he
> delibuh duh wings. Lots uh people gib deah awduhs fuh wings,
> cuz all deah libes dey been heahin bout folks wut could fly. Duh
> man jis go roun takin awduhs an collectin five dolluhs. Das duh
> las any ub us ebuh heah uh duh man aw duh wings. (*ibid.*: 42)

This commodification of diasporic African dreams into a mercantile scam illustrates their limitations in an American materialist capitalist reality. This cautionary tale highlights the dangers of believing in anything more than the allegorical nature of diasporic African dreams of flight, and how utopian desires can be taken advantage of by cynical charlatans. Told post-slavery, this narrative embodies a more cynical rendering of dreams of flight, revealing how their conjured freedom can be as chimeric as life after the Emancipation Proclamation of 1863. Future dreams harking back to an African past were tenable and held significant meaning for enslaved blacks, but in the post-emancipation maelstrom, where peonage had replaced chattel labour and lynchings were prevalent, these tales sometimes took a different and more realistic form. This does not mean that the symbol of flight became redundant, merely that its valencies changed.

The potency of myths of flying and transmigration after slavery is attested to by their prevalence in cultural forms ranging from post-emancipation dance forms through literature (both oral and written) to jazz music and film. These more recent manifestations of the mythologies inscribed a Modernist (and eventually postmodernist) symbolic meaning on the forms while retaining and reworking the link to the African past. Most recently, Julie Dash's monumental 1992 film, *Daughters of the Dust*, represents an artistic reworking of

Figure 8 Still from Julie Dash, *Daughters of the Dust* (1992). Reproduced by permission of Julie Dash. BFI Collections

African-American mythology surrounding migration. The film touches on many of the themes we have identified as central to African-American culture during slavery and its aftermath, especially in its multi-voiced discussion of the relevance and importance of the African presence in the New World. As Gloria J. Gibson-Hudson describes, 'the film unleashes the folklore and material culture, memories and heritage of Black women as they grapple with their destinies' (Gibson-Hudson, 1998: 50). Set on the Sea Islands, the film relates the events of one day, 19 August 1902, when many members of the

Peazant family were preparing for a move northward, leaving the matriarch, Nana Peazant, behind. Her belief in the ancestors is contrasted to Hagaar and Viola's espousal of Christianity. This is illustrated most dramatically when Nana's insistence on a 'pagan' leaving ceremony, in which everyone is urged to kiss a sewn hand containing a lock of her and her mother's hair strapped to a bible as a symbol of continuity between Africa, the South and the new life in the North, is seen by the Christian women as heretical. Nana's syncretic ceremony, in which she seeks to unite the word of God from the Bible with her ancestral traditions, is accepted by many of the Peazants as in keeping with their Sea Island heterodoxy, but this is under threat from a modernity which sees such beliefs as mere ignorant superstitions. Nana's incantation stresses links back to Africa that transatlantic chattel slavery had interrupted, and uses this past experience as an example of how traditional links must be continued in the new migration North to the cities:

> When I was a child, my mother cut off her hair when she was sold away from us. Now, I'm adding my own hair. There must be a bond ... a connection, between those that go North and those that remain ... between us that are here and us that are across the sea ... A connection! We are as two people in one body, the last of the old and the first of the new. We came here in chains and we must survive. We must survive. There's salt water in our blood ... (Dash, 1992: 151)

Continuity through remembered traditions and shared experience is at risk from this new migration, so Nana invokes cultural memory to remind those who are leaving of their links to their African homeland and the Sea Island culture which sustained many of its cultural traits; as Carol Smith and Jude Davies assert, 'The hand's synthesis of different signs of African American history and identity crystallizes Dash's practice in the film of seeking to make connections between disparate and often seemingly antagonistic constructions of African American identity' (Davies and Smith, 1998: 87).

It is the traditional ways that are most under threat, however, from the pressures of modernity, and the film constantly depicts the viability of their traditional way of life and how it has sustained the Peazants through slavery and its aftermath. The film employs various scenes and juxtapositions which emphasize African retentions, whether it is the spirit jars hanging in Nana Peazant's home, the Africanized graveyard with its scattered goods for the ancestors' use in the afterlife or the Peazant girls' ring-dancing. Most importantly for our discussion is the multi-telling of the narrative of a mass suicide by newly landed slaves. Dash's use of this legendary incident in Sea Island history and folklore attests to its power to symbolize the horrors of the slave past and survival through them. As Lawrence Levine stresses, such folk narratives and beliefs were crucial to the dynamic survival of black cultures in a fragmented diaspora:

Folk beliefs too provided hope, assurance and a sense of group identification, but they had another dimension as well: they actually offered the slaves sources of power and knowledge alternative to those existing within the world of the master class. (Levine, 1977: 63)

The multi-layered myth of the 'suicidal' Igbos is symptomatic of a counter-mythology that African Americans constructed both during slavery and in its aftermath as a form of 'identity formation and empowerment' (Gibson-Hudson, 1998: 50). In order to understand the resonances of these tales for the film, we need to establish the unique geographical and historical situation of the Sea Islands. The film often refers to 'salt-water negroes' whose arrival on the Sea Islands occurred long after the ending of the legal trade in slaves. Such a constant infusion of new Africans meant 'the coastal region was being supplied with Africans when much of older America was already sufficiently supplied or oversupplied with native born slaves bred for the domestic trade' (Granger, 1986: xli). This gave the Sea Islands their unique character, as a constant influx of new Africans guaranteed the survival of traditional customs. In fact, the last slave ship to dock there was *The Wanderer* in 1858, fifty years after the criminalizing of the trade in America. In their oral narratives and interviews from the 1930s, the Sea Islanders often refer to African progenitors who are only two generations removed from them. Thus, Jim Myers tells of his grandmother Bina who 'tell me how she got heah on a big boat and she lan down theah on Cumberland Ilun on a big dock ... ' (Georgia Writers' Project, 1986: 192). Of course in 1902, the setting for *Daughters of the Dust*, some of the African-born are still alive, represented by the Muslim, Bilal Muhammed, who had disembarked from *The Wanderer* forty-four years before, showing how in the Sea Islands 'culture [is] shaped as much by remembered traditions from Africa as by encountered traditions from elsewhere' (Joyner, 1986: x). Like the other salt-water Africans, he is lucky to have survived the horrors of the journey and the seasoning that followed it, and has maintained his own culture to such an extent that he has retained his Muslim religion. Oral narratives from the Georgia Writers' Project present the horrors such African arrivals had to endure, including a story related by Paul Singleton whose father had told him of a mass murder that occurred during the time of the illegal trade:

> Lots of time he tell me annudduh story bout a slabe ship bout tuh be caught by revenoo boat. Duh slabe ship slip tru back ribbuh intuh creek. Deah wuz bout fifty slabes on bode. Duh slabe runnuhs tie rocks roun duh slabes' necks and tro um ovuhbode tuh drown. Dey say yuh kin heah um moanin an groanin in duh creek if yuh goes neah deah tuh-day. (Georgia Writers' Project, 1986: 17)

The ghostly cries of the tethered Africans are much closer to these coastal African-Americans, both geographically and temporally, than they are to other enslaved blacks removed from such contact. The slave trade is not ancient history but part of an oral memory which remains relevant in the twentieth century.

If the latter tale memorializes the sacrifice of African lives for Anglo-American greed, the more prevalent story of Ibo's Landing exhibits multiple resonances that commemorate African survival as well as sacrifice. This tale of a cargo of Ibos who, once confronted with the realities of slavery onshore, just turned around, walked into the water and marched (or flew) right on back to Africa, is recalled in oral legends up and down the Sea Islands and is linked to many of the flying narratives I have already discussed. Julie Dash illuminates the importance of these legends for her film in an interview with bell hooks and makes the point that

> almost every Sea Island has a little inlet, or a little area where the people say, 'This is Ibo's Landing. This is where it happened. This is where this thing really happened.' And so why is it that on every little island – and there are so many places – people say, 'This is actually Ibo's Landing'? It's because that message is so strong, so powerful, so sustaining to the tradition of resistance, by any means possible, that every Gullah community embraces this myth. (hooks and Dash, 1992: 30)

However, the myth is not unidimensional, and much of the power of the film comes from the way Dash portrays different characters' reaction to, or use of, the myth. For instance, Bilal Muhammed tells the visiting photographer, Mr Snead, a pragmatic and realistic version of the myth which has much in common with the version told by Floyd White and collected by the Georgia Writers' Project. In this version, the drowning of the Ibo, though heroic, as it releases them from the horrors of slavery and destroys their value as chattels, is nevertheless not the prelude to a return to the homeland, but a more mundane welcoming of death. White recounts the story thus:

> Heahd bout duh Ibo's Landing? Das duh place weah dey bring duh Ibos obuh in a slabe ship an wen dey git yuh, dey ain lik it an so dey all staht singing an dey mahch right down in duh ribbuh tuh mahch back tuh Africa, but dey ain able tuh git deah. Dey gits drown. (Georgia Writers' Project, 1986: 185)

Note how the slaves all sing as they march into the water, an act that is reminiscent of Margaret Garner's wish to sing to the gallows in a jubilant display of delight at moving from death in life to life in death. Their sustaining belief in their ability to march back to Africa is undermined in this version by White's deadpan cynicism, and it is such a version which is surely the source for Bilal Muhammed's eyewitness account of the tragedy in his conversation with Snead:

> I came here on a ship called *The Wanderer*. I came with the Ibo.
> [recollecting the tragedy] Some say the Ibo flew back home.
> Some say they all joined hands and walked on top of the water.
> But, mister, I was there. Those Ibo men women and children, a
> hundred or more, shackled in iron ... when they went down in
> that water, they never come up. Ain't nobody can walk on
> water. (Dash, 1992: 152)

This version is dialogized in the film by other, different interpretations of the primal scene of the Ibo's landing. Just as in the folklore there are many different versions of the legend, so Dash does not allow one narrative primacy. It is not the facts of the event that create its resonances but the way it has become a symptomatic leitmotif of Sea Island culture, a story symbolic of the link to an African past and survival into the future on American land. This function is best adduced in Eula's retelling of the tale to her unborn child as she stands on Ibo's Landing. Dash places Eula with her back to the graveyard as she looks out across the water and tells a tale of the cheating of death which she hands on down the generations. This memory of African survival and triumph serves as a counterbalance to the dominant Anglo-American narrative of the elision of African culture in the progressive West. As she talks, her estranged partner Eli walks on the water, as though possessed by the Ibos that Eula describes, and becomes reconciled to his existence on the island. This act demonstrates his magical communion with his ancestors and illustrates the mythic potency of a narrative that provides emotional sustenance long after the events described. Eula's powerful voice describes how the Ibo, once on land and after 'studying the place real good', decided to turn back:

> When those Ibo got through sizing up the place real good and
> seeing what was to come, my grandmother said they turned, all
> of them, and walked back in the water. Every last man, woman
> and child. Now you wouldn't think they'd get very far seeing as
> it was water they was walking on. They had all that iron upon
> them. Upon their ankles and their wrists, and fastened around
> their necks like dog collars. But chains did not stop those Ibo.
> They just keep walking, like the water was solid ground. And
> when they got to where the ship was, they didn't so much as give
> it a look. They just walked right past it, because they were going
> home. (Dash, 1992: 142)

Just as 'chains did not stop the Ibo', so slavery could not sap the spirit of the Sea Islanders. Just as the Ibo 'chain-danced to freedom', so their memory, carried forward in mythic narrative, enables their ancestors to take their own steps to liberation. In these terms, the story of the Ibo is as much a triumphant myth for those survivors of slavery who remained true to a wide range of their African belief systems as it is for the walkers on water. As Dash comments, 'myth is very important in the struggle to maintain a sense of self and to move forward into the future' (hooks and Dash, 1992: 30). At this pivotal time, as many of the Sea Islanders prepare to move away from their roots Northward, the myth of the Ibo provides them with an allegorical touchstone to a coherent past that talks of survival and continuity. Together with Nana's ceremony, it provides a counter-mythology at a time of rapid technological progress. In Eula's retelling of the story, this is symbolized by the Ibos' rejection of the ship, their physical transporter, in favour of magical and imaginative links across the ocean. This is visually enhanced in the *mise en scène* as Eli walks on the water by a rotting slave ship's figurehead, exemplifying both the physical destruction of the actual ship and the symbolic death of the trade. In *Daughters of the Dust*, Dash 'demonstrate[s] how memory serves as a bridge to promote generational and cultural connections, encourages consciousness-raising, and functions as a cinematic device to foreground filmic representation' (Gibson-Hudson, 1998: 56). Dash's technical achievement (together with her collaborator, cinematographer Arthur Jafa) is in dynamically fusing the mythic and the realistic so that neither is given primacy. This is in keeping with an African womanist diasporan aesthetic that eschews Hollywood orthodoxies such as linearity, patriarchy and national exclusivity to create a 'sensual, inclusive and democratic' mode (Griffith, 1998: 166). As Ntongela Masilela comments astutely:

> by establishing an unusual rhythmic tempo and visual
> luminosity in *Daughters of the Dust*, Arthur Jafa and Dash were
> articulating a new aesthetics of cinematography consonant with
> the lived experience of time and consciousness by Africans in the
> Diaspora. (Masilela, 1998: 38)

If Paul Gilroy is right and 'routes' not 'roots' are the best descriptors of diasporan Africans' relationship across continents, then Julie Dash's film, with its insistence (both ideologically and stylistically) on a migration while consciously carrying the sounds of the past in your head, is surely a definitive black Atlantic film even though it never leaves the continental United States. The final scene, in which Nana Peazant, Yellow Mary and Eula walk across the beach where the Atlantic laps until 'each woman individually turns to dust and blows into the burning sun' (Dash, 1992: 164), captures this sense of lives lived on the Atlantic rim. Life continues through the Unborn Child who remains, 'growing older, wiser, stronger' (*ibid.*: 164) because of the doughty survival of African diasporan peoples and, most importantly, their knowledge of their complex heritage. The Ibo tale is crucial to this denouement, as it is 'recited and begins to function as both evidence of, and argument for, cultural continuity' (Bambara, 1992: 12). But it is not the only cultural form which provides such evidence. The basketwork that Nana works on is a quintessential African craft which the Sea Islanders brought with them across the water, while the dancing girls are evidence of the survival of African musicking traditions in the diaspora. By skilful cutting between dialogue and the depiction of such scenes, Dash establishes the centrality of such practices to the survival of African mores in America. Thus, as Nana Peazant impresses on her great-grandson Eli the importance of his African past, we cut back to the ring-dancing Peazant women and girls. Myown is possessed by an African spirit as Nana intones, 'Never forget who we are and how far we've come' (Dash, 1992: 96), 'spinning roun' and roun' dancing in the centre of the ring-and-line game' (*ibid.*: 93). Her possession illustrates the power of the African past in the here and now, and yet again it is dance which reveals this most appositely. It is the African-American form most dominated by an African aesthetic, as Brenda Dixon Gottschild has argued so eloquently in her book *Digging the Africanist Presence in American Performance: Dance and Other Contexts* (1996). It is this form I want to return to now.

African-American dance forms have always emphasized possession like that delineated in Dash's film. Sometimes this approximates flight, much to the amazement of white onlookers, and I would contend that such acrobatic delineations of leaping bodies were utopian responses to an American reality which sought to keep their bodies grounded in enforced labour. As the slaves gradually acculturated to the New World, these ceremonials became integrated into Christian worship, creating what Sterling Stuckey has called 'the Africanization of Christianity not only in emotive and intuitive force but in a larger religious sense' (Stuckey, 1987: 54). Stuckey quotes from Anglo-American and European witness accounts of such ceremonials to show just how African black American worship was. A hundred years later, Richard Wright, an African-American observer, was to discover in Ghana (then the British colony of the Gold Coast) how similar African and black American ceremonials still are even in the modern period. At a celebration held by future president Nkrumah's political party, spontaneous dancing breaks out. Wright describes a dancing aesthetic whose valencies have been translated virtually unchanged across the Atlantic:

> I was astonished to see women, stripped to the waist, their
> elongated breasts flopping wildly, do a sort of weaving, circular
> motion with their bodies, a kind of queer shuffling dance which
> expressed their joy in a quiet, physical manner. It was as if they
> were talking with the movement of their legs, arms, necks and
> torsos; as if words were no longer adequate as a means of
> communication; as if sounds could no longer approximate their
> feelings; as if only the total movement of their entire bodies
> could indicate in some measure their acquiescence, their
> surrender, their approval. (Wright, 1954: 56)

Here, the dancing aesthetic is seen as the primary artistic mode in a fundamentally oral culture, as important in expressing approval for a political ideology as a verbal response. There are links here to the dancing ceremonials which accompanied the eighteenth- and nineteenth-century slave rebellions I have discussed earlier in the chapter. However, Wright himself outlines another link to contemporary African-American forms:

> I'd seen these same snakelike veering dances before ... Where?
> Oh, God, yes; in America, in storefront churches, in Holy Roller

> Tabernacles, in God's Temples, in unpainted wooden prayer-
> meeting houses on the plantations of the Deep South ... And
> here I was seeing it all again against a background of a surging
> nationalist political movement! (*ibid.*: 56–7)

The African dance resembled the ring shout, with its shuffling feet and circular motion, and Sterling Stuckey, in his definitive study *Slave Culture: Nationalist Theory and the Foundations of Black America* (1987), has already substantively proved the African nature of this African-American form. Another pervasive element of this African aesthetic was a vigorous leaping dance in which the participants seemed to be virtually flying. Frederika Bremer describes an 1850s New Orleans worship where, in response to the preacher, members of the congregation

> began to leap – leaped aloft with a motion as of a cork flying out
> of a bottle, while in the air, as if they were endeavouring to bring
> something down, and all the while crying aloud ... And as they
> leaped, they twisted their bodies round in a sort of corkscrew
> fashion, and were evidently in a state of convulsion ... Whichever
> way we looked in the church, we saw somebody leaping up and
> fanning the air; the whole church seemed transformed into a
> regular bedlam, and the noise and tumult was horrible. (Bremer,
> quoted in Stuckey, 1987: 54)

One woman in close communication with the preacher is reported to have 'sprang aloft with such vehemence that three other women took hold of her by the skirts as if to hold her on the earth' (*ibid.*: 55). This ceremonial syncretizes African and Christian beliefs in the efficacy of flying (either back home or to Jesus). The leaping African Americans fly away (albeit momentarily) from a rocky American ground, from their position as lowly labourers in a slave state to the ecstasy of an imaginative communion with home. Thus, such a ceremonial is closely related to the folktales of flying Africans detailed earlier.

Flying is surely more than myth or symbol in African-American dance, highlighting through its acrobatic, leaping participants the desire to move beyond the physical constraints of the body to new gravity-defying feats: to fly home in the mind, while approximating such motions in the body. The trance-like state of many of the participants in both religious and secular dance in the African diaspora attests to this desire. African Americans often used such ceremonials to escape, albeit temporarily, the hegemonic power of their white masters. As Herbie Hancock was to say of contemporary break-dancers, such performers momentarily dominated, 'by the superior power of grace and invention', a hostile world which was designed to 'drain every atom of life and feeling' out of them (Lott, 1993: 43). Dancing ceremonials as radical counter-culture are not only the preserve of the contemporary ghetto, though, but were at work even in the ante-bellum church, as Sterling Stuckey emphasizes most strongly:

the community in which the celebrant attains such a [passionate] state basically rejects the authority of those who exercise control over it, since outbursts of general fervour, followed by the incapacitation of some worshipers through possession and convulsions challenge the master's sense of discipline. (Stuckey, 1987: 56)

Clearly, the mid-nineteenth-century participants were not literally flying back to Africa or to an ecstatic reunion with their ancestors in heaven, but their dancing equivalents of such freedom-loving leaps through the air allowed them to resist full acculturation to Anglo-American bourgeois ideals of sobriety and diligent adherence to the work ethic. At the same time, tales of flying Africans gave others hope of escaping the drudgery of everyday existence when they listened to them in the slave cabins. W. T. Lhamon probably expresses best the complex wishing of such gestures in dance and storytelling when he says, 'you can't go home again ... but you can sometimes palm the past, or dance it into the present – especially if no one is looking' (Lhamon, 1998: 218–19). The African homeland is recovered imaginatively through such autonomous cultural forms, which often have at their centre a flying motif.

The secular dance which incorporated most this 'air-mindedness' (as Ann Douglas would term it) was the Lindy Hop, which developed in the late 1920s. Allegedly named after Lindberg's famous transatlantic flight of 1927, though almost certainly predating it, the dance had its origins in pre-war dances like the Texas Tommy (first described in 1913), which incorporated kicks and hops. Most noticeably it incorporated breaks where one partner performed a solo. As Marshall Stearns notes, 'the breakaway is the time honored method of eliminating the European custom of dancing in couples and returning to solo dancing' (Stearns, 1956: 324). Such breaks had traditionally allowed the moment of ecstatic communion with the ancestors: as Robert Farris Thompson explains, participants 'break on into the world of the ancestors, in the possession state' (quoted in Malone, 1996: 33). As well as rediscovering an African form, the dance was performed with great athleticism by exponents like Shorty Snowden, whose description of his breaks illuminates the vernacular, improvised nature of the dance:

I've put together new steps in the breakaway by slipping and almost falling. I was always looking for anyone dancing in the street or just walking or doing anything that suggests a step. If I could see it, I could do it. (Stearns, 1956: 324)

This athleticism was mainly rooted to the ground until the development of the aerial Lindy in 1937. These new steps incorporated throws, leaps and jumps between the partners that established new parameters in popular dance. Now the Lindy resembled even more the flight it was purportedly named after, as we can see from contemporary descriptions:

> I saw girls grab men round the waist and slide to the floor like epileptic snakes. Maidens clasped hands behind men's necks, moaning with joy, while their feet dragged and their bodies wriggled to the drumbeat. I saw an Amazon in a red sweater get a standing scissors on her enchanted partner, throw her head back til it trailed near the floor, and dance with her arms. A blissful buck heaved his lady across his suspenders while she kicked ecstatic rhythms into space ... Then someone gave a Tarzan call, and the group went into an acrobatic furor. The whole maneuver ended with the she-devils taking an impulsive hop, skip and jump to their swains' shoulders, gripping the men's necks with their thighs, and laying on with hands – howling all the while. (Ross, 1993: 153–4)

The ecstasy of this secular dance is similar to the religious exultation in the nineteenth-century example discussed earlier. It has a similar utopic energy, albeit with a different purpose. The African-Americans, now having migrated to the North, are enmeshed in a modern capitalist exploitation and escape from their often mundane lives of domestic and factory labour by energetic aerial dancing. As Robin D. G. Kelley states, 'These urban dance halls were places to recuperate, to take back their bodies' (Kelley, 1994: 169).

The best re-creation of the vibrant energy of the performers appears in contemporary photographs, where the dancers' bodies are a whirl of motion. Albert Murray includes a wonderful example in his *Stomping the Blues*, where the female dancer is captured mid-leap, somersaulting over the fulcrum of her partner's hands (Murray, 1976: 28–9). In a gesture of homage to the possibilities opened up by such performances, Spike Lee's film *Malcolm X* (1992) re-creates the Lindy Hop in a wonderful kaleidoscopic presentation of the kinaesthetic forms in which black dance delighted during the 1930s and 1940s. The link between dancing, flying and African homecoming is captured most eloquently in the Robert Hayden poem, 'O Daedalus, Fly Away Home' (1962b). The first half of the poem establishes the site of flying legends as those ceremonies with African retentions, where Vodun magic prepares an escape route from a harsh Southern existence. There are echoes of Billie Holiday's wonderfully moving 'Strange Fruit' in the invocation of the Southern landscape in the poem; however, it rapidly becomes more optimistic, before drifting into an almost elegiac mode:

> Drifting night in the Georgia pines,
> coonskin drum and jubilee banjo.
>   Pretty Melinda, dance with me.
> Night is jubo, night is conjo.
>   Pretty Melinda, dance with me.
>
> Night is an African juju man
> weaving a wish and a weariness together
>   to make two wings

bad circumstances – and is a direct echo of an extant folktale which William A. Percy had published three years before, in which a black man hellraises round heaven wearing 'two left wings' (quoted in Dance, 1978: 13–14). The final lines comprise a dialogue with Saint Peter, who exclaims:

'Now look you niggers done tore up earth. You not coming up here and tear up heaven. Just gimme those wings!'
He say, 'Well, I had a flying good time while I had 'em on though.'
(*ibid*.: 14)

Ellison uses an extant comic tale to ground his story in African-American vernacular praxis. But as well as 'calling the culture', the finale highlights the tensions between the two generations of black men. Unable to recognize the wider relevancies of the premodern folktale, Todd, an aviator and a modernist *par excellence*, assumes that the comic ending and Jefferson's laughter are aimed just at him. The story has hit a raw nerve and he reacts angrily, demanding to know why blacks are restricted to a life as scavenging buzzards rather than soaring eagles. As a boy, Todd had been obsessed by flying and the futuristic possibilities it held out of rising beyond the limitations imposed by poverty and racism. Jefferson's story shows the illusive nature of such imaginings, but Todd does not want to hear, falling into a reverie about his boyhood love of flying that he believes has led to his 'escape from the limitations of race' (Callahan, 1996: xxxvii). Mechanized flying is not, however, the neutral arena Todd hopes for as he rediscovers when he remembers an incident from his own childhood in which a plane was used as a vehicle for racial terror:

the plane flying high, and the burst appeared suddenly and fell slowly, billowing out and sparkling like fireworks and he was watching and being hurried along as the air filled with a flurry of white pinwheeling cards that caught in the wind and scattered over the rooftops and into the gutters and a woman was running and snatching a card and reading it and screaming and he darted into the shower, grabbing as in winter he grabbed for snowflakes and bounding away at his mother's, 'Come on here, boy! Come on, I say!' And he was watching as she took the card away seeing her face grow puzzled and turning taut as her voice quavered, 'Niggers Stay from the Polls,' and died to a moan of terror as he saw the eyeless sockets of a white hood staring at him from the card and above he saw the plane spiralling gracefully, agleam in the sun like a fiery sword. And seeing it soar, he was caught, transfixed between a terrible horror and a horrible fascination. (Ellison, 1996: 170)

Here control of the sky is shown as being in the same hands as on the earth, as reactionary forces use the panoptical and propagandist possibilities of mechanized flight to maintain, through fear, their hegemony over the rural black underclass. The plane seems to exemplify Giraule's 1943 contention that the technology 'fixed the underlying structure both of topography and minds', creating a 'somewhat disturbing fantasy of observational power' (Clifford, 1988: 68–9). Todd's horror cannot obviate his fascination with the aeroplane, and the juxtaposition of 'terrible horror and a horrible fascination' exemplifies the dilemma of his double consciousness which desires the power of flight but recoils in horrific disbelief at its excesses. This is a lesson learnt very recently and it must have been in the forefront of Ellison's mind as he wrote the story, as the modern terror from the skies had destroyed a radical government in Spain and independent black government in Abyssinia in the 1930s, and was a significant element of Nazi terror. Childhood romanticism about flight was unsustainable in the face of such grim realities, as Todd realizes in the brute present, when white men arrive at the crash scene and peddle their racist distortions:

> This nigguh belongs in a straitjacket, too, boys. I knowed that the minnit Jeff's kid said something 'bout a niggah flyer. You all know you caint let the nigguh get up that high without his going crazy. The nigguh brain ain't built right for high altitudes. (Ellison, 1996: 171)

The irony of Mister Graves's white-trash folk wisdom is that he is entirely right. Flying has indeed sent this particular 'nigguh' crazy, as it has taught him to aspire beyond the straitjacket a Jim Crow society would put on him. As so often in African-American culture, flying is seen positively as a route to a life away from the restrictions of racism on the ground. What Todd has learnt by the end of his misadventure, however, is not the value of flying per se but that the folk wisdom of his people allows them to fly without even leaving the ground. Jefferson is 'the flyin'est son of a bitch what ever hit heaven' (*ibid.*: 160), as he shows by his calm dignity in the presence of the racist white men, which means he is able to help the aviator. As Todd is carried to safety by Jefferson and the boy, Teddy, he is reunited with his folk roots:

> it was as though he had been lifted out of his isolation, back into the world of men. A new current of communication flowed between the man and boy and himself. They moved him gently. Far away he heard a mockingbird liquidly calling. He raised his eyes seeing a buzzard poised unmoving in space. For a moment the whole afternoon seemed suspended and he waited for the horror to seize him again. Then like a song within his head he heard the boy's soft humming and saw the dark bird glide into the sun and glow like a bird of flaming gold. (*ibid.*: 172–3)

The buzzard, with which he had not wanted to be associated because of its carrion temperament, is now seen as a bird in flight as capable of beauty as any other. It is a symbol of the folk resources available to Todd in the South which can obviate the surrounding racism. The fellowship he finds with Jefferson and

Teddy can compensate for his failure to compete in a white man's world in the face of discrimination and prejudice and allows him 'to recognize where he is and who he is' (Callahan, 1996: xxxvii). Rooted solidly in the South, he is now buoyed by folk resources as the boy sings to him and he recognizes the song as his own ('within his head').

Flying is a complex trope in Ellison's short story, its use as a symbol for freedom deeply compromised by the realities of wartime, Jim Crow America. Todd had thought flying set him apart from the black peasantry, as indicated by his conversation with Jefferson early in the narrative:

> 'Son, how come you want to fly way up there in the air?'
> Because it's the most meaningful act in the world ... because it makes me less like you, he thought. (Ellison, 1996: 153)

However, Todd learns that flying does not allow him to escape Jim Crow America and that, just like the old man, he is regarded by white eyes as irredeemably black. This revelation leads not to despair, however, but to an inner peace created by his immediate acceptance into the communion of the old man and his son. That he moves to communion through the medium of a symbolic buzzard's flight in a sun-gelded landscape exemplifies a positive flying home that revels in Southern folk culture's dynamic resource which allows homecoming even to African-Americans born in the North.

This romantic ideology is taken to even greater lengths by Toni Morrison in *Song of Solomon* (1977). In brief, the novel relates the narrative of an African-American, Milkman Dead, whose dilatory bourgeois existence in urban America is transformed through the uncovering of his past. In discovering his heritage, he finds that a Southern no-count town was the home of his grandfather and great-grandfather, who are legendary figures in the community's folklore. He makes this discovery by decoding a children's song which names his ancestors as pivotal figures in a legend of flying Africans. This allows him to move from exasperation with the strange mores of these Southern folk to an acceptance of their culture as his own, of their equality with him. Just as his apparent lack of a name he could be proud of had frustrated him in the North (he wanted a name given with 'love and seriousness' [Morrison, 1980a: 17]), so now in his ancestors' homeland his movement from alienation comes from learning these ancestors' true names.

Hidden in the children's song he discovers that Jake, his grandfather, had been abandoned by his father Solomon, who had, according to legend, flown back to Africa. This is the first piece of the jigsaw of his family tree which the decoding of the whole song will eventually complete. As Alison Bulsterbaum asserts in her illuminating essay on the role of folklore in the novel, 'what began as a seemingly meaningless collection of lines is revealed to be the ballad story of a family ancestry' (Bulsterbaum, 1984: 16). Even at this late stage, Milkman's quest is not made easy, however, because he has no pen to transcribe the song, so must memorize it. Morrison's narrative ploy of having him use an oral technique to learn the song is a conscious foregrounding of African-American vernacular techniques of passing on a culture in which such oral modes of transmission are employed rather than written transcription. It stresses Milkman's absorption into vernacular culture, a literal return to his cultural roots As Deborah Clarke asserts, Morrison 'decentres written text, reduces its power, without eradicating it as a means of discourse' (Clarke, 1993: 276). While her written version of the incident is not eradicated, it is, however, radically deprivileged by the emphasis placed on Milkman's memorizing.

While Morrison uses repeated references to the song as a structured device, its role is mutifaceted and posits the various uses of musicking in African-American culture. The song is ultimately an encoding in myth of the legend of flying Africans, which was used to explain the absence of male slaves who had either run away or simply disappeared. As we have seen, such flying is regarded as a mythological return to Africa, and in using the image here Morrison is calling on a long tradition of folklore. As Bulsterbaum, quoting a passage from Harold Courlander's work, asserts: 'Morrison places this legendary black Solomon squarely into the middle of Negro storytelling tradition: "flying Africans" were those slaves who, as the story goes, would endure just so much of an overseer's cruelty ... ' (Bulsterbaum, 1984: 21).

Morrison is concerned to situate the myth centrally in African-American lived history and, as we have seen, other stories of flying Africans attest to the widespread telling of the myth. For instance, a typical legend recounted by Rosa Grant from Georgia, whose grandmother Ryna and great-grandmother Theresa were captured in Africa and brought to America, shows how specifically Morrison used folklore from these Georgia archives:

> Attuh dey bin yuh a wile, duh mothuh git to weah she caahn
> stan it an she wannuh go back to Africa. One day muh gran
> Ryna wuz standin wid uh in duh fiel. Theresa turn roun – so –
> ... She stretch uh ahms out – so – an rise right up an fly right
> back to Africa. Muh gran say she wuz standin right deah wen it
> happen. (Georgia Writers' Project, 1986: 145)

Ryna's appearance here as the daughter left behind and Morrison's use of the same name for the wife deserted by Solomon could indicate the centrality of this particular mythical example as a source for the novel. As discussed earlier, the flight of African Americans from the white man's yoking and enchaining arms is an analogy of their escape from slavery. Similarly, Solomon's 'flying' was actually a 'fleeing' transmogrified into flight by the power of myth. The great courage and fortitude needed to escape is celebrated in the myth, which also mourns the need for leave-taking. The constant refrain of 'You can't just go off and leave a body' throughout the novel is Morrison's way of emphasizing the consequences of their actions on those left behind. The song itself can function as a blues lament for those abandoned, and highlights the dysfunctional nature of a system of slavery which only allowed freedom to African Americans if they were prepared to leave their families. Morrison shows how the legacy of slavery persists in the racist structure of society in the post-slavery world, ensuring that some black men are unable to commit themselves entirely in their relationships with women. She illustrates the continuing 'fleeing/flying' through Milkman's abandonment of his lover and cousin, Hagar. Milkman writes a thank-you letter to Hagar:

> And he did sign it with love, but it was the word 'gratitude' and the flat-out coldness of 'thankyou' that sent Hagar spinning into a bright blue place where the air was thin and it was silent all the time, and where people spoke in whispers or did not make sounds at all and where everything was frozen except for an occasional burst of fire inside her chest that crackled away until she ran out into the streets to find Milkman Dead. (Morrison, 1980a: 99)

Hagar's painful lost love is allied to the plight of Ryna, left behind by the flying African, Solomon. Morrison achieves this by the use of an imaginative instance of call and recall, where Hagar's 'spinning' is recalled later in the description of Ryna in the children's song as 'Black lady fell down on the ground/Threw her body all around' (*ibid.*: 307). Such cut backs and instances of call and recall link passages from the present to the past, so that the aerial imagery in the description of Hagar's madness anticipates the aeroplane actions which accompany the children's song and solidifies the links between past and present leave-takings. These aeroplane actions represent contemporary transformations of the children's song that allow it to survive into the modern period and still appear relevant to the new generation who sing it, even though its lyrics refer to incidents predating mechanized flight. Morrison makes the link between passages explicit in Milkman's response to Hagar's death:

> now she was dead – he was certain of it. He had left her. While he dreamt of flying, Hagar was dying. Sweet's voice came back to him: 'Who'd he leave behind?' He left Ryna behind and twenty children. Twenty-one since he dropped the one he tried to take with him. And Ryna had thrown herself all over the ground, lost her mind, and was still crying in a ditch. Who looked after those twenty children? Jesus Christ, he left twenty-one children! Guitar and the days chose never to have children. Shalimar left his, but it was the children who sang about it and kept the story of his leaving alive. (*ibid.*: 336)

As well as the link between Hagar and Ryna, Morrison draws parallels with modern resistance to oppression in her reference to Guitar and his comrades in the Seven Days organization (a radical Black Nationalist group whose ethos was to even up the numbers by killing whites whenever blacks were killed, and who chose not to have children to avoid compromising their ability to revolt).

The many resonances of the song are highlighted throughout the text, as it adduces different meanings depending on context, revealing the malleability of the African-American cultural tradition. As the song enters and re-enters the narrative, it provides a flexible form in which the characters can place their own specific meanings while the song itself always contains the historical cadences it has accrued. As Paul Berliner explains in talking about the jazz solo: 'In a sense each solo is like a tale within a tale, a personal account with ties of varying strength to the [original] ... composition' (Berliner, 1995: 205). When Reba and Pilate sing a version of the song to a teenage Hagar early in the narrative, it serves a dual purpose – to lament her fatherlessness (for her father had just 'gone on and left her body') and to reimagine their family's place at the centre of a living Southern heritage with links back to an African tradition. Bulsterbaum makes this point well by describing how the Sugarman song is 'stylistically similar to authentic Afro-American folk songs' (Bulsterbaum, 1984: 22), such as those described by Du Bois as 'Sorrow Songs' in *The Souls of Black Folk* (1965), and at the same time exhibits a quintessentially African form of 'alternating lines of improvisation and a reiterated burden' (*ibid.*: 22–3). In the conversation with her mother and grandmother, Hagar had complained that 'Some of my days were hungry ones' (Morrison, 1980a: 48); eventually Pilate and Reba understand this hunger to be an emotional rather than physical lack, and they sing their version of the song as compensation for the loss of a father figure in her life. The narrative continues: 'Pilate began to hum as she returned to plucking the berries. After a moment, Reba joined her, and they hummed together in perfect harmony until Pilate took the lead: *O Sugarman don't leave me here* ... ' (*ibid.*: 49).

Such compensatory blues singing is a central part of African-American musicking as well as a key and foundational mode in the jazz tradition. Its functional nature here is revealed when Hagar joins in the chorus, her hunger in part assuaged by the power of the song. As Joseph Skerrett Jr asserts, the women's song 'functions as a blues, allowing Pilate, Reba and Hagar to finger the jagged edge of their unhappiness as a way of mastering it' (Skerrett, 1985: 200); Morrison's foregrounding of such musicking is one instance among many where the song is given relevance well beyond its Southern nineteenth-century roots. To echo Amiri Baraka's apposite phrase, the song, like much African-American music, is a 'Changing Same' which is always there for the next generation to pick up and utilize. Morrison's use of oral folktales about flying and their transmogrification in her novel exemplifies this process, which treats the past not as history but as a living resource. The flying tales might not have the same valencies today, but they are still relevant to a developing African-American culture because of their pedagogical function. They teach Milkman Dead about his culture and allow him to reconcile this past and use it to become more acculturated to his African-American heritage.

Pilate had felt the urge to sing the Sugarman song earlier in the novel following the suicide of Robert Smith, the insurance agent who had thrown himself from the 'No Mercy' whites-only hospital when the stress of belonging to the Seven Days organization had become too much for him. Jacqueline De Weever correctly cites as a source for this leap 'the orthodox ending of the myth of Icarus' (De Weever, 1980: 133). However, Morrison uses the white myth as a base line to signify on. She exhibits the full resources of African-American vernacular culture to figure the Icarus myth in specifically cultured ways. For instance, Pilate's rendition of a portion of the Solomon/Sugarman song as a poignant blues lament for Robert Smith provides the soundtrack to his leap:

> Her head cocked to one side, her eyes fixed on Mr Robert Smith, she sang in a powerful contralto:
>
> *O Sugarman done fly away*
> *Sugarman done gone*
>
> *Sugarman done cut across the sky*
>
> *Sugarman gone home …*
>
> A few of the half hundred or so people gathered there nudged each other and sniggered. Others listened as though it were the helpful and defining piano music in a silent movie. (Morrison, 1980a: 5–6)

Note how Morrison figures the song as a literally 'defining' mode that helps to explain the troubling scene for some of those present. Black music is seen here as literally interpretive, as definitive as a good film soundtrack in establishing mood and meaning. The singing of the song at this moment is particularly apt, and Bulsterbaum's contention that Pilate sings it 'for reasons that not even she fully understands' (Bulsterbaum, 1984: 16) is surely untenable, as the song's theme of the leave-taking of black men is the perfect accompaniment to Robert Smith's suicide, linking him to a tradition of flying Africans escaping the rigours of a society where their manhood is not respected. Morrison links Robert Smith directly to the music when she describes his leap:

> Mr Smith had lost his balance for a second, and was trying gallantly to hang on to a triangle of wood that jutted from the cupola. Immediately the singing woman began again:
>
> *O Sugarman done fly*
>
> *O Sugarman done gone*
>
> Downtown the firemen pulled on their greatcoats, but when they arrived at Mercy, Mr Smith had seen the rose petals, heard the music and leaped on into the air. (Morrison, 1980a: 9)

The phrase 'leaped on into the air' will be recalled at the end of the novel when Milkman leaps into the air toward Guitar. But this is not the only call and recall pattern initiated in this early part of the narrative. A more subtle pattern is established by the rose petals Robert Smith sees as he prepares to leap. These have been made by Milkman's sisters, Lena and Corinthians, and scattered by his mother, Ruth, who is about to give birth to him. Shocked by the appearance of Robert Smith with his blue silk wings, 'she dropped her covered peck basket, spilling red velvet rose petals. The wind blew them about, up, down and into small mounds of snow. Her half-grown daughters scrambled about trying to catch them … ' (ibid.: 5). These rose petals are recalled twice in the text: once by Corinthians who, in retrospect at least, had enjoyed the moment, as it had scattered the red velvet, symbol of the middle-class strictures on her life, to the four winds (ibid.: 199); and more significantly, by Guitar, a later member of the Seven Days, whose memory of the petals is associated with a bombing atrocity he must avenge:

> Every night now Guitar was seeing little scraps of Sunday
> dresses – white, purple and voile, velvet and silk, cotton and
> satin, eyelet and grosgrain. The scraps stayed with him all night
> and he remembered Magdalene called Lena and Corinthians
> bending in the wind to catch the heart-red pieces of velvet that
> had floated under the gaze of Mr. Robert Smith. Only Guitar's
> scraps were different. The bits of Sunday dresses he saw did not
> fly; they hung in the air quietly, like the whole notes in the last
> measure of an Easter hymn. (ibid.: 174)

This recollection links Guitar to Smith and to a whole history of vengeance against racist murder which the narrative details as debilitating to those who undertake it. Guitar has reworked this pivotal memory of his childhood and integrated it into a nightmare of his present.

Another significant example of the use of call and recall in the text occurs when one of Guitar's admonitions to Milkman is recalled in a later scene. Guitar's speech is about the travails of the black man: 'Everybody wants the life of a black man. Everybody. White men want us dead or quiet – which is the same thing as dead. White women, same thing … And black women, they want your whole self' (ibid.: 224). Guitar posits a situation in which all sections of society seek to control the lives of black men, so that danger comes not only from those who threaten his life but also from those who apparently care for it. Here, black women are characterized as dangerous to black men because of the demands they make on them as breadwinners. It is telling that the symbol Morrison reaches for to show how the creative possibilities of black men are undermined by such economic demands is that of the musician. After detailing black women's hamstringing of masculine possibility, Guitar moves to the final musical example:

> Buy a horn and say you want to play. Oh, they love the music,
> but only after you pull eight at the post office. Even if you make
> it, you stubborn and mean and you get to the top of Mount
> Everest, or you do play and you good, real good – that still ain't
> enough. You blow your lungs out on the horn and they want
> what breath you got left to hear about how you love them. They
> want your full attention. Take a risk and they say you're not for
> real. That you don't love them. They won't even let you risk

your own life, man, your own life – unless it's over them. You can't even die unless it's about them. What good is a man's life if he can't even choose what to die for. (*ibid.*: 224–5)

Note how the black man is always an object of 'they' in this passage, stressing his lack of agency. A possible escape route is offered through music, but this is in turn undermined by capitalism (having to 'pull eight at the post office') and the voracious demands of black women. The extended riff on the bleakness of the black man's life is emphasized later on when an extended description of the skinning of a bobcat is interspersed with reiterations of Guitar's ruminations on the status of a black man's lot:

His knife pointed upward for a cleaner, neater incision.
'*Not his dead life; I mean his living life.*'
When he reached the genitals he cut them off, but left the
    scrotum intact.

'*It's the condition our condition is in.*'
Omar cut around the legs and neck. Then he pulled the hide off.
'*What good is a man's life if he can't even choose what to die
    for.*' (*ibid.*: 285)

Morrison invokes the earlier passage here, because Guitar, thinking Milkman has betrayed him by stealing gold needed for Seven Days' vengeance, has just attempted to kill him. The precariousness of the black man's life here is equated with that of the bobcat which the hunters are skinning. The call and recall technique illustrates the perverseness of Guitar's philosophy, which would have him kill Milkman despite his constant avowal of the need to preserve the lives of black men. As the novel closes, it is now Milkman who assumes a position as mentor and teacher (a position that Guitar has hitherto held), for he has learnt that his life is incomplete without connection to others, that his ancestors could fly beyond the limitations of Anglo-American hegemony because of their links to an African past and that his responsibility to Guitar is greater than his own survival. Milkman's grandfather had leapt to escape slavery and had been forced to fly from his family responsibilities as a result. Milkman, in a conscious inversion, leaps towards responsibility to his community:

'You want my life?' Milkman was not shouting now. 'You need it? Here.' Without wiping away the tears, taking a deep breath, or even bending his knees – he leaped. As fleet and bright as a lodestar he wheeled toward Guitar and it did not matter which one of them would give up his ghost in the killing arms of his brother. For now he knew what Shalimar knew: If you surrendered to the air you could ride it. (*ibid.*: 341)

Note the recall not only of Solomon's leap but also that of Robert Smith which opened the narrative. Such surrendering to the air recalls the improvisatory leaps made by jazz musicians, which, though apparently selfish and egocentric, have the potential to be communal acts of artistic delight if a responding musician catches and returns them. As J. A. Rogers articulated in the 1920s: 'the jazz musician could release all the suppressed emotion at once, blow off the lid, let off musical fireworks [and] revolt joyously against everything that would confine the soul of man and hinder its riding free on the air' (quoted in Douglas, 1997: 433). Morrison's invocation of African-Americans surrendering to the air mirrors the jazz praxis of improvisation as articulated by Rogers and, intriguingly, in very similar terms, describes Milkman's leap as a jazz-like improvisatory gesture which is both consciously wrought and located within a communal context. Milkman has come a long way to be capable of initiating such a communal rite. He has found a liberating chorus in a song about his ancestor which memorializes a leap the African had made for freedom, and it is this song which provides an apt soundtrack for his own leap of commitment to his fellow African-Americans. As Joseph Skerrett Jr asserts, Milkman 'has become an improvising bluesman denying the finality of death through the continuity of his art' (Skerrett, 1985: 201). Morrison has reworked the legend of flying Africans and shown its relevance for contemporary African-Americans. For in the novel, as Robert O'Meally incisively asserts, the flyer 'learns that to be a great solo flyer he must be connected with others and mindful both of history's imposed limitations and of its invitation to soar' (O'Meally, 1994: 253).

Contemporary writers in other diasporic African traditions have also used legends of flying Africans as themes in their work. Earl Lovelace begins his 1996 novel, *Salt*, with a description of the ramifications of a solo flight in a Trinidadian context. After a failed rebellion,

> Guinea John, with his black jacket on and a price of two
> hundred pounds sterling on his head, made his way to the East
> Coast, mounted the cliffs at Manzanilla, put two corn cobs
> under his armpits and flew away to Africa, taking with him the
> mysteries of levitation and flight, leaving the rest of his family
> still in captivity mourning over his selfishness ... (Lovelace,
> 1996: 3)

Here we see again the themes of selfishness through flight and the way legends of flight are often told in the context of rebellion. Although flight is not such a central concern of the novel, it does provide the pivotal folkloric background of the plot.

Another twentieth-century artist acutely aware of the power of the flying symbolic was the avant-garde jazz musician Sun Ra. Born Herman Blount in Birmingham, Alabama, in 1914, he became one of the most charismatic African-American musical performers in a career which lasted from the 1930s to his death in 1993. His Arkestra, which he gathered together to play with him from the 1950s onward, was a close-knit family unit whose members often stayed in the group and lived together for years at a time. The Sun Ra Arkestra gained a reputation for solipsistic avant-gardism from many traditional jazz critics, who disliked their space-age costumes and what they saw as a wilful obscurantism that encompassed lyrics shot through with references to intergalactic travel and Egyptology. However, as Graham Lock has shown in his excellent *Blutopia* (1999), far from abandoning his solid Southern cultural roots, the Arkestra's music and the accompanying dancing actually paid homage to them. In analysing the lyrics of the songs, Lock reveals how derivative they are of the spirituals and how the counter-clockwise dancing of the Arkestra in performance, as they 'travelled the spaceways from planet to planet', is similar to Southern Baptist praxis and its development of the ring-shout tradition (Lock, 1999: 34–43). He shows how Ra's lyrics virtually paraphrase preachers such as the Reverend Nix, and are 'deliberately based on the heavenly journey of the Baptist sermon Tradition' (Lock, 1999: 32). What these lyrics share is an involvement in the flying symbolic, which as we have seen is a constant utopic theme in African-American culture. Sun Ra urges his 'congregation' (*ibid.*: 31) to follow him to all the planets in order, including Venus, Jupiter, Neptune and 'Pluto too' (Sun Ra, 1990b). In his sermon 'The White Flyer to Heaven' (1927), the Reverend Nix describes a train which seems to transmogrify into a flying machine as it takes communicants on a journey through the heavens. This bears a striking resemblance to Sun Ra's later journey:

> Higher and higher! Higher and higher!
> We'll pass on to the second Heaven,
> The starry big Heaven and view the flying stars and dashing
>   meteors
> And then pass on by Mars and Mercury, and Jupiter and Venus
> And Saturn and Uranus, and Neptune with her four glittering
>   moons.
> ... beyond the sun, moon and stars, back behind God's eternal
>   Word ... (Oliver, 1984: 153)

This interplanetary spiritual flying clearly represents an imaginative leap that has developed from the flying myths discussed earlier. However, such performances are linked to these myths by their demands for utopia (in this instance, heaven) and the imaginative transportation to another world away from the travails of life in Jim Crow America. As we have seen, the flying symbolic suffuses both the secular and spiritual culture of African Americans. Sun Ra taps into both modes in his adaption of the symbol in concert performances and in recordings throughout his career.

However, Sun Ra also taps into secular flying myths to delight in the freedom flight affords, even if there is no interplanetary goal. While he performs exactly the same counter-clockwise shuffling dance on these occasions, giving them the appearance of the ring shout of the Baptist tradition, the lyrics are less immediately profound. At a concert as part of the Frog Island Jazz/ Blues Festival at Ypsilanti, Michigan, in 1990, and during his set at the Edinburgh Jazz Festival in the same year, Sun Ra used the children's song 'Let's Go Fly a Kite' as a celebratory incantation of the possibilities of flight. The performance of the song, which lasted at least twenty minutes, on both occasions was led by Ra, who marched around the audience, with his band in tow, pointing skywards at the imaginary path of the kites. This juxtaposition of a children's secular song with a spiritual tradition is typical of Sun Ra's inclusivity and illustrates how jazz uses both spiritual and secular modes to create new melded forms which combine energy and reverence. Of course, this reverence is never po-faced, and there is much postmodern irony, not least in the juxtaposition of the innocent song with Sun Ra's deadly seriousness about its message. Through such performances, Sun Ra continues a tradition of using the flying symbolic into the postmodern age. No longer concerned merely with flying back to Africa or to outer space (though both are referenced by the African modes of the music and the space-age costumes), Sun Ra's space-age journeys delight in flying for flying's sake, like a children's kite going 'up to the highest point'. Such 'radical alterity' is key to our understanding of artists like Ra, and Paul Gilroy, in his latest study *Between Camps: Race, Identity and Nationalism at the End of the Colour Line* (2000), highlights how a space-age flying symbolic is a crucial element of postmodern black Atlantic culture:

> Barred from ordinary humanity and offered the equally
> unsatisfactory roles of semi-deity, janitor or pet, artists seek, like
> Sun Ra, another mode of recognition in the most alien identity
> they can imagine. The momentum they acquire in moving from
> the infrahuman to the superhuman finally carries them beyond
> the human altogether. You will believe a man can fly. That
> critique is still lived and enjoyed as both counterculture and
> counterpower, formulated at the junction point, the crossroads
> of diaspora dwelling and diaspora estrangement. (*ibid.*: 348–9)

The flying imaginary is also used by African-American artists like Adrian Piper to describe her movement beyond the racial stereotyping that pigeon-holes and restricts her. In her writings, she describes flying dreams that lift her from everyday reality and lead to philosophizing about the conceptual nature of a flying symbolic that she relates to abstraction – getting away from the barriers of social realism:

> Abstraction is flying ... Abstraction is also flight. It is freedom
> from the immediate spatiotemporal constraints of the moment;
> freedom to plan the future, recall the past, comprehend the

present from a reflective perspective that incorporates all three; freedom from the immediate boundaries of concrete subjectivity, freedom to imagine the possible and transport oneself into it ... Abstraction is freedom from the socially prescribed and consensually accepted, freedom to violate in imagination the constraints of public practice, to play with conventions, or to indulge them. Abstraction is a solitary journey through the conceptual universe, with no anchors, no cues, no signposts, no maps, no foundations to cling to ...
(Piper, 1996: 224)

Here, flying becomes an extended metaphor for a specific postmodern artistic mode, but it also bears uncanny similarities to Sun Ra's notions of a flying symbolic which stretches humdrum reality and moves Africans in the diaspora beyond mere definition by the racist social reality that constricts and confines. The 'freedom to violate in imagination the constraints of public practice' could be an epigraph to Sun Ra's intervention in African-American musical praxis that his travel through the spaceways opens up. As esoteric as it appears, his flying is hardly a unique praxis in African diasporan cultures, merely an extension of the flying symbolic into outer space.

At Sun Ra's graveside, the Baptist preacher Reverend Pherelle Fowler invoked the spiritual part of this flying tradition, 'call[ing] on those assembled to ask the Lord that Sun Ra be raised on eagle wings and taken on high where he might shine like the sun' (Szwed, 1997: 381); however, as Lock contends, Sun Ra had subverted and transformed this myth so that it would have additional meanings for his friends and followers who were present (Lock, 1999: 233). Hence, like the flying symbolic throughout its transfigurations in African-American culture, its use by Sun Ra exhibits a multivalency which allows it to become a dynamic explicator of a multitude of diasporan lives. The theme of intercontinental travel is essential to an understanding of Africans in the diaspora: what the flying symbolic shows is that such travel is not confined to the physical movement between continents, but includes the imaginative flying leap across oceans and even upwards into space. Far from pursuing a dilettante avant-gardism, Sun Ra indulged, through the flying symbolic, in communal rites from the centre of his cultural background that explain his people's doughty survival despite centuries of oppression.

An illustration of the all-pervasiveness, both geographically and chronologically, of such a symbolic occurs in the realm of sport, where 'air-mindedness' links African diasporan sportsmen across the generations. The first famous black footballer in Britain has recently been rediscovered by Phil Vasili's intriguing study (1998). Not only was Arthur Wharton, born on the Gold Coast in 1865, a skilled goalkeeper for a variety of northern English teams but he had also held the world record for the 100 yards sprint in 1886. His goalkeeping style had an athletic dynamism and playfulness which drew much comment from his contemporaries. Fifty years later, T. H. Smith recalled a match between Rotherham and Sheffield Wednesday, where he saw

> Wharton jump, take hold of the cross bar, catch the ball between
> his legs, and cause three onrushing forwards – Billy Ingham,
> Clinks Mumford and Mickey Bennett – to fall into the net. I have
> never seen a similar save since and I have been watching football
> for over fifty years. (quoted in Vasili, 1998: 200)

Such airborne athleticism was his trademark, as was a 'coolness' or 'detached
nonchalance ... bordering on arrogance' (*ibid.*: 68). This combination of
detachment and athleticism creates a virtual 'aesthetic of the cool', exhibiting
amazing athletic feats while appearing unhurried and uninterested. In this he
can be compared to Michael Jordan, whose athletic feats, which approxi-
mated flying on the basketball court a full century later and reflected 'the
stylization of the performed self' (Dyson, 1998: 374), led to Nike naming Air
Jordan sneakers after him. Nike's commodification of Jordan's actions
demonstrates how such black performance is appropriated by multinational
capitalism. However, it should not blind us to the liberatory potential of the
acts themselves. For instance, Jordan's 'will to spontaneity' leads to similar
performative acts as Wharton's deceptive save. Witness Michael Dyson's
description of his basket against the Los Angeles Lakers in 1991:

> Jordan made a dive toward the lane, gesturing with his hands
> and body that he was about to complete a patent Jordan dunk
> shot with his right hand. But when he spied defender Sam
> Perkins slipping over to oppose his shot, he switched the ball in
> midair to his left hand to make an overhead scoop shot instead,
> which immediately became known as the 'levitation shot.' Such
> improvisation, a staple of the will to spontaneity, allows Jordan
> to expand his vocabulary of athletic spectacle ... (*ibid.*: 375)

These sportsmen perform flying feats to gain advantage. Such modes are
developed through a black cultural style that relies on improvisation, coolness
and stylization. These two examples reveal 'air-mindedness' as central to
African diasporan culture and delineate a continuum in black Atlantic culture
in the use of a flying symbolic that includes oral literature, dance, music and
performance as well as sport. As W. T. Lhamon Jr asserts of Africans in the
diaspora (in a comment of particular relevance to Wharton, whose role in
British sport had been almost totally erased):

> Cultural history should record and analyze their astounding
> capacity to maintain meaning down the years against the
> physical erasure, the constant covering over, and the disdain
> even of those who chronicle them. They tell a history that does
> not belong to the apparent winners. (Lhamon, 1998: 26)

Flying Africans (both real and imaginary) constantly show up links beyond
an alienating slave and Jim Crow reality to a utopian African past and present
and to an imagined utopian future elsewhere that helps to explain the nuances

of the struggle for dignity in the here and now (whether that happens to be in the seventeenth or the twentieth/twenty-first century). To paraphrase Ralph Ellison's character Jefferson in 'Flying Home', black people were 'the flyin'est son[s]-of-bitches what ever hit heaven' (Ellison, 1996: 160).

=== 5 ===

'WHO'S EATING WHOM?'

THE DISCOURSE OF CANNIBALISM IN NARRATIVES OF THE BLACK AND WHITE ATLANTIC

> the cannibal black, the devourer, the black plague, insatiable men and women free-ranging through (or buried within) the white jungle of psyche
>
> a thirties Max Fleisch cartoon: Betty Boop pursued by the round black sun of Louis Armstrong – 'I'm Gonna Get You, You Rascal, You' – chasing her from the cannibal kitchen stew-pot through a rippling jungle phantasm
>
> if the black's a cannibal, the white becomes what's beheld; in the frenzy of what is blissfully dubbed postmodern is a trophy room of cannibalized cultures; to consume is to be consumed (Meltzer, 1993: 13)
>
> Tell the people in Europe who enjoy chocolate, that they are eating my flesh. (Comment from contemporary enslaved child in the cocoa plantations of the Ivory Coast, quoted in *Slavery: A Global Investigation*, 2000)

The response to stereotyping is as important an area of study as stereotyping itself. The ways in which oppressed people react and survive in the face of exploitation and colonization is manifested in part through a stereotyping discourse. Toni Morrison is only the latest black artist to take back the malevolent jungle and primitive imagery which has been used to demean her and her race, employing it instead to make polemical points about racial, sexual and class conflicts in American, African-American and black Atlantic culture. This tradition has encompassed (among others) Quobna Ottobah Cugoano, Olaudah Equiano, Frederick Douglass, Henry Bibb, Charles Chesnutt, Oscar Michaux, Claude McKay, Zora Neale Hurston, Duke Ellington, Malcolm X, Chester Himes, Ishmael Reed, Archie Shepp and Spike Lee, in addition to a whole host of oral artists/practitioners. This chapter will concentrate on the transatlantic manifestations of this counter-hegemonic discourse as it has manifested itself in the work of black writers of the Enlightenment period and beyond and in the discourse of the mid-nineteenth century as refracted through Toni Morrison's late-twentieth-century writing. I aim to contextualize Morrison's use of the primitivist trope by placing it in a historical and avowedly Atlanticist framework to demonstrate its significance for both black Atlantic conceptions of oppression and Euro-American conceptions of non-white savagery. Indeed, I want to show how these two impulses have fed upon each other to create modes of expression that can explicate the colonial and postcolonial relationship in a dynamic new way.

At the centre of the white-held stereotype of the bestial other, as promulgated in a variety of discourses from the academic/anthropological to the cartoon character, is the figure of the cannibal. It should be no surprise, then, that cannibalism is a central motif running through Toni Morrison's historical novel about slavery and its aftermath, *Beloved* (1987). However, it is one that is rarely discussed by her critics. One of the few to talk about cannibalism in Morrison's oeuvre is Barbara Hill Rigney, who discusses its use in *The Bluest Eye* (1970), and we shall return to this interesting passage from Morrison's early writing in the next chapter. More specifically in relation to *Beloved*, Barbara Offutt Mathieson and Christiana Lambidis also explore the issue of cannibalism, but concentrate more on the relationship between mothers and daughters within African-American families than the inter-communal discourse around cannibalism which is my interest here. In particular, they discuss the way in which Sethe's daughter Beloved seems to prey on her mother in a cannibalistic manner – as Mathieson puts it: 'The infant literally devours its mother's sustenance' (Mathiesen, 1994: 225).

While Beloved preys on her mother, as the narrative develops, she is shown to be obsessed by the fear of becoming the prey of others. Beloved 'had two dreams: exploding and being swallowed' (Morrison, 1998: 133). The critics have written much on the first dream, relating it to oppressive practices of slavery, and writing myriad papers on the idea of dismemberment in the text and Morrison's emphasis on the need to remember in order to heal the legacy of slavery (see, for example, Goldman, 1990; Rushdy, 1990; Henderson, 1991; Keenan, 1993; Hamilton, 1996). However, the implications and contextualization of Beloved's second dream of being eaten remain, with the exception of Lambidis and Mathieson, largely unexplored. I want to map the history Morrison is drawing on through this trope of cannibalism, showing how her use of the discourse surrounding the cannibal is reliant upon earlier black Atlantic discourse and illuminates our understanding of African–European encounters from as far back as the sixteenth century through emancipation and beyond.

To understand the power of Morrison's development of the cannibal trope as a key to the exploration of slavery and racism, it must first be established that Beloved is more than just a character of the same name as the novel; she is literally the haunting ghost of slavery, describing a middle passage she was far too young to experience in reality. As her mother, Sethe, describes, it is Beloved's grandmother who has experienced the horrors of the journey across the Atlantic, during which Sethe herself was born and retained, even while her siblings were 'thrown away' because their fathers were white (Morrison, 1988a: 62). In her short life, Beloved has no direct experience of such a middle passage, having been born in Kentucky before escaping with her mother to Ohio. However, in an extended stream-of-consciousness monologue towards the end of the novel, Beloved describes the experience of the middle passage as though she too has experienced it:

> there will never be a time I am not crouching and watching
> others that are crouching too   I am always crouching   the man
> on my face is dead   his face is not mine   his mouth smells
> sweet but his eyes are locked   some who eat nasty themselves I
> do not eat   the men without skin bring us their morning water
> to drink   we have none   at night I cannot see the dead man on
> my face ... (*ibid.*: 210)

The racial memory of the horrendous voyage is so deeply woven into the slaves' consciousness that when the dead child Beloved returns as a grown-up ghost she has literally imbibed it with her mother's milk; it is part of this frightening legacy of a slave past that Beloved represents in the novel. I will return to depictions of the middle passage later in this chapter, but first I want to place her discussion of this horrendous journey in the context of African-American history so that I can move to an interpretation of the more specific topic of cannibalism.

As I have discussed in Chapters 3 and 4, many African slaves used different methods of resistance during transportation across the Atlantic: ranging from suicide and refusal to comply with orders to outright rebellion. Jumping overboard was a method frequently chosen in preference to the horrors of present captivity and an uncertain future. However, when the slavers under-took to lessen the dangers of losing such valuable cargo in this way, the Africans were forced to try new ways of easing their passage to the spirit world. One method was to refuse food, so that the slavers were often driven to force-feed their valuable slaves. This was taken to extreme lengths on some ships, where the refusal to eat even the smallest amount of food was punished by a force-feeding regime which matched the other horrors of the middle passage. On the *Amistad*'s now famous voyage of 1839, depositions from the slaves, who were later to revolt, revealed the harshness of this regime:

> They had rice enough to eat, but had very little to drink. If they
> left any of the rice that was given to them uneaten, either from
> sickness or any other cause, they were whipped, it was a
> common thing for them to be forced to eat so much as to vomit.
> (Barber, 1840: 19)

These vicious acts were misinterpreted by many of the victims, who felt that the only reason for such diligence on the part of these usually indifferent men must be that they were being fattened up to be eaten. Such perceptions did not occur in a vacuum, as rumours and myths about light-skinned cannibals were present in Africa during (and indeed after) the slave trade, and in fact were multiplied by the very operations of the trade itself.

Throughout the slave trade and particularly in the eighteenth and nineteenth centuries, there is much evidence that rumours and folktales abounded in Africa about the incidence of cannibalism on the slave ships. What other explanation could there be for the disappearance of their kinfolk? John Thornton shows how these rumours were prevalent even in the early years of the slave trade. Alonso De Sandoval describes how the slaves who landed in Cartagena in 1622 were unwilling participants in a 'form of witchcraft' in which 'upon their arrival they would be made into oil and eaten' (Thornton, 1992: 161), while Job Ben Solomon's return to The Gambia in 1734, having been enslaved by Mandingoes in 1729 and sold to traders to be shipped to America, was greeted with astonishment in his home territory, as they expected all slaves taken by white men to be murdered or eaten (Austin, 1995: 60). Participants in the slave trade often reported their 'cargo's' fears of cannibalism and the dangers these fears posed to good order among the captives. William Bosman, who was chief factor at Elmina Castle, reported in 1699 on such folk beliefs: 'We are sometimes sufficiently plagued with a parcel of slaves which come from a far in-land country, who very innocently persuade one another, that we buy them up only to fatten and afterwards eat them as a delicacy' (quoted in Kaplan, 1969: 292).

In his intriguing study *Black Legacy: America's Hidden Heritage* (1993), William D. Piersen outlines these African folk myths Bosman refers to which talk of a race of light-skinned cannibals who stole away black men for their repasts (Piersen, 1993: 5–12), while W. Arens, in *The Man-eating Myth* (1979), shows how such myths were used by slavers as late as the midnineteenth century for their own ends. Arab slavers exploited both black and white fears of cannibalism to increase their monopoly power over slavery in the Congolese area. They kept whites away from the area with tales of the cannibalistic habits of many of its tribes; at the same time, they dissuaded the Congolese tribesman from helping white traders by warning them of white cannibalistic practices (Arens, 1979: 88). As Sam Shepperson and Thomas Price have discovered, similar rumours were being spread in East Africa too (Shepperson and Price, 1987: 9). Many distinguished historians of Africa have followed this gruesome gastronomic trail, revealing how rumours of white cannibals helped to shape colonial and postcolonial relations between Africans and Europeans, in the same way that myths of African savagery and cannibalism construct European attitudes to Africans. Initial rumours about white cannibals were given added credence by the dynamics of sacrificial cults like the Aro cult of the Ibo people, whose delivery of slaves into the transatlantic system through tributes from religious followers meant they were symbolically consumed as a precursor to their enslavement. Basil Davidson explains:

> Any man who should offend the oracle – and the Aro priests saw
> to it that nothing was easier – was mulcted of a fine: but it was a
> fine that was paid in slaves. Once paid the fine was supposed to
> be eaten by the oracle: in truth, of course, the captives were

simply handed along the Aro network to the traders of the coast
who sold them to Europeans. Perhaps this was one reason why
the Ibos thought the Europeans were cannibals. (Davidson,
1968: 189)

Africans are eaten by the oracle and then 'spewed out as slaves and marched
to the coast for export' (Manning, 1992: 57–8). It is hardly surprising that this
'eating' of the slaves by the oracle became transformed into rumours of
European cannibalism, for white men were, after all, at the end of this particular food chain. The rumours (or at least traces of them) were not confined
to the West of Africa but can be tracked in the south and east of the continent
and well into the nineteenth century, as Neil Parsons and Sam Shepperson's
research reveals. In *King Khama, Emperor Joe and the Great White Queen*
(1998), Neil Parsons relates the visit of the Bechauna chiefs (of present-day
Botswana) to London in 1895 in an effort to forestall the sale of their lands to
a private company run by Cecil Rhodes. A petition from King Khama and 135
others to the imperial government, which predated their departure for Britain,
uses imagery of cannibalistic capitalism that indicts the company as voracious
devourers of their land:

> your petitioners have heard much of the injustice and oppression
> which the Chartered Company inflict upon the tribes who live in
> the north; and your petitioners fear very much lest they should
> be killed and eaten by the Company. For the petitioners see that
> the company does not love black people; it loves only to take the
> country of the black people and sell it to others that it may see
> gain. (quoted in Parsons, 1998: 60)

While Parsons rightly warns us against taking the 'Setswana idiom of being
devoured ... literally' (*ibid.*), its use here to symbolize the rapacious nature of
unbridled imperialism illustrates how Khama and his fellow leaders felt that
the cannibal metaphor accurately described evil white men long after the
abolition of the slave trade. Such symbolic cannibalism is surely related to the
history of white cannibals deduced throughout this chapter. Sam Shepperson
and Thomas Price's research is even more clearcut. They relate how in 1892
Jessie Monteith Currie, a Scottish missionary's wife in Southern Nyasaland,
hears how

> It was commonly asserted [she said] that our chief ... had eaten
> his child by a slave wife. Some of our boys believed us capable of
> this abominable practice ourselves. When a very stout white
> man, a land surveyor, called by the natives 'Che Chimimba' [Mr
> Big Stomach] visited our station and stayed in the doctor's
> house, [the] table-boy there fled in terror lest he should be eaten
> by the fat man. And another time when the Msungu [European
> in charge] was smoking a piece of wild boar in a barrel, a boy

believed firmly that the 'nyama' [meat] was one of his comrades.
(quoted in Shepperson and Price, 1987: 10–11)

Even the most innocent (and loving) of gestures by the Europeans were
open to misinterpretation, so that when the famous missionary Joseph Booth
risked his life to rescue a woman and child stolen into slavery in 1893, Arab
traders wilfully misconstrued his actions as selfishly acquisitive, informing
four Yao chiefs 'that the whites were cannibals, that their pretended friendship
toward the slaves was only so as to get them for food' (quoted in *ibid.*: 86–7).
When his daughter Emily kissed the black baby, it only added to the unease
felt by some of the Africans, as she reveals: 'the story went round that the
white man [Booth] and the little girl took the black baby and ate it' (quoted in
ibid.: 87). As described by Emily, the baby is 'sweet enough to kiss' (*ibid.*), but
her innocent remark betrays the interpenetration of gastronomic vocabulary in
descriptions of affection that have implications for the colonial relations that I
explore elsewhere in this study.

Of course, the Europeans are no innocents in this manufacturing of
rumours of cannibalism to the unsophisticated. For instance, in the Caribbean
in the eighteenth and nineteenth centuries, the English played on black fears of
the cannibalistic other to help control revolt by accusing the few native Caribs
who were left of anthropophagy so that slaves were less inclined to flee into
the hinterland – better the devil you know than the possibility of a man-eating
devil who lives on the far side of the island. As Carib chief Irvince Auguiste
from Dominica commented in a 1990 interview:

> when they first brought in Black slaves, the English told them we
> Caribs ate Black people, so that the maroons would not seek to
> join us when they ran away and would fight us when they did.
> Like that they kept us divided a long time. (Hulme and
> Whitehead, 1992: 350)

From narratives such as these, we can tell that the discourse surrounding
cannibalism was never straightforward or related simply to one race or tribe,
but a complex mythology used in an attempt to explicate new or strange
occurrences on the borders of communities which was sometimes coopted by
powerful forces as a useful method of control over the conquered. Taking this
view, the cannibalistic nature of the other is almost always a myth, which,
despite bearing little relation to historical reality, contains and transmits significant cultural messages for those who maintain it. Peter Hulme has usefully
defined cannibalism as 'the image of ferocious consumption of human flesh
frequently used to mark the boundary between one community and its others –
a term that has gained its entire meaning from within the discourse of European colonialism' (Hulme, 1992: 86). For instance, the discourse around
cannibalism allowed the whites, during the Atlantic slave trade, to promulgate
an ideology of civilizing the primitive, of saving the African from an
unchristian savagery. More pointedly, as can be seen in the final example
above, it was used by slavers themselves to augment their dominance over

their slaves. Jan Nederveen Pieterse summarizes cannibalism's centrality to white imperial conquest most succinctly: 'When new lands were found and strange peoples encountered, whether in America, the Pacific or the African interior, the accusation of cannibalism served to affirm and secure the central place of Christian civilization' (Pieterse, 1992: 116). Such salvational and pragmatic reasons for the discourse were always buttressed by what might be termed the psychological needs of the imperialists. Maggie Kilgour posits this most astutely, describing how 'the cannibal is the individual's "alien" against which he constructs his identity, and whose threat to his identity is represented as literal consumption' (Kilgour, 1990: 147). Identity formation is literally dependent on demonizing the other, and Kilgour's definition can clearly be extended to Africans who, in demonizing their oppressors as cannibals, constructed themselves as always the innocent victims despite African involvement in the trade. However, this illusionary psychological equivalence should not blind us to the operation of political and economic power, which meant that Europeans generally exerted definitional power in their relations to the other throughout the period of European imperialism. Kilgour acknowledges this in describing how 'the definition of the other as cannibal justifies its oppression, extermination, and cultural cannibalism (otherwise known as imperialism) by the rule "eat or be eaten"' (*ibid.*: 148). Conquest is the answer to the danger posed by a cannibal other and was one which Europeans initiated with great zeal throughout the imperial phase.

In the wake of such brutal imperialism and the transportation of over eleven million Africans across the Atlantic, counter-mythologies developed: for many of the Africans left behind, the myth of white cannibals provided an explanation for the loss of friends and loved ones, and accounted for such a large-scale tragedy as the transatlantic slave trade. Such depictions of Europeans as cannibals did more than this, though, as the 'evidence would seem to allow for its use as a figure for the destruction of native social systems by European presence' (Hulme, 1992: 289). If we follow this logic, the whites assumed the mantle of cannibal and were cast as such in the written and spoken narratives of the colonized and enslaved because they literally ate away at the cultures of native peoples. I shall return at length to some of these narratives later, but first we must address the origins of the mythology in European cultures.

The European view of cannibalism expressed in the images of Africans and native others as cannibals existed almost from the beginning of colonial contact and became a staple of imperialist discourse in the cartoons of the nineteenth and early twentieth centuries. These were buttressed by the pseudo-scientific writings of the leaders of the Enlightenment, such as Thomas Jefferson and David Hume, who compared Africans to animals and denied their ability to think rationally, implying a bestiality which was linked directly to cannibalism. Contemporary chroniclers of West Indian slavery, such as Bryan Edwards in the 1790s, indicted whole African nations as cannibalistic without any evidence. He contended that the 'Eboes are in fact more truly savage than any nation of the Gold Coast; inasmuch as many tribes amongst them ... have been without doubt, accustomed to the shocking practice of feeding on human flesh ... ' (quoted in Carretta, 1999: 293). When James Riley was captured and enslaved in Morocco in 1815, his description of his 'African captor as a subhuman cannibal' (Baepler, 1999: 29) is obviously influenced by the whole discourse of the African as inferior delineated by Jefferson and Hume:

> his face resembled that of an ourang-outang more than a human being; his eyes were red and fiery; his mouth which stretched nearly from ear to ear, was well lined with sound teeth; and a long curling beard, which depended from his upper lip and chin down and gave him altogether a most horrid appearance, and I could not but imagine that those well set teeth were sharpened for the purpose of devouring human flesh. (quoted in Baepler, 1999: 29–30)

Such views were not confined to the African continent. American examples of the dominance of popular views of the African as bestial and cannibalistic are prevalant throughout the yellow press, and we can follow them in responses to the capture of the *Amistad* by the American authorities and subsequent court cases. The New York press was particularly scathing about the nature of the cargo on board the *Amistad*, which was of poor quality because the blacks, according to the *New York Daily Express*, were 'hardly above the apes and monkeys of their own Africa and the language they jabber [was] incomprehensible here' (Jones, 1986: 48). Abolitionists who helped them were labelled as naive innocents who needed to be protected from themselves. According to the *New York Advertiser and Express*, only time would show 'what mischievous consequences may follow their ridiculous fraternising with the barbarians who would probably eat them, if they could catch them in their native country' (*ibid.*: 84). The yellow press, then, used the image of the African/ black man as cannibal to further its agenda of demonizing the *Amistad* captives.

However, and interestingly for my argument here, the discourse surrounding the incident was so replete with references to cannibalism that those defending the *Amistad* blacks appropriated a language which posited rapacious American slavers as cannibalistic in much the same way as the captured Africans had described their white enslavers. Thus, Amos Townsend, in anticipating legal action to free the captives, declares, 'if anything can be done legally to pluck the prey from the jaws of human tigers I hope it will be done' (*ibid.*: 165). Even John Quincy Adams in his famous disposition could not resist a sarcastic reference to the cannibalistic natures of Spain and the United States. Discussing a treaty obligation to return impounded merchandise to port officials intact, he declared that 'a stipulation to restore human beings entire might suit two nations of cannibals but would be absurd and worse than absurd, between civilised and Christian nations' (*ibid.*: 179). By indicting Christian nations for their cannibalistic interest in the slaves, Adams introduces an element of cultural relativism into the debate that is reminiscent of Michel de Montaigne in his famous 1580 essay, 'Of the Cannibales', which had highlighted the 'primitive' nature of the cannibalistic other in order to shed light on the savage practices of so-called civilized Western nations in such institutions as the Inquisition. Montaigne asserts:

> I think there is more barbarisme in eating men alive, than to feed upon them being dead; to mangle by tortures and torment a body full of lively sense, to roast him in peeces, to make dogges and swine to gnaw and teare him in mamockes (as wee have not only read but seene very lately, yea and in our owne memorie, not amongst ancient enemies, but our neighbours and fellow-citizens; and which is worse, under pretence of pietie and religion) than to roast and eat him after he is dead. (Montaigne, 1928, Vol. 1: 223–4)

Such cultural relativism is almost entirely absent from Daniel Defoe's famous eighteenth-century novel *Robinson Crusoe* (1719), which illustrates white fears of a savage other with cannibalistic desires in the passages which precede Crusoe's meeting with Friday. When he first discovers the footprint that shows he is not alone on the island, Crusoe experiences 'dread and terror of falling into the hands of savages and cannibals' (Defoe, 1982: 162). Such fears had been a staple of a European psychosis since Columbus had first encountered what he described as 'cannibals' in his 'discovery' of the Americas in 1492. Then, as later in the eighteenth century, proof of cannibalism was required to taint whole tribes with similar accusations, merely rumours from those willing to point the finger at people who pursued a different way of life in a neighbouring region. On his voyage Columbus encountered many rumours of cannibalism, but absolutely no concrete evidence. He reports that the natives on one island 'further informed him that at a distance there were men with one eye only, and others with faces like dogs, who were man-eaters, accustomed upon taking a prisoner to cut his throat, drink his blood and dismember him' (Columbus, 1994: 122–3).

Columbus, of course, had as much difficulty finding the men with one eye as he did the fictitious cannibals. However, despite the non-appearance of actual cannibals, it was Columbus's voyage which established the term 'cannibalism' (deriving from the descriptive term 'Carib') in the discourse of European colonialism. As Eric Cheyfitz elaborates:

> After ... Columbus ... cannibal will come to mean one thing in Western languages: a human who eats another's flesh ... part of a diverse arsenal of rhetorical weapons used to distinguish what they conceive of as their civilised selves from certain savage others, principally Native Americans and Africans. (Cheyfitz, 1991: 42)

The term 'cannibal' had other uses too: it distinguished those peoples who acquiesced to colonial rule from those who fought against it. The former were patronized and enslaved, the latter demonized and murdered. As Peter Mason contends, 'those who accept the Spaniards on [their] terms are labelled Arawak, while those who defend their territory and way of life are labelled Carib' (Mason, 1990: 22). Even a commentator such as Philip P. Boucher, who is sympathetic to evidence that some Carib people were anthropophagous, is clear that the evidence for such practices was out of all proportion to the level of vilification meted out by the European colonialists:

> What is clear about the issue of cannibalism is that starting with Columbus and the Spaniards Europeans levelled grossly distorted charges of man-eating against potentially enslavable peoples who ferociously resisted incursions into their island homelands. Whatever the reality of Island Carib practices Europeans created the myth of Caribs as ferocious, insatiable cannibals. (Boucher, 1987: 7)

Although the non-white fear of cannibalism is less well documented in the discourse of European colonialism, its presence is evident in texts with as wide a geographical and historical range as Ralegh's discovery narrative of Guiana where the Arawaks 'feared that we would have eaten them' (quoted in Whitehead, 1997: 84), mythology from Amerindians like those in Surinam, who believed that the whites who invaded their country were assimilated to a neighbouring tribe whose priests were cannibalistic (Mason, 1990: 163) and travelogues such as that written by Mungo Park, which details African fears of the cannibalistic other. In view of its African provenance, this last example deserves more attention:

> they viewed me at first with looks of horror and repeatedly asked if my countrymen were cannibals ... A deeply rooted idea that the whites purchased Negroes for the purpose of devouring them, or of selling them to others, that they might be devoured hereafter, naturally makes the slaves contemplate a journey to the coast with great terror. (Park, 1954: 390)

For those left in Africa, rumours of cannibalism were thankfully confined to folktales; however, for the Africans on the ships to the Americas, the rumours seemed far too close to reality for comfort. As Joseph Wright is loaded onto a ship in Lagos in the 1820s, he describes his feelings and those of his fellow captors: 'We were all very sorrowful in heart because we were going to leave our land for another ... [and] we had heard that the Portuguese were going to eat us when they got to their country' (quoted in Thomas, 1997: 714–15).

Speculation as to their intended fate led to dire consequences for some Africans who, on nearing landfall and anticipating that they were to be the white man's next meal, took drastic action to escape their fate. There are, for instance, incidents of mass suicide attempts which were caused by fears of cannibalism. Over a hundred slaves jumped overboard from the *Prince of Orange* at St Christopher in San Domingo in 1737, and thirty-three were drowned (Piersen, 1993; 10–11). The slave captain commented:

> The reason (I have learned since) of this misfortune was owing to one of their countrymen who came on board, and told the slaves, in a joking manner, that they were first to have their eyes put out and then to be eaten ... (Donnan, 1969, Vol. 2: 460)

Other evidence of how the fear of cannibalism impacted on relationships between slavers and their 'cargo' comes from depositions about revolts: witness the *L'Annibal* revolt of 1729, where the ship's captain 'hear[ed], furthermore, their constant complaints that we kept them on board in order to eat them' (D. M. Hall, 1992: 91). That cannibalism was prevalent on these phantasmagoric sailing machines off the coast of Africa is a matter of written record. John Atkins, a Royal Naval surgeon, reports how as punishment for the unsuccessful revolt on the *Robert of Bristol* in 1721, African captors were made into cannibals: 'three other, Abettors, but not Actors, nor of strength for it, he sentenced to cruel Deaths; making them first eat the Heart and Liver of one of them killed ... (quoted in Kaplan, 1969: 295). This incident showed that rumours of cannibalistic practices on the ships were, to an extent, justified and exemplified a slave system which literally ate up Africans. Such barbarous episodes and their retelling throughout the African continent were crucial to the development of definitive myths, which sprang up to explicate aspects of European cultural praxis that according to legend were reliant on the use of the African bodies taken away from the continent. Joseph Miller summarizes these common myths from the eighteenth century which involved the Lord of the Dead, Mwene Puto, whose subjects were the white slavers:

> The bodies of the blacks taken off to those regions of the dead far beyond the water Mwene Puto pressed to extrude the cooking oil that his subjects brought back to Africa for their own use in settlements at the edge of the ocean where they lived. The blood of Mwene Puto's black victims also returned to Africa as the deep red wine the strangers sold. The foreigners' cheeses, it was further said, were made from blacks' brains. The fires of Hell also flared in the Land of the Dead where the followers of Mwene Puto burned the bones of the blacks to yield the ashlike, lethal gray powder that, when placed in iron tubes, transformed itself back into the flames from which it had come and spewed pain and destruction against any who tried, unprepared to resist their demands. (Miller, 1988: 5)

That gunpowder and other purely European goods should be imagined as products of African bodies exemplifies how the myth speaks to the truth, that the surplus value of the slaves is used to aggrandize the Europeans and is crucial to their dominance over a long period. The technological superiority of gunpowder is reliant first on the operation of the barbarous trade of slavery which allows its purchase. Legends such as these are closer to the truth of how the slave economy works than the Western demonization of heathen African beliefs would give them credit for. Their prevalence is shown most interestingly in the *Amistad* revolt of 1839.

The *Amistad* incident is probably the most famous instance of how the fear of cannibalism led to a revolt on board a slave ship. I have documented earlier in this chapter how the fear of cannibalism was spread by force-feeding, which indicated to many slaves that they were being fattened up in order to be eaten. Such fears were compounded as they neared land and their treatment became worse, as is related in their depositions:

> there was much whipping and the cook told them that when
> they reached land they would all be eaten. To avoid being eaten
> and to escape the bad treatment they experienced, they rose
> upon the crew with the design of returning to Africa (Barber,
> 1840: 19)

The testimony of one of the African captives, Fuliwa, was even more explicit, repeating the claim that the cook gloated that they would all be eaten after their heads had been cut off. Hence, when they rose against the sailors, the cook was the first to be killed. The fear of being killed and consequently eaten continued when (and maybe even especially when) they were in jail in New Haven. Four thousand visitors came to view the captives, a legion of white faces that convinced the frightened blacks they were in imminent danger of death. These fears were compounded when their previous owner, Jose Ruiz, paid a visit. The African captives took fright asking, 'If they don't mean to kill us, why are so many people here to see us?' (Jones, 1986: 164). Once on shore and under white control fears of entering his bodily economy came to the fore.

Thus, rumours of cannibalism were a fundamental cause of one of the major slave rebellions in the history of the Atlantic slave trade and continued to haunt the Africans during their imprisonment. The preponderance of such rumours and their effect on the slaves shipped to the Americas are confirmed, not only by European writers like Park and the Scottish missionaries discussed by Shepperson and Price, but also by early African writers on the Atlantic slave trade. Thus, an anonymous black poet in a 1793 *Gentleman's Review* outlines the basic rudiments of the myth that slavery was effectively a form of cannibalism:

> Here de white man beat de black man
> Till he's sick and cannot stand.
> Sure de black man be eat by white man!
> Will not go to white man land. (quoted in Pieterse, 1992: 120)

More substantively, in his autobiography, Quobna Ottobah Cugoano attests to the widespread influence of folktales claiming the existence of white cannibals. After first using a rhetorical reversal by positing white slavers as literal white devils that undermines the stereotypical depiction of blackness as inherently devilish (Cugoano, 1999: 12), he moves to a narrative that describes the voracious appetite of these devils for black flesh. After he has been captured by African slavers, he comes into contact with white men:

> Next day we travelled on, and in the evening came to a town,
> where I saw several white people, which made me afraid they
> would eat me, according to our notion as children in the inland
> part of the country. (*ibid.*: 14)

Such folktales provide what I will term a cannibalistic symbolic which emerges in Cugoano's work, so that slavers are often described as voracious monsters preying on innocent Africans. Thus, even African slave-catchers are perceived as 'villains [who] meant to feast on us as their prey' (*ibid.*: 13). The slave narrative of Olaudah Equiano, *The Interesting Narrative of the Life of Olaudah Equiano ...* , published in 1789, shows the influence of such a symbolic to an even greater extent. He constantly harps upon his fear of being eaten, which repeated assurances from some of his fellow sufferers do little to assuage. One of his first sights on boarding the ship is a boiling copper cauldron surrounded by chained black people. To Equiano this can only mean one thing:

> I no longer doubted of my fate, and, quite overpowered with
> horror and anguish, I fell motionless on the deck and fainted.
> When I recovered a little, I found some black people about
> me ... I asked them if we were not to be eaten by those white
> men with horrible looks, red faces, and long hair. (Equiano,
> 1995: 55)

As on the *Amistad* in the nineteenth century, the fear of cannibalism was reinforced by a force-feeding regime which seemed to Equiano to be part of a strategy to deliver plump and edible bodies to the white man's homeland. He details how they are denied the option of suicide by the constant vigilance of the crew, which is accompanied by care over their eating habits:

> I would have jumped over the side, but I could not; and, besides,
> the crew used to watch us very closely who were not chained
> down to the decks, lest we should leap into the water; and I have
> seen some of these poor African prisoners most severely cut for
> attempting to do so, and hourly whipped for not eating.
> (*ibid.*: 56)

Cugoano also 'refused to eat or drink for whole days together' (Cugoano, 1999: 14) after being captured, revealing the widespread nature of such strategies to forestall the cannibalistic enslavers. Although I wish to use these passages to show how genuine was the fear of white cannibals among those Africans transported to the New World, Equiano's and Cugoano's repeated use of the trope of cannibalism is also a polemical and strategic one in the context of eighteenth-century writing. Their narratives are anti-slavery tracts and their depiction of slavers as inhuman, cannibalistic demons works at both a rhetorical and realistic level. The enforced removal of Africans from their stable and civilized environments in the belly of ships which often become literal graves is thus equated to the barbarism of cannibalism. As Piersen contends: 'As a mythopoeic analogy it does not seem farfetched to portray chattel slavery as a kind of economic cannibalism' (Piersen, 1993: 12). European colonialism and New World slavery were after all literally to consume generations of Africans. Following on from this, the repeated reference by eighteenth-century African writers to their cannibalistic fears could surely be seen as a sophisticated device to illustrate the realities of the Atlantic slave trade. This is emphasized when the ship reaches Bridgetown and Equiano reiterates his fears of cannibalism:

> Many merchants and planters now came on board, though it was in the evening. They put us in separate parcels, and examined us attentively. They also made us jump, and pointed to the land, signifying we were to go there. We thought by this we should be eaten by these ugly men, as they appeared to us ... at last the white people got some old slaves from the land to pacify us. They told us we were not to be eaten, but to work, and were soon to go on land, where we should see many of our country people. (Equiano, 1995: 60)

Once on land, the slaves' fears of cannibalism are reawakened for, as Park relates, the legends had talked about being sold to other white men to be eaten. Equiano's reference to cannibalism at the point of sale testifies to the accuracy of Park's information about the legend, but it also illustrates Equiano's polemical point that slavery is a cannibalistic process, a form of economic cannibalism (or vampirism) that sucks at the life-blood of the enslaved Africans. This is also emphasized by the interaction of significations of the gastronomic and labour in the phrase 'we were not to be eaten, but to work'. The replacement of the fear of incorporation with the actuality of the exploitation of the labouring body in the slave system should not blind us to equivalencies between whites as cannibals and whites as users of forced labour which Equiano's juxtaposition illuminates here. Crystal Bartolovich usefully distinguishes this 'cannibal/parasite distinction' that enables the slaveholder to see himself as the civilized partner in the exchange. He outlines how 'on the side of civility is placed consumption of human labour power; on the side of savagery consumption of human flesh' (Bartolovich, 1998: 214). Equiano's juxtaposition does more than link these imagined binaries; it shows how incorporation is not merely a function of individual cannibalistic physical bodies but also of a whole system which exploits black bodies until they are used up, which literally consumes their labour power. However, this knowledge of consumption being more metaphorical than actual does not completely assuage his fears of being eaten. Even after he has completed the middle passage and been sold, his return to the sea in the company of his master brings up old nightmares. As they run out of food on the long voyage, his fear of the cannibalistic whites is once again roused: 'In our extremities the captain and people told me in jest they would kill and eat me, but I thought them in earnest and was depressed beyond measure, expecting every moment to be my last ... I did not know what to think of these white people; I very much feared they would kill and eat me' (Equiano, 1995: 65). These fears are reinforced by his master's casual discussion of cannibalism as though it were an everyday practice. Equiano reports how his friend Richard Barker often ate with his master:

> My master had lodged in his mother's house in America: he respected him very much, and made him always eat with him in the cabin. He used often to tell him jocularly he would kill and eat me. Sometimes he would say to me – the black people were not good to eat and would ask if we did not eat people in my country. I said, No: then he said he would kill Dick (as he always called him) first, and afterwards me. Though this hearing relieved my mind a little as to myself, I was alarmed for Dick, and whenever he was called I used to be very much afraid he was to be killed. (*ibid.*: 65–6)

As an owned man, Equiano fears entering the bodily economy of the white man just as easily as he had been consumed by the economy of his state. As discussed earlier, Houston Baker Jr has noted how 'it is absolutely necessary for the slave to negotiate the economics of slavery if he would be free' (Baker, 1987: 39), and Equiano successfully negotiates his way through this grotesque economy without being consumed either literally or metaphorically. He makes it to Britain whole in body and not driven mad by his awful experiences. In a sense, his master's jocularity about his cannibalistic desires is Equiano's first hint that his fears are exaggerated, and could be seen as a rhetorical device designed to show his maturation. He now understands cannibalism as a function of power and fears of it as a weakness that stems from the impotence of the slave position. As the narrative unfolds, Equiano does more than just negotiate his own way out of the 'economic cannibalism' of the Atlantic world, indicting the slave trade by linking it with a cannibalism which is held in horror by both white and African cultures. However, he uses the white fear of cannibalism not to indict a savage other race, to which he of course belongs, but to point out the savagery at the heart of the Europeans' own everyday practices, a savagery that would even play on the cannibalistic fears of a young boy for the entertainment of his oppressors.

The equation of white men and a savagery that could include cannibalism meant that the latter became a staple terror for African peoples on long voyages where food shortages were always possible. After the *Tiger* shipwreck in 1766, for instance, there was little doubt who would be the first to die so that his blood could be drunk and his flesh eaten: as one narrative relates, 'it came into Viauld's recollection that mariners had cast lots who should die to keep their comrades from famine. His eyes lighted on the negro youth' (quoted in Simpson, 1986: 125). A year earlier, the crew of the damaged *Peggy* mid-

Atlantic, having run out of leather, candles, tobacco, cats, pigeons, but still with a supply of alcohol on board, finally cast lots. It is related that 'the lot had fallen on the negro who was part of the cargo' (*ibid.* 124); as Simpson comments, 'it strains credulity to suppose that lots were fairly cast' (*ibid.*). Nathaniel Philbrick relates a different version in which no lots were cast and the slave was butchered and eaten against the wishes of the captain (Philbrick, 2001: 171–2). Having consumed the unfortunate slave, they used his body 'with the utmost economy' making it last for ten days (Simpson, 1986: 124). This slave had truly entered the bodily economy of the white man, and his unfree status made him an easy victim.

The evidence of Africans being the first to be eaten in survival cannibalism shows how the Atlantic slave-trade economy disregarded the humanity of African peoples, treating them not only as 'beasts of burden' to drive the engine of commerce but as an ancillary food source at times of disaster. In 1820–1, adrift in the Pacific in boats from the doomed whale ship *Essex*, African-American sailors were the first to die and be eaten, butchered (though in this case, most reluctantly) by their white and black comrades. Ironically, the captain and mates had decided not to steer to the Society Islands, because, in the words of the captain George Pollard Jr, 'we feared we should be devoured by cannibals' (Philbrick, 2001: 165). These instances of actual white cannibalism, though rare, are in contradistinction to the typical discourse about the practice, which, as we can see from Pollard's comment, invariably indicts primitive others as cannibalistic.

African folktales are testament to the close relation between the economic and the cannibalistic. Patrick Manning relates a tale from Benin which describes how

> cowries were obtained by the use of the slaves. A slave was thrown into the sea and allowed to drown. Then cowries would grow over the body of the slave, and after a time the body would be dredged up and the cowries collected from it. (Manning, 1992: 61)

As Manning points out, cowries actually grew in the Indian Ocean, not the Atlantic. They were, however, a crucial trading commodity, acting as a currency in the transatlantic and internal slave trades. The folktale, then, reflects an obvious symbolic truth, as numerous African bodies were literally traded away for the economic gain of a few; as Manning asserts, 'the myth of collecting cowries off the cadavers of slaves evokes the crass and cruel mentality of the era' (*ibid.*: 64). African slaves are an expendable item in a trade that literally feeds off their productive bodies. Just as those Africans who were left behind recognized the economic value of black flesh and constructed myths to explicate the strange custom of trading in human beings, so early European opponents of the trade realized that metaphors of voraciousness accurately indicted an international trade which debased civilized human values. Guillaume Raynal, in his *A Philosophical and Political History of the Settlements and Trade of the Europeans in the East and West Indies* (1776), delineates the exchange of cowries for black bodies in terms of European capitalist imperialism:

> Slaves are to the commerce of Europeans in Africa, what gold is in the commerce we carry on in the New World. The heads of our Negroes represent the stock of the state of Guinea. Every day this stock is carried off, and nothing is left of them, but articles of consumption. (quoted in Thomas, 2000: 26)

Consumed by the ravenous machine of the slave trade, the black bodies become mere 'stock' who are exchanged for material goods. Voracious consumption affects both those who take the black bodies away and those Africans who exchanged them. The former use the slaves as farmers use stock, while the latter conspicuously consume the European goods they have exchanged for the human cargo. Symbolic cannibalism afflicts all traders in the hellish trade. Thus, the anonymous author of the 1735 poem 'An Essay on Humanity. Inscrib'd to the Bristol Captains' describes the hateful symbolic cannibalism of Bristol slave traders as far worse than any actual cannibalism conducted by Africans:

> Kind are the Cannibals compar'd with you,
> For we must give to every one his Due;
> They are by Hunger prompted to destroy;
> You murder with a Countenance of Joy;
> They kill for sake of Food, and nothing more,
> You feed your Cruelty with Christian Gore;
> Then talk no more of Savages for Shame,
> All Men agree that you are most to blame,
> And as a Punishment so justly due,
> Which you deserve, henceforward each of you,
> As a Reproach, shall be nick-nam'd all
> An unrelenting Bristol-Cannibal. (quoted in Ferguson, 1992: 16)

In discussing this poem, Moira Ferguson laments the way it 'fortified distorted views of Africans by suggesting cannibalism was common practice' (*ibid.*), but surely its exploration of cannibal praxis takes after Montaigne's strategic use of cannibalism to indict a far worse economic cannibalism perpetrated by slavery and imperialism. If the European readership, however unfortunately and erroneously, believes in a savage non-Western cannibalism, then this can be skilfully used to indict nefarious practices perpetrated by men far closer to home. It is intriguing that the poem was published in the same year as John Atkins's *A Voyage to Guinea, Brasil and the West Indies* ... (1735), which had related the enforced cannibal activities on the Bristol slaver *Robert* in 1721, and we can only speculate on whether or not the anonymous poet's designation of Bristol slave traders as cannibals was related to that particular incident. As Jan Nederveen Pieterse asserts: 'Cannibalism is an allegory which establishes a centre and a periphery within a moral geography' (Pieterse, 1992:

116). Just as European stereotyping designated Africans as outrageous others capable of an immoral man-eating, so Africans, both on the continent and in the diaspora, and Europeans actively opposed to the slave trade replied with their own interpretation of a rapacious, cannibalistic, imperial polity feeding off the surplus value of black bodies. Such language around cannibalistic whites continued into the nineteenth century and expanded to critique a savage plantocracy that threatened even their fellow whites, as descriptions by Baptist missionaries of planter behaviour towards non-conformists and their black congregations in Jamaica highlight. In the wake of the slave rebellion there in 1831, many planters intensified their physical opposition to their slaves' autonomous activities and what they saw as the encouraging of such behaviour by missionaries. Appalled by the behaviour of this planter class, Thomas Burchell wrote in 1832 how

> the most furious and savage spirit was manifested by some of [what were called] the most respectable white inhabitants, that ever could have been discovered amongst civilised society. They began to throng around me, hissing, groaning and gnashing at me with their teeth. Had I never been at Montego Bay before, I must have supposed myself among cannibals, or in the midst the savage hordes of Siberia or the uncivilised tribes of central Africa … I am fully persuaded, had it not been for the protection offered me by the colored part of the population – natives of Jamaica – I should have been barbarously murdered – yea, torn limb from limb, by my countrymen – by so-called enlightened, RESPECTABLE! CHRISTIAN BRITONS! (quoted in C. Hall, 1992: 212)

Burchell consciously invokes a cannibalistic discourse as an ironic symbol. Unusually, his fear of a cannibalistic other is related to those racially most like him, as the savagery of these white planters is ironically compared to the behaviour of the Africans who now ensure his safety. The multiple ironies of this piece work because it invokes the usual stereotype (the black as cannibal, savage, other) in order to undermine it by pointing to a reality which is the opposite of the norm (the white as savage, other and cannibal). As civilized behaviour is discussed, the designation of who is the cannibal establishes the very moral geography Pieterse describes above, indicting white imperialists and slave-owners as the rapacious savages; however, imperial power means that dynamic critiques of European 'cannibal' activities are all too often marginalized in Western discourse. The history of the discourse surrounding savagery has usually privileged the centre as the civilized and morally correct metropolises controlled by Europeans, while the periphery is home to the outlandish, immoral African continent whose interior remained a mystery to Europeans ensconced in coastal trading forts. However, as this chapter shows, such morality has often been contested both from the peripheries and by opponents of imperial hegemony in the metropolises.

Of course, responses to the African other were not confined to the African continent, and the dispersal of Africans to the Americas and Europe, and the proximity of the races that this ensured, meant that the boundaries between white civilized self and black savage other increasingly broke down. The discourse surrounding the *Amistad* captives discussed earlier illustrates this, but so too do a number of nineteenth-century slave narratives, which, as Henry Louis Gates Jr and Marcus Wood discuss, sometimes contain similar cannibalistic imagery. In his famous 1845 *Narrative*, Frederick Douglass coins the expression 'human flesh-mongers' to describe callous masters who will even sell their own flesh and blood if they are the product of liaisons with female slaves (Douglass, 1986: 49). As Gates says: 'Douglass has here defined American cannibalism, a consumption of human flesh dictated by a system that could be demonic' (Gates, 1987: 93). Later, Douglass describes how slave escape is fraught with dangers that seem to reimagine the middle passage through descriptions of the privation attendant on flight. In returning to the middle passage as a leitmotif of slave terror, it is not surprising that voracious and savage white cannibals reappear, now as slave-catchers and their hounds rather than slave traders and slaver-captains. Douglass describes a hypothetical escape and the effect that such fantasies have on his co-conspirators, and his own imaginations:

> there stood slavery, a stern reality glaring frightfully upon us, – its robes already crimsoned with the blood of millions, and even now feasting itself greedily upon our own flesh ... Upon either side we saw grim death, assuming the most horrid shapes. Now it was starvation, causing us to eat our own flesh; – now we were contending with the waves, and were drowned; now we were overtaken and torn to pieces by the fangs of the horrible blood hound. (Douglass, 1986: 123)

Clearly, here, the trope of cannibalism is used as an exemplary rhetorical and polemical weapon against the excesses of a system that preys on the minds of slaves just as much as their bodies. But its power is double-edged. For, images of escape are always already implicated in images of recapture and reincorporation into the body of the slave polity which foregrounds the enormous power of the institution in the minds of enslaved blacks. Douglass means to demonize the institution by reference to its voracious use of black bodies, and he succeeds brilliantly in portraying slavers as cannibals. In doing so, though, he also shows the debilitating effect of such ideas on African Americans, for, as Marcus Wood incisively comments:

> Slavery as a cannibalistic metaphor implicates both slaves and enslavers. Slavery, personified in ensanguined robes devouring its own kind, like some latter-day Saturn, merges into the slaves, who as starving fugitives are forced to literalise the cannibalistic excesses metaphorically applied to the slave power, and to eat each other. (Wood, 2000: 101–2)

A savage institution creates excesses beyond civilized thought and praxis, and Douglass, through his cannibalistic imagery, proclaims the existence of a nihilistic amoral dog-eat-dog world in the Southern states which the abolition of the slave trade has done nothing to obviate. The monsters eating black flesh portrayed in Turner's famous slave painting discussed in Chapter 3 are at work on land too, as they are, crucially, in the imaginations of enslaved African Americans. The ravenous cannibalistic pleasure afforded the enslavers is a central trope elsewhere in these narratives, though not always expressed as obviously as in the example above. Henry Bibb, in describing how his owner, Madison Garrison, whipped his wife, says: 'I have often heard Garrison say that he had rather paddle a female, than eat when he was hungry – that it was music for him to hear them scream, and to see their blood run' (quoted in *ibid.*: 126). Here, the sadistic abuse of a female slave is regarded as more satisfying than assuaging his hunger. His bodily needs for food are met by the abuse of a black female body. He is involved in a symbolic cannibalism, an ocular incorporation of black female flesh that describes his control over her purely in sensual terms. The transposition of eating imagery with sadistic abuse reveals the centrality of metaphors of incorporation in all aspects of the institution of slavery, as the slave-owners' complex fantasies of control are expressed in the language of basic needs such as that for food. While Garrison might not be literally eating his slave here, in Bibb's description his cannibalistic desire runs alongside his sado-masochistic praxis, creating an image of abuse that chimes with critiques of slavers stretching back to Blake's images of dismembered bodies produced for the 1796 edition of John Stedman's *Narrative of a Five Years' Expedition against the Revolted Negroes of Surinam* ... Here, Blake's engraving of *A Negro Hung Alive by the Ribs to a Gallows* is given added piquancy by the skulls and bones that surround the unfortunate victim, as though a cannibal ritual has already taken place under the control of the white abusers. In a significant reversal, the detritus of the cannibal meal relates to white abuse rather than black savagery.

Such images of white abuse were rare in the eighteenth and nineteenth centuries. Hence, before moving ahead to look at Toni Morrison's specific use of cannibalism as a trope to indict the slave trade, it is important to show how she illustrates this dominant hegemonic view of cannibalism and the primitive other in the mid-nineteenth-century Eurocentric world in which her novel is set. For it is in the juxtaposition of the African myth of the white cannibal with the white fear of the primitive other as cannibal that Morrison follows the example of Equiano, Cugoano, Blake, Douglass and Bibb to illustrate the economic and psychic horrors of slavery and the racism that follows it. The principal character through whom she expresses white racist conceptions of the African American as cannibal is the eponymous Schoolteacher, who is obsessed by the differences between the races and how physical characteristics illustrate the closeness of African Americans to the animalistic. He teaches his nephews to outline the characteristics of all his slaves, differentiating between their human and animal features. This obsession with a division between African and European peoples in terms of hierarchy dominated the discourse on race in the eighteenth and nineteenth centuries, leading to pseudo-sciences like phrenology which sought to differentiate between race types on the basis of the shape and size of their heads – hence Schoolteacher's use of a measuring string in his experiments to prove white superiority. Schoolteacher's ultra-rationalist ideas of division and hierarchy between the races in a direct line up from (and down to) the beasts is used in the novel not only satirically to show the ludicrous nature of racism but because such views were legion in America both during and after the Atlantic slave trade. The nineteenth-century science of phrenology was only the latest methodology to be used, and 'mark[ed] the beginning of biological attempts to locate the differential "capacities" in the brains of men and women, Negro and white, the Irish and the English ... [it] not only rearticulated old hierarchies but also worked to secure scientists' place in them' (Doyle, 1994: 60–1). It represented a scientific gloss on former differentiations between the races which had relied on pure metaphysics. Thomas Jefferson, for instance, in his *Notes on the State of Virginia* (1787), outlines how there was 'a preference of the Oranatoon for the black woman over those of his own species' (Jefferson, 1944: 256); this is only one of many unsubstantiated opinions expressed in the Enlightenment by figures such as Hegel, Hume and Kant who identify a much narrower gap between the bestial and the African than between the bestial and the civilized European (Gates, 1992: 43–69).

All markers of the bestial are habits that civilized Europeans regard as taboo, vices which differentiate the civilized from the primitive. The triangle of vices includes 'idolatry, cannibalism and sexual excess' (Mason, 1990: 63). All three vices are alluded to in the discourse around slavery, but it is canni-balism that I would like to highlight in this chapter. It appears in writings by pro-slavery apologists such as William Gilmore Simms, the South Carolina novelist, who in a lecture on 'The Morals of Slavery' (1837) stated that, 'the negro comes from a continent where he was a cannibal destined ... to eat his fellow or be eaten by him' (Fredrickson, 1971: 52). Later, in 1867, his fellow Southerner, Mark Twain, in commenting on Henry Inman's crayon portrait of Abd ar-Rahman, illustrates the prevalence of this view in mid-nineteenth-century America even among those with less dogmatic opinions. Clearly, satirical, his remarks are designed to undermine the romanticism that dogged progressive thought and that refused to see anything other than an idyllic African continent of victims, despite evidence to the contrary. However, his depiction of the Muslim as a cannibal is gratuitously offensive:

> I, for one, sincerely hope that after all his trials he is now
> peacefully enjoying the evening of his life and eating and
> relishing unsaleable niggers from neighbouring tribes who fall
> into his hands, and making a good thing out of other niggers
> from neighbouring tribes who are unsaleable. (quoted in Austin,
> 1995: 79)

With such views legion among Southerners in the ante- and post-bellum periods, it is unsurprising that Morrison has Schoolteacher, her cipher for such views in the novel, associate the actions of Sethe in murdering her children to prevent them being re-enslaved with the bestiality of a cannibalism which the civilizing effect of slavery had kept at bay. Morrison's text editorializes:

> Then with the sun straight up over their heads, they trotted off leaving the sheriff behind amongst the darndest bunch of coons they'd ever seen. All testimony to the results of a little so-called freedom imposed on people who needed all the guidance in the world to keep them from the cannibal life they preferred. (Morrison, 1988a: 151)

In such a world-view, slavery is seen as a positive institution, because it prevents Africans from falling back into the bestiality from which they have been forcibly rescued. Morrison's use of pro-slavery rhetoric here is surely a conscious gloss on such texts as E. N. Elliot's edited collection of pro-slavery documents, *Cotton Is King* (1860), and *Cannibals All!* (1857) by George Fitzhugh. The former's introduction contains passages which bear a striking resemblance to Schoolteacher's discourse on black barbarism. Elliot contends that the African 'by himself was never emerged from barbarism, and even when partly civilised under the control of the white man, he speedily returns to the same state if emancipated' (Fredrickson, 1971: 83). It is too much freedom which leads to a barbarism that slavery had prevented. Fitzhugh's text is a more subtle exposition on the relationships between races. He contrasts a wage-slave's hard life in the North with the carefree lives of the Southern slaves, the Northern capitalist's exploitative regime with the comforting plantation system of the South, where all a slave's physical needs are taken care of:

> The negro slave is free too when all the labors of the day are over, and free in mind as well as body; for the master provides food, raiment, house, fuel and everything else necessary for the physical well-being of himself and family. The master's labors commence just when the slave's end. (Fitzhugh, 1960: 16)

Under Schoolteacher's tyranny, the plantation Sweet Home, far from illustrating Fitzhugh's idealistic picture, reverses it. Fitzhugh's text, though, is interesting for the purpose of this essay because of its intriguing title. His 'cannibals', however, are not the indolent slaves enjoying a carefree life saved from bestiality by civilizing slavery, but the vampiric Northern capitalists who exploit their workers. Early on in his text he addresses this readership:

> You are a Cannibal! And if a successful one, pride yourself on the number of your victims, quite as much as any Fiji chieftain who breakfast dines and sups on human flesh – and your conscience smites you, if you have failed to succeed, quite as much as his, when he returns from an unsuccessful foray. Probably you are a lawyer, or a merchant ... (*ibid.*: 17)

According to this view, true cannibalism exists in the dog-eat-dog world of Northern capitalism rather than the paternalistic South of the plantocracy. An escape from slavery would only leave the slaves as vulnerable to the 'moral cannibals' of Northern capitalism. Reading Schoolteacher's glossed comments in the light of Fitzhugh's revision of cannibalism adds to Morrison's text, so that the idea that African-Americans 'needed every guidance in the world to keep them from the cannibal life they preferred' takes on a double meaning. While clearly it refers to the supposed bestial cannibalism of a primitive African existence, it also highlights the potential for a descent into cannibalistic practice that might result if free labour rather than slavery were to be the dominant mode of production in the South.

Morrison, though, has her own opinion about the identity of the cannibals in the ante-bellum and Reconstruction South. It is those white racists who literally cook African-Americans, dismembering and burning them in brandings, punishments and lynchings which mirror the very cannibalistic practices Columbus had heard tell of in his journeys to America and which have subsequently been the staple of European discourse around cannibalism. Like Equiano, Cugoano *et al.* before her, Morrison reverses this stereotype of primitivistic black cannibals, showing how European colonialism and the slave trade and its aftermath created bestial whites who committed economic cannibalism on non-white peoples, stopping just short of actual cannibalism. In her interpretation, as in Equiano's, it is little wonder that Africans feared cannibalistic whites. In a key passage of *Beloved*, Paul D., who has avoided the Sweet Home massacre instigated by Schoolteacher in the wake of a mass escape attempt, outlines his fears of white oppression in terms which invoke cannibalism when he talks of the dangers faced by black people alone in a racist America. He wants Beloved to leave Sethe's house but cannot bring himself to throw her out:

> He wanted her out, but Sethe had let her in and he couldn't put her out of a house that wasn't his. It was one thing to beat up a ghost, quite another to throw a helpless colored girl out in territory infected by the Klan. Desperately thirsty for black blood, without which it could not live, the dragon swam the Ohio at will. (Morrison, 1988a: 66)

Here, Morrison reverses the stereotype of black bloodthirstiness by showing the actual bloodthirsty character of white racists. Its equivalence to cannibalistic practices is repeated later in the text when Stamp Paid, who had been instrumental in helping Sethe escape slavery, approaches her haunted house. He interprets the sounds in the house as those of the victims of slavery and racism, again seeing in these actions forms of symbolic cannibalism:

> So in spite of his exhausted marrow, he kept on through the voices and tried once more to knock at the door of 124. This time, although he could not cipher but one word, he believed he knew who spoke them. The people of the broken necks, of fire-

cooked blood, and black girls who had lost their ribbons. What
a roaring. (*ibid*.: 181)

These three examples from *Beloved* reveal both how the whites label the
African as primitive cannibal to justify their enslavement of him and the extent
of the African-Americans' transplanted fears of cannibalistic whites. For
African-Americans are as justified in their depiction of racists as cannibalistic
as Africans had been of slavers. These victims of racist violence are portrayed
in terms of a cannibalism ('fire-cooked blood') which links this passage to
earlier parts of the text and to a whole discourse of cannibalism which
Morrison's work seeks to foreground. Such short passages, though, are merely
a coda to the extended musings on cannibalism and savagery of Stamp Paid as
he tries to make sense of the strange happenings at 124. For here, Morrison
highlights white fears of the bestial other (the African in this case) as cannibal,
how these fears make 'whitefolk' act in uncivilized ways towards the African
and the debilitating effect of such a stereotyping discourse not only on those
who are stereotyped but also on those who frame such a limited vision. In her
critical essays, Morrison highlights the importance of addressing such issues.
In *Playing in the Dark* she articulates it thus:

> A good deal of time and intelligence has been invested in the
> exposure of racism and the horrific results on its objects ... that
> well-established study should be joined with another equally
> important one: the impact of racism on those who perpetuate
> it ... to see what racial ideology does to the mind, imagination
> and behaviour of masters. (Morrison, 1993: 11–12)

As we can see from this discussion of primitive stereotyping in *Beloved*,
Morrison had already been involved in articulating the debilitating effects of
this racist ideology in her novels, describing the 'fabricated brew of darkness,
otherness, alarm and desire that is uniquely American' (*ibid*.: 38). This following passage does more, however, moving to a depiction of the 'whitefolk'
as the actual cannibals in the historical relationship between the races. This
inevitably leads us back to Equiano and Cugoano's vision of white cannibals,
and to Douglass's depiction of a cannibalistic South, and reveals how Morrison was drawing on a legacy of inscribing the white man as a savage man-
eater which has always coloured Eurocentric discourse about savage
man-eating Africans:

> Whitefolk believed that whatever the manners, under every dark
> skin was a jungle. Swift unnavigable waters, swinging,
> screaming baboons, sleeping snakes, red gums ready for the
> sweet white blood. But it wasn't the jungle blacks brought with
> them to this place from the other (liveable) place. It was the
> jungle whitefolks planted in them. And it grew. It spread. In,
> through and after life, it spread until it invaded the whites who
> had made it. Touched them every one. Changed and altered

them. Made them bloody, silly, worse than even they wanted to be, so scared were they of the jungle they had made. The screaming baboon lived under their own white skin; the red gums were their own. (*ibid*.: 198–9)

Here, Morrison employs two tropes familiar in discussions of race – the bestial and the cannibal – exemplifying the racist myths of black beasts and cannibals as the starting point in her own agenda to expose these stereotypes as the reflection not of biological reality but as a construction of white Eurocentric cultural hegemony at a particular juncture in historical relations between peoples. In foregrounding this stereotyping, Morrison makes a political intervention, revealing how these images are constructed out of imperial power. In this, she follows Marcus Garvey, who used the trope of the savage cannibal to attack European imperialism in a 1925 pamphlet: 'their [white] cannibalism was more prolonged than ours; when we were embracing the arts and sciences on the Nile their ancestors were still drinking human blood and eating out of the skulls of their conquered dead (quoted in Howe, 1998: 76). The stereotype is exposed by both Morrison and Garvey as a mere construction to justify power over an alien people at a time of European ascendancy. But Morrison does more: while exposing the obvious dangers of the stereotypes for African-Americans, she also shows how dangerous such a limiting vision is to those who propagate it. The language Morrison uses here is surely a conscious gloss on the primitivist stereotyping that has been so much a staple of the discourse around race. Her depiction of a whitefolk associating African and African-American experience with the jungle, and through their hegemonic control dissipating this view and inculcating it throughout the culture of the black Atlantic, exemplifies the ignorance of those who perpetuate the stereotype, for, as Marianna Torgovnick discusses, the jungle is a fraudulent construction:

The *jungle*, for example, is a term popularly used to describe the locale of the primitive. And yet, in a strict geographical sense, it is a term most applicable to parts of Southeast Asia, not to African savannas, plains, deserts, forests, or rain forests ... (Torgovnick, 1990: 22)

The term invented to describe the ignorant savagery of the other in fact exhibits the wilful ignorance of European intellectuals. Morrison's reworking and signification on the term 'jungle' can be usefully compared to, and may even originate from, Frantz Fanon's seminal work on the psychology of racism, *Black Skin, White Masks* (1952). In the following passage, Fanon is talking about colonized peoples, but surely it could also describe the cultural alienation experienced by African Americans in the aftermath of slavery and in the midst of a racist nineteenth-century America. Morrison definitely thinks so, describing an American-Africanism '[rising] up out of collective needs to allay internal fears and to rationalize external exploitation' (Morrison, 1993: 38) in American literature being linked to a European Africanism which manifests itself in colonial literature. It is little wonder, then, that Morrison's passage uncannily echoes and expands on the jungle symbolism of Fanon:

> Every colonized people – in other words, every people in whose soul an inferiority complex has been created by the death and burial of its local cultural originality – finds itself face to face with the language of the civilizing nation; that is with the culture of the mother country. The colonized is elevated above his jungle status in proportion to his adoption of the mother country's cultural standards. He becomes whiter as he renounces his blackness, his jungle. (Fanon, 1970: 14)

For Fanon, the 'jungle' is a positive which stands for the adoption of local, 'native' values in contradistinction to European value systems. For Morrison, there are significant dangers in such adoption, because of the ambiguity of such essentialist racial values. Hence, she exposes the dangers of such stereotypes for African Americans and the perils attendant on those Anglo-Americans who propagate such a limited Manichean vision. Its poisonous nature literally infects those who indulge in it, so that they become the monsters they fear. To return specifically to the passage in *Beloved*, Stamp Paid (and through him Morrison) signifies on the 'jungle' as the home of African-Americans and creates a different reality – the jungle as a limiting concept which constrains and undermines the development of the minds of whitefolk. In the final sentence here Morrison imagines whitefolk as having become the cannibals they had earlier feared. The 'red gums' which had been ready for the 'sweet white blood' in a deliberate parallel now belong to the whites who had originally seen themselves as intended victims. By creating the stereotype of the cannibal other, 'whitefolk' become the very beast which they feared through their bestial treatment of the African other. As David Meltzer succinctly remarks: 'if the black's a cannibal, the white becomes what's beheld; in the frenzy of what is blissfully dubbed postmodern is a trophy room of cannibalized cultures; to consume is to be consumed' (Meltzer, 1993: 13).

Morrison's warning about the dangers of stereotyping is not ossified in the racial past of the United States but has relevance for the age in which she is writing too, as Meltzer's comment reveals; while stereotyping might be more subtle now, it is just as dehumanizing to victim and perpetrator. By her inversion of the signifiers 'cannibal' and 'jungle', so that the former describes white oppression and not black gastronomy and the latter is shown to infect whites, not blacks, Morrison makes what Henry Louis Gates Jr would call a Signifyin(g) retort to the stereotyping discourse of Anglo-America. To quote Gates, her reply could be interpreted in the following way: 'that by which you intend to confine or define me, I shall return to you squarely in your face' (Gates, 1988: 66). Her 'in the face' retort, though, should not be seen as an isolated response to the limiting stereotype but the latest salvo in a battle over meaning and interpretation which began with African folktales of white cannibals and was adapted during the period of the Enlightenment by the earliest black writers in the Western tradition. Historically, as Morrison's character Schoolteacher reminds us, 'definitions belong to the definers – not the defined' (Morrison, 1988a: 190); however, Morrison, along with Equiano, Cugoano, Douglass and Garvey before her, through their ingenious reworking of the trope of cannibalism, undermine such a limited vision, showing us that the definers' power is far from ubiquitous. On the contrary, it is heavily circumscribed by the power of the defined to reply in kind.

= 6 =

FUNKY ERUPTIONS AND CHAIN-DANCING TO FREEDOM

THE IMPLICATIONS OF TONI MORRISON'S RADICAL STYLE IN *THE BLUEST EYE*, *TAR BABY* AND *BELOVED*

> The silence of the ethnographic workshop has been broken – by insistent, heteroglot voices, by the scratching of other pens. (Clifford, 1988: 26)

> You have to give up the idea that culture exists in neat pockets. Culture is exchange. (Ralph Ellison, quoted in West, 1990: 41)

> The Negro enslaved by his inferiority, the white man enslaved by his superiority alike behave in accordance with a neurotic orientation. (Fanon, 1970: 44)

As with many writers from a wide range of communities, a close attention to Toni Morrison's style helps uncover her radical politics and poetics. One of the most influential and radical Morrison critics has been Susan Willis, who in her excellent study of African-American women novelists, *Specifying* (1987), discusses the concept of 'funk' at length, though with very little reference to musical style. Her materialist feminist approach ably shows how Morrison indicts the hegemonic forces of capitalist America for making many African-Americans ashamed of their vernacular culture and anxious to disown it. As internally colonized subjects, the African-Americans' predicament can be linked to the position of other colonized peoples who are encouraged to disown their vernacular culture in order to progress within the majority culture. Morrison's foregrounding of vernacular modes is a 'funky', decidedly political response to demands for conformity to Anglo-American modes. As Stelamaris Coser says of such gestures by African-American women writers, 'Rooted in culture and community [they are] an attempt to counter the version of truth and facts presented by the colonizer of yesterday and today with the view from the dominated' (Coser, 1994: 16). I hope to show how a critical paradigm mindful of vernacular black aesthetics in a postcolonial context enhances Willis's critique and that, far from aestheticizing a materialist paradigm, such a methodology contributes to strengthening a materialist reading of Morrison's work; in effect, that Morrison's concern to write a vernacular form itself comes from a political and internationalist imperative which, in the light of Paul Gilroy's work, we could call a black Atlantic paradigm. We have seen this political imperative at work in Morrison's use of the cannibal trope to critique slavery and racism in *Beloved*; this chapter will explore more fully how Morrison's radical politics is matched by a radical poetics. The best place to start is with Morrison's revisioning of the concept of 'funk'.

The very history of the word 'funk' attests to the political nature of language and the way in which African-American peoples have reconstructed language literally from the verbal detritus of their former 'masters'. 'Funk' was at one point African-American slang for a bad smell before becoming a term used to describe the particular soul quality in black music (Major, 1971: 56 and 70). Amiri Baraka notes the political nature of the African-American adoption of this term when he talks about jazz musicians' concept of the term in the late 1950s:

> In jazz, people started talking about funk and the white man had
> always said: the negro has a characteristic smell, but then
> the negro takes that and turns the term round, so that if you
> don't have that characteristic smell, that funk, then the music, or
> what you are is not valuable. The very tools the white man gave
> the negro are suddenly used against him. (quoted in Harris,
> 1985: 33)

I will return later to the way such language use and inversion is also part of a vernacular aesthetic Morrison employs by virtue of its sounding of a Signifyin(g) discourse, but for now it is sufficient to know that 'funk' is not presently confined to a musical signification, and that many African-Americans, including Toni Morrison, use it to indicate a particular lower-class and radical African-American attitude to the world. Thus, as Willis points out, when Morrison uses images of 'funkiness', she is envisioning an alternative social milieu. Willis's idea that 'funk' erupts in order to project a different reality to the black bourgeois world seems to me very astute, if a little close to an essentialism which undermines the force of her argument. She examines how Morrison uses 'eruptions of funk' to posit an alternative to the alienation many African-Americans encounter when they move North, away from the wellspring of their culture. 'The problem at the centre of Toni Morrison's writing is how to maintain an Afro-American cultural heritage once the relationship to the black rural South has been stretched thin over distance and generations' (Willis, 1984: 264).

The 'eruptions of funk' literally juxtapose an alternate reality to that bourgeoisification which encourages African-Americans to forget their cultural roots. In using such 'eruptions of funk', Morrison follows in the African-American tradition epitomized by Zora Neale Hurston, whose *Their Eyes Were Watching God* (1937) critiques middle-class African-Americans (even those still resident in the South) for their ludicrous vanities. These satirical passages are given added potency because Hurston 'turns the trick' on the middle-class blacks, who are equated with animals – an equation usually reserved for the lower-class blacks. Joe Starks is the mayor and store owner, the big man in town, a status he displays by a conspicuous consumption that even extends to spitoons:

> And then he spit in that gold-looking vase that anybody else would have been glad to put on their front-room table. Said it was a spitoon just like his used-to-be-bossman used to have in his bank up there in Atlanta. Didn't have to get up and go to the door every time he had to spit. Didn't spit on his floor neither. Had that golden up spitting pot right handy. But he went further than that. He bought a little lady-size spitting pot for Janie to spit in ... It was bad enough for white people, but when one of your own color could be so different it put you on a wonder. It was like seeing your sister turn into a 'gator. A familiar strangeness. You keep seeing your sister in the 'gator and the 'gator in your sister, and you'd rather not. (Hurston, 1978: 76)

The Starks's embourgeoisification is portrayed as dehumanizing, as it distances them from African-American folk culture and the townspeople. In Hurston's conceit, they literally transmogrify into reptilian shapes whose human status is at risk. Hurston's critique of such bourgeois values runs right through the novel and reaches its apogee in the character of the light-skinned Mrs Turner, whose hatred of dark-skinned (generally characterized as lower-class blacks) is virulent:

> dey makes me tired. Always laughin'! Dey laughs too much and they laughs too loud. Always singin' ol' nigger songs. Always cuttin' de monkey for white folks. If it wuzn't for so many black folks it wouldn't be no race problem. De white folks would take us in wid dem. De black ones is holding us back. (*ibid.*: 210)

Mrs Turner's obscene hatred of her own folk is parodied in the book by her logical inexactitude and her lonely seclusion, neither accepted by the blacks she despises nor the whites she aspires to join. Through this grotesque character, Hurston lampoons the aspirations of middle-class blacks who wish to distance themselves from the folk-life of African-Americans in the South. Their demands to 'lighten the race' and 'class off' (*ibid.*) from lower-class blacks are dynamically critiqued by Hurston's savage satire.

Right from her early fiction, Morrison poses the same dialectical struggle, foregrounding the importance of class in African-American culture and satirizing middle-class aspirations. For instance, the character of Geraldine in *The Bluest Eye* (1970) is portrayed as a typical bourgeois African-American. In counterpoint to her desire for refinement and moderation is the alternate lower-class mode of 'funkiness'. Morrison describes how middle-class blacks learn

> the rest of the lesson begun in those soft houses with porch swings and pots of bleeding heart: how to behave. The careful

development of thrift, patience, high morals and good manners. In short how to get rid of the funkiness. The dreadful funkiness of passion, the funkiness of nature, the funkiness of the wide range of human emotions.

Wherever it erupts, this Funk, they wipe it away; where it crusts, they dissolve; wherever it drips, flowers, or clings, they find it and fight it until it dies. They fight this battle all the way to the grave. The laughter that is a little too loud; the enunciation a little too round, the gesture a little too generous. They hold their behind in for fear of a sway too free; when they wear their lipstick, they never cover the entire mouth for fear of lips too thick, and they worry, worry, worry about the edges of their hair. (Morrison, 1972: 78)

Such bourgeois African-American women demonize their lower-class sisters through a discourse of primitivism learnt from the dominant Anglo-American culture. As Valerie Lee asserts, 'these are women who have internalized stereotypes of black people to the point where they see a constructed notion of funk as a symbol for a latent primitivism, a beast in the jungle needing to be civilized' (Lee, 1996: 54). Morrison's critique of these bourgeois women is reinforced by her stylistic genius. In the first paragraph of the above passage, the repetition of 'funkiness' ironically builds up a wonderful rhythm or riff on the very 'funkiness' which Geraldine is striving to deny. In this context, 'riff' refers to the repetition of lexical phrases analogous to the repeated background phrases that form a 'foundation' in many types of jazz solo (Berliner, 1995: 300). The free-flowing riff on 'funkiness', and the attempt to suppress it, is continued in the second paragraph by an involved passage that uses repetitions of words and phrases ('worry, worry, worry'), assonance to connect the gestures which highlight 'funkiness', ('loud', 'round', 'generous') and parallelisms ('wherever', 'where', 'wherever') to build up a musical rhythm which reveals a funkiness just beneath the surface of even the most uptight bourgeois African-American. The rhythmic style here exemplifies a funkiness which complements and enhances the theme of Geraldine's entrapment within a working-class cultural milieu from which she hoped her light skin would save her. Like Mrs Turner, she cannot escape an African-American folk culture she despises and thinks she is too good for.

Morrison's riff on funkiness here is given added power by the force of the word in the black vernacular, exemplified by Baraka's anecdote about the musicians' theorizing on 'funk' which I quoted earlier. Its resonances, though, stretch throughout the African-American community, while its power to range over a whole welter of African-American experiences, from physical appearance through fashion to musical style, could justify the appellation 'mascon' word to the term 'funk'. The concept of mascon words was developed by Stephen Henderson in his seminal analysis *Understanding the New Black Poetry* (1973) and can, I believe, be extended to other African-American artistic practices. A mascon word is one that carries '*a massive concentration of Black experiential energy*' (Henderson, 1973: 44; original emphasis). Funk is such a word, as it carries 'an inordinate charge of emotional and psychological weight, so that wherever ... [it is used it sets] ... all kinds of bells ringing, all kinds of synapses singing, on all kinds of levels' (*ibid.*). By her riffing on the word Morrison alerts the reader to a phrase she discusses as key to an understanding of black reality. She does this elsewhere in her work with riffs on such concepts as naming in *Song of Solomon* (Morison, 1980a: 17–18) and cannibalism or the jungle in *Beloved* (Morrison, 1988b: 198–9), the latter of which we have already discussed. As Henderson is quick to point out, though, the repetition of mascon words or phrases has parallels in jazz history, where repeated boogie-woogie or blues phrases embody similar charges of emotional and psychological weight (Henderson, 1973: 45).

Morrison, then, in using such mascon words, is adapting a technique developed in the musical culture which she utilizes. The riffing on a mascon word like 'funk' is analogous to a jazz form at a stylistic level. Surprisingly, Willis all but ignores this, preferring to concentrate on the implications of the passage for Morrison's major themes. However, it is precisely by foregrounding Morrison's stylistic riffing and use of mascon words that the vernacular aesthetic helps the critic to underpin Willis's critique, showing how the passage's rhythmic nature and literal worrying around a key concept in the culture (just as a blues man or jazz musician slurs or slides on a phrase or end line they want to accentuate) emphasizes the very funkiness that middle-class blacks seek to deny. Thus, even a cursory look at the mechanics of this short passage reveals how the alternative mode is not just present thematically but also at a stylistic level.

'Eruptions of funk', then, not only pose an alternative social world through their thematic undermining of African-American middle-class (and even light-skinned) values but also provide an alternative discourse through which this world can best be imagined. Of course, this is not the only occasion in Morrison's oeuvre where such eruptions occur. In *Jazz*, Alice Manfred's fear of such eruptions of funk is even more blatantly related to the 'playing of lowdown stuff', and again the style of the passage mirrors its jazzy theme (Morrison, 1992: 57). Morrison uses specifically African-American stylistic devices to create this alternative world. In doing so, she is engaged in a radical restructuring of the traditionally Anglo-American novel form, in effect 'colouring' the language with the timbre of a jazz-inflected mode. African-American writers like Toni Morrison resist being confined by the language of the oppressive white culture and seek to create from its ashes a musically inflected language of their own. In her headlong rush to materialize Morrison's radical gesture, Willis does her a disservice by ignoring the wonderful use of riffing that makes the passage (and others in Morrison's oeuvre) work so well. Morrison's jazz-inflected language has brought a literal funkiness to the Anglocentric form of the novel through its use of such extended riffing passages.

Willis's partial identification of the vernacular mode is valuable, though her painting of it as merely a nostalgic harking back to a Southern past undermines its wilful doubleness which envisions a modernist urban future at the same time as it invokes a Southern rural idyll. There is radical possibility in the 'funkiness' too, which the riff's energy points to. For instance, as the vernacular and, in particular, jazz hark back to a premodern rural past, they simultaneously, through their syncopation and poly-rhythms, respond effectively to a contemporaneous modernist cityscape as is exemplified in Morrison's novel *Jazz* (Rice, 1994b). Willis's 'eruptions of funk' should, then, not merely be seen as the nostalgic interventions of a primal folk culture fighting a rearguard action against a bourgeois ideology beholden to Anglocentric modes of behaviour, but as vital emancipatory tools for the modern African-American in his/her desire for a voice in the cityscape. In her *Granny Midwives and Black American Women's Literature* Valerie Lee appositely describes the radical nature of funk in African-American culture: 'funk is a subversive discursive practice, a destabilizing of what is expected because of an alternative cultural matrix' (Lee, 1996: 54). This 'alternative cultural matrix' has diasporan valencies, as it can be related to what has come to be known as a Signifyin(g) discourse.

Morrison, along with many other black writers and artists, uses this technique to create passages which posit a different reality from that which the dominant Anglocentric culture is used to hearing. This Signifyin(g) mode is outlined in Henry Louis Gates Jr's *The Signifying Monkey*. He describes the specific term 'Signifyin(g)' to foreground instances where 'the absent (g) is the figure for the Signifyin(g) black difference' (Gates, 1988: 46), but other critics talk of Signifyin' or sigging. Gates shows how the mode is a retention from an African, specifically Yoruban, past which valued smart talking and moralistic storytelling above other communicative modes. When retained in the African-American community in extended oral narratives known as toasts (like the *Titanic* toasts discussed in Chapter 2) and in verbal jousts such as the dozens, this Signifyin(g) mode developed into a core oral technique in African-American culture. Geneva Smitherman defines it thus:

> the verbal art of insult in which a speaker humorously puts
> down, talks about, needles – that is signifies on – the listener.
> Sometimes signifyin (also siggin) is done to make a point,
> sometimes it's just for fun ... [it is] characterized by exploitation
> of the unexpected and quick verbal surprises. (Smitherman,
> 1985: 118–19)

Morrison's use of it, then, should not surprise us as it is a core African-American verbal and musical praxis. It merely reveals her desire to privilege an African diasporan cultural form and highlights the presence of a black Atlantic paradigm in her work. The analysis of cultural theorists such as Henry Louis Gates Jr and Ingrid Monson details its use in a jazz context. Gates's description of a Signifyin(g) mode in jazz highlights the centrality of the praxis in jazz composition and improvisation. In a jam session and in performance, jazz players take a tune, a previous performance of it or a solo that one of their colleagues has just completed and respond by transforming the raw material into a new composition on the spot. Such Signifyin(g) has been a constant of jazz history, from Louis Armstrong's deliberate use of spirituals in the 1920s to Charles Mingus's adoption of a gospel mode in the 1950s to the radical revision of popular Broadway tunes by the Free jazz players of the 1960s and 1970s.

In her discussion of John Coltrane's legendary recordings of the Rogers and Hammerstein tune 'My Favourite Things' (1960), Ingrid Monson follows on from Gates's (1988: 105), discussion of the tune outlining the methods by which 'a sentimental, optimistic lyric is transformed into a more brooding, improvisational exploration' (Monson, 1994: 298). Coltrane's performances often lasted twenty minutes or more, as he remade the tune in his own image. As Monson goes on to say: 'In the core of "My Favourite Things" the transformation of the tune simultaneously communicates the resemblance between the two versions and the vast difference of the Coltrane version' (*ibid.*: 305).

Coltrane uses the seemingly predictable pop tune for his own artistic practices, creating a whole new meaning for the tune through irony, parody and even burlesque, until it becomes secondary to his flagrant revision of it. Such Signifyin(g) practices were brought across the Atlantic by Africans and informed many of their early cultural practices. Thus, in slave times, the cakewalk burlesqued the apparently high seriousness of Southern plantation life. As Stearns notes, '[they] take off the high manners of the white folk in the big house, but their masters who gathered round to watch the fun missed the point' (Stearns, 1956: 116). Such irony and parody, such doubleness, of appearing to do one thing while doing another, are 'central and expected means of aesthetic expression in the African American tradition' (Monson, 1994: 303) and can be traced throughout the history of the jazz form, including Louis Armstrong's version of 'All of Me' in 1931 (Armstrong, 1983). Marshall Stearns comments on this performance:

> given the most banal of tunes to record and with impressive consistency, he transformed them into something else, something intensely appealing ... He makes fun of the tune, sharing with his listener his insight into the silliness of the whole expression and at the same time, he improvises with such gusto and imagination that a tawdry ballad emerges as a thing of beauty. (Stearns, 1956: 318)

Morrison's use of a Signifyin(g) mode is wide-ranging and is present in all the novels, an indication of how African diasporan vernacular praxis informs her poetics throughout her oeuvre. In *Tar Baby* (1981), for instance, the 'waste' riff is key to an understanding of the novel as an intervention in the debate around the exploitation of resources by multinational companies as the latest stage in the far-reaching abuse of African peoples in the diaspora. It is the centrepiece of a Signifyin(g) rebuke from Morrison to an exploitative and ecologically damaging capitalist system. Here, and throughout the novel, the inversion and exaggeration which exemplify Signifyin(g) are used not in intra-communal contestation but as a marker of inter-communal disputation between Anglo-American and African-American value systems. It marks an intervention in the struggle between the colonized and the colonial/neocolonial power which questions the legitimacy of the latter. As Michael Cooke explains:

> Signifying always involves questions of power on two levels, the social and the mental, the signifier is the one who as best he can makes up for a lack of social power with an exercise of critical or intellectual power. (Cooke, 1984: 26)

Son is a character at the bottom of the neocolonial pyramid (a casual wage-labourer), but through effective Signifyin(g) he, and through him Morrison, is able to indict the system which continues to oppress many African diasporan people throughout the circum-Atlantic region. He does this by indicting the capitalist oppressors as supremely wasteful, a charge which, as I will show later, had typically been directed against the labouring African:

> That was the sole lesson of their world: how to make waste, how to make machines that made more waste, how to make wasteful products, how to talk waste, how to study waste, how to design waste, how to cure people who were sickened by waste so they could be well enough to endure it, how to mobilize waste, legalize waste and how to despise the culture that lived in cloth houses and shit on the ground far away from where they ate. And it would drown them one day, they would sink into their own waste and the waste they had made of the world and then finally they would know true peace and the happiness they had been looking for all along. (Morrison, 1983: 204)

This extended solo on the riff of 'waste' is intentionally hyperbolic. The use of 'waste' in as many contexts as possible, moving from generalized waste to particular human waste products, approximates the improvisation on a series of notes in a jazz solo (the riff); the riff (word) remains the same but it is stretched by the various interpretations of it. Just as Albert Ayler (or any other jazz musician) creates solos which elaborate on a musical concept before returning to it – as, for instance, in his seminal tune 'Truth Is Marching In' (1967), which constantly returns to the riff based on the traditional spiritual 'When The Saints Go Marching In' in order to flesh out all its meanings – so Morrison's prose takes a word and deconstructs all its meanings while the word itself remains lexically unchanged, the rhythmic constant to which she continually returns, as James Snead explains, 'The repetition of words and phrases rather than being overlooked is exploited as a structural and rhythmic principle' (Snead, 1994: 151). Notice also the internal rhymes ('mobilize', 'legalize' and 'despise') which add rhythmic complexity to a brilliantly achieved jazzy passage. Again, Morrison's stylistic virtuosity is at the service of a polemical message about the brutality of Western exploitation and its misuse of others' resources. The 'waste' she plays on here is a by-product of the neocolonial relationship between the Caribbean islands and American (and increasingly global) capitalism in the latter half of the twentieth century.

Morrison's commentary on the abuse of the natural resources of the islands and Anglo-American creation of 'waste' is so powerful because it signifies on a widespread nineteenth-century colonial discourse which had indicted the lazy 'Negroes' as the creators of waste. Thomas Carlyle's 'Occasional Discourse on the Negro Question' (1850) would later be retitled 'Occasional Discourse on the Nigger Question' (1853), and its virulent racism is best prefigured by the latter title. Catherine Hall has delineated brilliantly the essay's relevance for nineteenth-century race relations and its crucial intervention in developing the ruling British imperial hegemony, from the sympathetic sentimentalism of the 1840s to 'the articulation of a new racism' in the 1860s (C. Hall, 1992: 286). In her dynamic refiguring of the word, Morrison highlights the continuing relevance of the discourse of 'waste' inaugurated by Carlyle.

Carlyle had described the consequences of letting 'Negroes' have more freedom in the Caribbean as being tantamount to wasting its opportunities, as they were too lazy to take advantage of its benefits. The proof of this, according to Carlyle's diabolic vision, could be seen in the collapse of the Haitian economy in the decades after the successful slave revolt of the 1790s and subsequent establishment of a black government in 1802. The alternative to the 'beneficient whip' of the planters was the 'far sterner prophecy of Haiti', which existed as a dire warning to ungrateful Africans. Carlyle continued:

> Let him, by his ugliness, idleness and rebellion, banish all White
> men from the West Indies and make it all one Haiti, – with little
> or no sugar growing, Black Peter exterminating Black Paul, and
> where a garden of the Hesperides might be, nothing but a
> tropical dog-kennel and pestiferous jungle. (Carlyle, 1964: 327)

Carlyle's splenetic attack on the waste of an uncultivated land of bestial, fratricidal blacks is a Manichean vision that denies any middle way between an illusory plantation utopia and an autonomous black hell. Before the arrival of the 'Saxon-British', according to Carlyle, the land had produced only 'reeking waste and putrefaction' (*ibid.*: 326). Morrison's passage answers such a charge by indicting the colonialists and their ancestors as the true creators of waste by their pursuit of profit at all cost. Carlyle, though, is not content merely to use the symbol of waste to stand for a past which must make way for inevitable Anglo-Saxon capitalist progress, but employs it to point to an inevitable future of British dominance in the wake of Africans' inability to make anything of the land. Again, an image of 'waste' is central to the development of his argument:

> Before the West Indies could grow a pumpkin for any Negro,
> how much European heroism had to spend itself in obscure
> battle; to sink, in mortal agony, before the jungle, the
> putrescence and waste savageries could become arable, and the
> Devil be in some measure chained there ... Not a square inch of

soil in those fruitful Isles purchased by British blood, shall any Black man hold to grow pumpkins for him, except on terms that are fair towards Britain. (*ibid.*: 327)

By using the phrase 'waste savageries', and in demonizing the land for its lack of civilization, Carlyle also critiques the savages who live there. The Devil in chains is a necessary prelude to the taming of the lands. Thus, symbolically, slavery here is figured as necessary for the proper exploitation of the land and to move it from a state of 'waste savagery'. Morrison's passage critically inverts such a discourse and, in an exemplary anti-colonial move, reveals the real wasters to be the colonial exploiters who lay waste to the land, before literally defecating on it. Morrison takes a phrase which has been developed to demonize diasporan Africans as uncivilized and dramatically reverses its meaning. Her intervention is best understood by reference to the Russian language philosopher M. M. Bakhtin's work in *The Dialogic Imagination*, which argued that there is a constant struggle over language within and between social, cultural and racial groups:

> The word in language is half someone else's. It becomes one's own only when the speaker populates it with his own intention, his own accent, when he appropriates the word, adapting it to his own semantic and expressive intention. Prior to this moment of appropriation, the word does not exist in a neutral and impersonal language, but rather it exists in other people's mouths, in other people's contexts serving other people's intentions: it is from there that one must take the word and make it one's own. (Bakhtin, 1981: 293–4)

Morrison takes the word 'waste' out of a colonial and neocolonial hegemonic use and adapts it to critique that hegemony. But her intervention is not just radical in terms of content: it is her intention to make the word her own, to appropriate the literary tradition for her own vernacular purpose. The language of the literary tradition has inevitably often been used to serve the intentions of the powerful; Morrison's desire is to use it to relate the untold stories of a diasporan people who had been denied the power of literary language through legalized oppression and poor educational opportunities during and after slavery. This radical intention, though brilliantly codified by Bakhtin, does not come from Russian language theorists or even deconstructionists, postmodernists or poststructuralists, but from the core traditions of her people who had to 'make a way out of no way', and did so by taking the words out of white people's mouths and adapting them for their own purposes – literally Signifyin(g) on them. Morrison's 'dialogization' (an expression coined by Bakhtin) of key phrases of the imperial power such as 'waste' is a dynamic example of this tradition. It also links her to an African diasporan tradition of writers who have taken the English language by the scruff of the neck and made it work for them. M. Nourbese Philip, a Caribbean poet based in Canada, codifies this move most appositely. Her comments on African-

Caribbean writers apply to Morrison and African-American writers too, especially at those moments when Morrison is dialogizing on the English language:

> The place African Caribbean writers occupy is one that is unique, and one that forces the writer to operate in a language that was used to brutalize and diminish Africans so that they would come to a profound belief in their own lack of humanity. No language can accomplish this – and to a large degree English did accomplish it – without itself being profoundly affected, without itself being tainted. The challenge, therefore, facing the African Caribbean writer who is at all sensitive to language and the issues it generates is to use the language in such a way that the historical realities are not erased or obliterated, so that English is revealed as the tainted tongue it truly is. Only in so doing will English be redeemed. (Philip, 1997: 117)

Black writers throughout the diaspora have had a troubled relationship with the language that has been used, through its stereotyping discourse, as a tool to oppress them. This 'tainted' language must be reclaimed by the formerly colonized writer and made to work for her/him. As we have seen, Morrison is exemplary of black Atlantic writers, as she redeems the English language by Signifyin(g) on Carlyle's use of the term 'waste savageries' to reveal the tortured history of racial stereotyping and to propose a counter-hegemonic riposte. This becomes clearer as the novel develops. Morrison's 'waste' passage itself is connected to a whole series of other passages which link a critique of the European and American waste of resources in the colonial and neocolonial world to the impoverishment and exploitation of African peoples throughout the diaspora. As Evelyn Hawthorne states succinctly, '*Tar Baby* is a contemporary revisioning of racial history' (Hawthorne, 1988: 100). Valerian, the retired candy manufacturer, is used by Morrison as symptomatic of the exploitation such a revisioning of racial history exposes, and in a passage of great emotive force she indicts him for his crimes against African and working-class peoples. He has just dismissed his servants for thieving apples, a product that would not even have entered the local economy without his intervention (*ibid.*: 102). Morrison condemns him through Son's perception of his calm manner after he has sacked the servants:

> Son's mouth went dry as he watched Valerian chewing a piece of ham, his head-of-a-coin profile content, approving even of the flavour in his mouth although he had been able to dismiss with a flutter of the fingers the people whose sugar and cocoa had allowed him to grow old in regal comfort; although he had taken the sugar and cocoa and paid for it as though it had no value, as though the cutting of cane and picking of beans was child's play and had no value; but he turned it into candy, the invention of which really was child's play, and sold it to other

> children and made a fortune in order to move near, but not in
> the midst of, the jungle where the sugar came from and build a
> palace with more of their labour and then hire them to do more
> of the work he was not capable of and pay them again according
> to some scale of value that would outrage Satan himself ...
> (Morrison, 1983: 203–4)

Son strips away colonialism's illusory mask here, showing how the matter-of-fact, seemingly common-sense nature of progress and capitalism is based on the stealing of resources and selling them back as finished goods either to those from whom they had been stolen originally, or to the children of those whose labour power had been utilized to produce them. The passage is also a response to the charge from Carlyle and other imperialist apologists that the waste land would be unimproved without European intervention, showing that it is crucially labour power which makes the land productive. Hence, Valerian's designation of his servants as thieves is a function not of some abstract philosophical notion of right and wrong but of his power in an exploitative relationship, where their thieving is, in fact, a justifiable response to years in which their labour power and other resources have been stolen by greedy colonial and neocolonial exploiters just like Valerian. It is a modern version of the African-American myth in which the slave, accused of stealing his master's chicken, which he has eaten, replies that he has merely been improving the master's most important human resource by feeding it sufficiently. Such decoding of the reality lurking beneath the illusory is a dynamic intervention in the discourse of colonialism, only with a voice that is often marginalized – the exploited and dispossessed. Such a siren voice destabilizes and dialogizes language within the colonial linguistic economy. This becomes even clearer as the passage continues:

> and when those people wanted a little of what he wanted, some
> apples for their Christmas, and took some, he dismissed them
> with a flutter of the fingers, because they were thieves, and
> nobody knew thieves and thievery better than he did and he
> probably thought he was a law-abiding man, they all did, and
> they all always did, because they had not the dignity of wild
> animals who did not eat where they defecated, but they could
> defecate over a whole people and come there to live and defecate
> some more by tearing up the land and that is why they loved
> property so, because they had killed it soiled it defecated on it
> and they loved more than anything the places where they shit.
> Would fight and kill to own the cesspools they made, and
> although they called it architecture it was in fact elaborately
> built toilets, decorated toilets, toilets surrounded with and by
> business and enterprise in order to have something to do
> between defecations since waste was the order of the day and
> the ordering principle of the universe. And especially the
> Americans who were the worst because they were new at the

business of defecation spent their whole lives bathing bathing
bathing washing away the stench of the cesspools as though
pure soap had anything to do with purity. (*ibid.*: 204)

Once Morrison has elaborated on theft so that it reaches its logical conclusion – namely, that the whites are the thieves in the colonial context – the
passage becomes even more breathless and animated, linking such thievery to
the laying waste of the resources of the colonized world. She uses riffs on
lexical items like 'defecation' and 'toilets' to emphasize the link between such
scatological terms and the whites who are used to blaming the Africans for a
lack of hygiene. Such inversion is a Signifyin(g) response which means that
white Americans in this vision can never be clean because of the dirt they have
created in other cultures. No amount of 'bathing' can wash away the stench
they cause. The Americans, though a relatively recent colonial power, have
become particularly adept exponents of exploitation. The criticism in this
section of the novel is one strand of an avowedly political and polemical
theme; however, Morrison uses the full resources of her stylistic range to
create an insistent, riffing and Signifyin(g) response that helps to make the
charge stick. Her radical anti-colonial polemic is underpinned by a poetics
which comes from vernacular African diasporan routes.

The dysfunctional nature of Valerian's family is a product of their colonizing status and is shown most clearly by his wife Margaret's abuse of their
son. This is linked to Valerian's involvement in the sugar trade by Margaret's
use of a language of satisfying ingestion to describe her torture of Michael:

> Nothing serious though. No throwing across the room, or out of
> the window. No scalding, no fist work. Just a delicious pin-stab
> in sweet creamy flesh. That was her word 'delicious'. 'I knew it
> was wrong, knew it was bad. But something about it was
> delicious too.' She was telling him, saying it aloud at the dinner
> table after everyone had gone. His knees were trembling and
> he'd had to sit down again ... She was serene standing there
> saying it, and he agreed with that, thought it could be, must be,
> true – that it was delicious, for at that moment it would have
> been delicious to him too if he could have picked up the carving
> knife lying on the platter next to the carcass of the goose and
> slashed into her lovely Valentine face. Delicious. Conclusive and
> delicious. (*ibid.*: 233–4)

'Delicious' is repeated and debated (or in Bakhtin's language, 'dialogized')
by Morrison in this passage so that its provenance escapes this section of the
novel, becoming not merely a word concomitant to Margaret's individual
pathology but to a whole culture that expropriates delicious goods (like sugar)
from the third world to underpin a market economy whose destructive nature
eventually distorts and undermines, even makes pathological, the lives of those
who colonize as much as it does the colonized peoples. Of course, Morrison
would return to this theme in *Beloved*, as I outlined in the previous chapter.

Margaret's 'pin-stab in sweet creamy flesh' exhibits a greedy invasion and expropriation of her son's body that is equivalent to the invasion and exploitation of colonial resources by her husband, while Valerian's 'delicious' anticipation of violent revenge stresses the simmering brutality that exists in a family made dysfunctional by their central position in the colonial economy. The riffing on 'delicious' here is Morrison's Signifyin(g) retort to a world-view which sees the continuation of market and colonial relationships as natural and unproblematic while they apparently satisfy common human needs. In contrast, she figures them as being as abusive as violence against an innocent child, and at the same time shows how the powerful are undermined by this abuse of their power. She takes a word like 'delicious' out of the mouths of the exploiters and reveals its multiple negative valencies. Such an inversion is quintessentially a Signifyin(g) gesture, albeit a subtle and complex one.

It is not only to Caribbean islands that the tentacles of the world capitalist system, as exemplified by sugar production, reach. In her first novel, *The Bluest Eye*, Morrison shows how the consumption of finished goods is as much dictated by the forces of racial exploitation and capitalism as the production of raw materials. This is best illustrated when the main protagonist Pecola, whose desire to have blue eyes is the central concern of the text, buys candy from Mr Yacobowski. As so often in her novels, Morrison illustrates the ramifications of the commercial transaction at the level of style. Mr Yacobowski regards the black girl with 'glazed separateness' (Morrison, 1972: 47), yet his look is strong enough to be a controlling look, for it is this look which undermines Pecola's humanity:

> She does not know what keeps his glance suspended. Perhaps because he is grown, or a man, and she a little girl. But she has seen interest, disgust, even anger in grown male eyes. Yet this vacuum is not new to her. It has an edge; somewhere in the bottom lid is the distaste. She has seen it lurking in the eyes of all white people. So. The distaste must be for her, her blackness. All things in her are flux and anticipation. But her blackness is static and dread. And it is the blackness that accounts for, that creates, the vacuum edged with distaste in white eyes. (*ibid.*: 48)

Madonne M. Miner, in her apposite discussion of Mr Yacobowski's look in terms of gender politics, sees it as another instance of a male denying presence to a female which 'parallels previously described rape scenes' (Miner, 1985: 185). However, it achieves more than this. As in so much of Morrison's prose style, it is the repetitions and dialogization of words that create meaning here. 'Distaste' and 'blackness' are repeated to stress Pecola's entrapment in a white-dominated world which does not allow her to fulfil her human potential. In the bottom lid of Mr Yakobowski's eyes is a distaste which constructs her blackness as her all-important signifier. The constant linking of the two lexical terms here as riff and counter-riff elides their difference in meaning, so that the blackness for which Yakobowski has distaste becomes that which *creates* the distaste. For Yakobowski, who in the final part of the paragraph becomes representative of white folk, distaste and blackness become interchangeable and an inevitable function of the dominant white gaze, which through the operation of racial and colonial power constructs black people as inferior.

On leaving the shop, Pecola strives to overcome the shame and anger caused by the encounter with the racist shopkeeper by eating the candy he has sold her: literally to taste sweetness as an antidote to the 'distaste' of the transaction. Barbara Hill Rigney rather excessively sees this passage as an assumption of cannibalistic power, as she symbolically eats those who have dominion over her. In Rigney's interpretation, the Mary Janes (candy with wrappers showing a perfect white girl) become a symbol of the white body, and she contends that by eating them Pecola liberates herself. Rigney comments that the young black girl 'perhaps enacts a primitive rite of passage, a cannibal feast as she gorges herself on the body of the enemy in order to assume its power' (Rigney, 1991: 85). Unfortunately, such a passing reference fails to acknowledge Morrison's much more foregrounded discussion of cannibalism in *Beloved*, which might have warned Rigney against such oversimplification. Even more regrettably, by privileging a positive reading of the eating of the sweets, Rigney actually misreads Morrison's intentions. Pecola's consumption of the candy is not a liberating act, but a sign of her entrapment in a globalized capitalist system in which intensively plantation-farmed sugar and its teeth-rotting products symbolize the exploitation of third world peoples, as both workers and consumers.

Rigney's liberationist interpretation ignores the troubled history of candy and its major component, sugar, which Susan Willis so brilliantly foregrounds in her analysis of *The Bluest Eye*. Willis's discussion uses Sidney Mintz's scholarship, from his magisterial study *Sweetness and Power* (1985), to show how sugar production oils the wheels of the systems of both slavery and capitalism, so that sugar becomes 'a substitute for real food' and an 'opiate of the working class under capitalism' (Willis, 1987: 177–8). As Mintz argued, 'Sugar led all else in dramatising the tremendous power concealed in mass consumption' (Mintz, 1986: 185). Morrison's use of sugar to highlight the dynamics of power between exploiter and exploited shows how exploitation occurs not only at the point of production but also at the point of consumption. The theme suffuses her novels, from Yakobowski's candy shopkeeper in *The Bluest Eye* to Valerian's status as a candy manufacturer in *Tar Baby*. In all cases, the diasporan African is shown as part of a producing and consuming mass that is controlled by desires for products which literally rot their bodies. Far from being a liberating gesture, then, the eating of candy shows how Pecola is entrapped by Anglo-American value systems in a capitalist economy. A close look at the style of the passage which describes Pecola gorging on the Mary Janes shows how Willis's reading (after Mintz), is more pertinent:

> Each pale yellow wrapper has a picture on it a picture of a little Mary Jane, for whom the candy is named. Smiling white face. Blonde hair in gentle disarray, blue eyes looking out of a world of clean comfort. The eyes are petulant mischievous. To Pecola they are simply pretty. She eats the candy, and its sweetness is

good. To eat the candy is somehow to eat the eyes, eat Mary
Jane. Love Mary Jane. Be Mary Jane.
   Three Pennies had brought her nine lovely orgasms with Mary
Jane. Lovely Mary Jane for whom a candy is named.
(Morrison, 1972: 49)

The language of the passage, with its simple sentences and imperative clauses,
resembles not one of Morrison's spectacular anti-capitalist or anti-colonial
passages, which she would surely have used had she meant the eating of the
candy to be a liberatory gesture coming from the assumption of cannibalistic
power, but that of the reading primer, the 'Janet and John book' which frames
the novel. As Inger-Ann Softing contends, 'here the language of the narrative
significantly adopts the rigid and lifeless style of the pre-text' (Softing, 1995:
87). So Rigney's assertion of the potential radicalism of the cannibalistic feast
at a thematic level appears misguided, because the passage is couched in the
language which Morrison uses to show the working of Anglo-American
hegemony. Willis's astute reading of the passage as a negative one, then, is
buttressed by paying close attention to Morrison's stylistic praxis.
   Other clues to the negative interpretation of the eating of the candy appear
earlier in the passage as Pecola surveys the sweets. The narrator notes, 'A peal
of anticipation unsettles her stomach' (Morrison, 1972: 47). The peal here is
figured as negative and literally unsettling. Moreover, as Shelley Wong notes,
"the peal" anticipates the "high yellow" character Maureen Peal, who
represents the closest a black girl can get to a white appearance and who will
unsettle Pecola later by screaming insults at her' (Wong, 1990: 479). Thus,
Morrison's introduction of an unsettling 'peal' is merely the coda to the
human Peal to come. Such a subtle pattern of 'call and recall' (O'Meally,
1989: 198) links this passage to the later passage about Pecola's perceived
ugliness in a world which values light colouring above all else. Such connections reveal the all-pervasive nature of a racist hegemony, which stretches
from commerce (the general store) to education (the school playground) and
pervades black experience throughout the diaspora.
   Morrison shows that African-Americans are not totally dominated by an
oppressive culture through the set-piece confrontations of some of her other
characters. For instance, Claudia attempts to assert her autonomy from the
oppressive white standards of beauty that constrict Pecola by her destruction
of white dolls. This allows her the satisfaction of destroying these key icons of
Anglo-American standards of beauty. As Softing contends, 'Claudia is the only
character in this novel who consciously makes an attempt at deconstructing
the ideology of the dominant society' (Softing, 1995: 90). Her dismemberment
of a doll is an act of demystification which emphasizes the fact that this object
of veneration is nothing more than a squalid consumer item:

I had only one desire: to dismember it. To see of what it was
made, to discover the dearness, to find the beauty, the
desirability that had escaped me, but apparently only me ... I
could not love it. But I could examine it to see what it was that

all the world said was loveable. Break off the tiny fingers, bend
the flat feet, loosen the hair, twist the head around, and the thing
made one sound – a sound they said was the sweet and plaintive
cry 'Mama,' but which sounded to me like the bleat of a dying
lamb, or, more precisely, our icebox door opening on rusty
hinges in July. Remove the cold and stupid eyeball, it would
bleat still, 'Ahhhhhh,' take off the head, shake out the sawdust,
crack the back against the brass bed rail, it would bleat still. The
gauze back would split, and I could see the disk with six holes,
the secret of the sound. A mere metal roundness. (Morrison,
1972: 23)

Claudia's dismemberment of the doll is her way of uncovering the falsity of
Western values of beauty. Her recognition of its sounds as mere bleatings
indicates how her growing awareness of the object's falsity has emerged
through the rupture of its sound: the way the sound does not signify what the
world has told her it does. The signifier literally becomes detached from the
signified, so that the cry of 'Mama' the world hears is just a bleating lamb or a
rusty hinge. Such signification means that the doll is not merely negatively
dismembered; once destroyed, it is used to illustrate the hollow nature of
Anglo-American social and cultural hegemony. As Softing describes it, the
destruction of the doll deconstructs the white cultural myth which is syn-
onymous with 'the text's act of undressing the inadequacy of the pre-text (the
primer)' (Softing, 1995: 90). The novel had begun with a realistic portion of a
primer which, by the end, is reduced to gobbledygook by Morrison: so
Claudia is indulging in the same kind of uncovering as Morrison, showing
how stylistic praxis is mirrored within the narrative itself. It is telling that
Morrison portrays Claudia's discovery of the truth about the doll through
sound; such demystification lies at the heart of a jazz praxis which likewise
takes Western pop tunes and dissects them before composing a new tune
rather than merely reproducing what is written. The demystification of the
popular tune is here paralleled by the demystification of the popular icon, and
Morrison's final comment on it – 'A mere metal roundness' – stresses the
pathetic nature of the object that enthrals. Its falseness and inauthenticity is
contrasted almost immediately by the blues songs which Claudia's mother
sings on a lonesome Sunday:

She would sing about hard times, bad times, some-body-done-
gone-and-left-me times. But her voice was so sweet and her
singing eyes so melty I found myself longing for those hard
times, yearning to be grown without 'a thin di-i-me to my
name'. I looked forward to the delicious time when 'my man'
would leave me, when I would 'hate to see the evening sun go
down ... ' 'cause then I would know 'my man has left this
town.' Misery colored by the greens and blues in my mother's
voice took all of the grief out of the words and left me with a

conviction that pain was not only endurable, it was sweet.
(Morrison, 1972: 27)

Here, blues lyrics are embedded in the text to show how African-Americans
have coped with the constrictions that the hegemony of Anglo-American
values has imposed on them; how the misery of racism and poverty has been
turned on its head by the blues impulse, which makes an art out of suffering
and elevates African-Americans beyond the conditions that undermine their
humanity. As Ralph Ellison has said, 'the blues ... are an art form and thus a
transcendence of those conditions created within the Negro community by the
denial of social justice' (Ellison, 1972: 257). In the novel, the 'mere metal
roundness' which bleats out of the prized white doll is contrasted to the
quality of the human voice, which has the power to make pain seem sweet. It
is such human voices from the vernacular culture of black America which
Morrison seeks to foreground through her use of a musical mode.

The best illustration of Morrison's acknowledgement of the resilience of the
musical tradition and its central place in her people's history comes in *Beloved*
when Paul D. is imprisoned in a chain gang. A deluge turns the Georgia
countryside where the gang is located into a watery simulacrum of the conditions on board a leaky slave ship:

> It rained.
>   In the boxes the men heard the water rise in the trench and
> looked out for cottonmouths. They squatted in muddy water,
> slept above it, peed in it. Paul D. thought he was screaming; his
> mouth was open and there was this loud throat-splitting sound –
> but it may have been someone else. Then he thought he was
> crying. Something was running down his cheeks. He lifted his
> hands to wipe away the tears and saw dark brown slime.
> (Morrison, 1988a: 110)

The disorientating experience of being caged in a dark confined space in close
proximity to others links this experience to Beloved's account of conditions on
board the slave ship. Thus, Morrison makes links across the black Atlantic
between those exploited in the transatlantic trade and those trapped in the
slave system of the Americas. The escape from this literal watery grave is
achieved by an inspired piece of collective improvisation. Morrison first
establishes the forty-six imprisoned men as archetypal African-Americans
engaged in musicking. They perform on a functional level to help them get
through their dull work and to explicate the joyful and pained lives, they have
all enjoyed and endured. Also, through musically encoding and thus remembering such lives, they revel in their joys and ameliorate their sorrows. Music
functions as a link to past struggles and allows them to pass the time cre-
atively, as James Baldwin recognizes when he consisely sums up a pragmatic
philosophy of black musicking:

Music is our witness and our ally. The beat is the confession

which recognises changes and conquers time. Then, history
becomes a garment we can wear and share, and not a cloak in
which to hide; and time becomes our friend. (quoted in Gilroy,
1993a: 203)

Through song they gain an agency their situation as chained prisoners
would seem wholly to negate. It also allows them to glory in their communal
culture, as music is a witness to their shared cultural praxis. More prag-
matically (and here crucially), they use music as a tool of communication to
encode messages between themselves that white men are unable to decipher.
During their work, their leader Hi Man establishes a call to which they
respond, apparently effortlessly, establishing a repetitive rhythm which Morrison mirrors in her riffing prose style:

With a sledge hammer in his hands and Hi Man's lead, the men
got through. They sang it out and beat it up, garbling the words
so they could not be understood; tricking the words so their
syllables yielded up other meanings. They sang the women they
knew; the children they had been; the animals they had tamed
themselves or seen others tame. They sang of bosses and masters
and misses; of mules and dogs and the shamelessness of life.
They sang lovingly of graveyards and sisters long gone. Of pork
in the woods; meal in the pan; fish on the line; cane, rain and
rocking chairs. And they beat. The women for having known
them and no more, no more; the children for having been them,
but never again. They killed a boss so often and so completely
they had to bring him back to life to pulp him one more time.
Tasting hot mealcake among pine trees they beat it away.
Singing love songs to Mr Death, they smashed his head.
(Morrison, 1988a: 108–9)

Immobilized by chains, the men take control in the fantasy world of the song,
beat out their frustration and take revenge on those who have oppressed them
in the past or incarcerate them now. The release valve of the song is stressed by
Morrison through her direct paralleling of the song and its functions at the
stylistic level. There is a syntactic parallelism between the repeated 'they sang'
phrases of the first paragraph, which help to establish the rhythm, and the
echoing phrase 'and they beat'. Both are followed by a string of dependent
nouns that emphasizes the link between the vocal sounds and the rhythmic
noise of the hammers which accompany the singing. Note too the repeated 'no
more' phrase which adds a song-like refrain to the second half of the passage.
Hi Man sets up a call and response pattern that allows space for them all to
sing of their individual situations within a collective musicking. It also allows
them to enjoy a repetitive activity which is meant to degrade them. Morrison's
description of the men's transformation of their monotonous labour into
liberational joy through song and rhythmic gesture is not merely a romanticized interpretation: for, African Americans who have survived on the chain

gang attest to the importance of communal singing to their survival. Lonnie Elder describes the way humdrum and back-breaking work is made bearable and even enjoyably therapeutic through communal musicking:

> The chain gang they put us on was a chain gang and a half ... I would do it like this! I would hit the rock and the hammer would bounce-bounce so hard it would take my hand up in the air with it – but I'd grab it with my left hand and bring it down like this: Hunh! (Carried away by the rhythm of his story, he starts twisting his body to the swing of it.) It would get so good to me, I'd say hunh! Yeah! Hunh! I'd say OoooooooooOweeeee! I'm wide open now. (Swinging and twisting.) Yeah baby, I say Hunh! Sooner or later that rock would crack. (quoted in Floyd, 1995: 230)

Through the singing of the song and the rhythmic actions, chain-gang participants move from a position as helpless victims beholden to Anglo-American power to autonomous individuals who survive as part of a wider community. As Olly Wilson points out, the work and the song interpenetrate so that they become indistinguishable:

> The sound produced by the ax creates a component of the music which is essential to the structure of the song. The music, then, is not simply accompanying the work, but the work becomes the music, and the music becomes the work. (Wilson, 1998: 91)

Their labour is transformed through song from creating a surplus value in goods at the mens' expense, to the creation of music that transcends their situation as convict labourers. Through such communal musicking the men literally remove themselves from victimhood, something that James Baldwin was well aware of in his discussion of the mental chains that afflict African Americans:

> I refuse absolutely to speak from the point of view of the victim. The victim can have no point of view for precisely so long as he thinks of himself as a victim. The testimony of the victim as victim corroborates simply, the reality of the chains that bind him – confirms, and, as it were consoles the jailer. (Baldwin, 1985a: 78)

Their singing liberates them from the mental chains, from victimhood, enabling them to be 'free in their mind' and retain their sanity despite hideous privations. As feelings produced in song are for themselves and not for the ears of listening whites, they make these deep musings on life appear nonsensical – 'garbling the words so they could not be understood; tricking the words so their syllables yielded up other meanings'. Such masking is a quintessential feature of African-American musicking which was commented on by Frederick

Douglass and W. E. B. Du Bois in their discussion of slave songs, and by Duke Ellington in his discussion of both ante- and post-bellum work songs. Ellington describes how such workers sang not because 'it is the nature of the Negro to sing at his work' but at the behest of their masters who wanted to eliminate communication between them by busying them at song:

> Fearful of the silence of these groups of blacks, their masters
> commanded them to raise their voices in song, so that all
> opportunity for discontented reflections or plans for retaliation
> and salvation would be eliminated. (quoted in Ulanov,
> 1998: 166)

Of course, far from inhibiting autonomous communication, these songs actually provided the occasion for it. Morrison's positing of such cultural strategies here is important, as it reveals how African-American musicking establishes a communication system which exists parallel to, but distinct from, Anglo-American society. As Timothy L. Parrish asserts in drawing a parallel with the singing slaves described by Frederick Douglass in his *Narrative of the Life of an American Slave* (1845), 'Morrison's singing prisoners create an identity separate from their imprisonment. This separate identity enables them to survive their imprisonment' (Parrish, 1997: 87). The independence from hegemonic beliefs that speaking a different language can develop, and Morrison's foregrounding of it here as a key element in the survival of African-Americans in dreadful conditions, shows how she employs diasporan African vernacular aesthetic not only to structure her texts but also as an underpinning philosophy that sustains them. As Gilroy asserts, 'the means of cultural representation available to racially subordinate peoples' are limited because 'denied access to particular cultural forms (like literacy)' they utilize others which '(like song) are developed both as a means of transcendence and as a type of compensation for very specific experiences of unfreedom' (Gilroy, 1993a: 123). Clearly, these vernacular forms are functional in the context of oppression that Morrison describes in *Beloved*.

The songs have a base-line function, which is to support those who sing them through the terrible conditions of the chain gang, providing a communal and collective response to help those individuals most affected by the harsh regime. The more experienced or hardy help the new or weaker members of the gang through the medium of song:

> More than the rest, they killed the flirt whom folks called Life
> for leading them on. Making them think the next sunrise would
> be worth it; that another stroke of time would do it at last. Only
> when she was dead would they be safe. The successful ones – the
> ones who had been there enough years to have maimed,
> mutilated, maybe even buried her – kept watch over the others
> who were still in her cock-teasing hug, caring and looking
> forward, remembering and looking back. They were the ones
> whose eyes said, 'Help me, 's bad'; or 'Look out,' meaning *this*

> *might be the day I bay or eat my own mess or run*, and it was
> this last that had to be guarded against, for if one pitched and
> ran – all, all forty-six, would be yanked by the chain that bound
> them and no telling who or how many would be killed.
> (Morrison, 1988a; 109)

The collective here is seen to be key, for if one breaks, then all are endangered.
The importance of a communal response is shown when the men actually
escape, for it is in their ability to communicate with one another through the
chains that bind them that they are able to break out. As the flood levels rise,
the opportunity of flight comes closer:

> It started like the chain up but the difference was the power of
> the chain. One by one from Hi Man on down the line, they
> dove. Down through the mud under the bars, blind, groping ...
> Some lost direction and their neighbours, feeling the confused
> pull of the chain, snatched them round. For one lost, all lost. The
> chain that held them would save all or none, and Hi Man was
> the delivery. They talked through that chain like Sam Morse
> and, Great God, they all came up. Like the unshriven dead,
> zombies on the loose, holding the chain in their hands, they
> trusted the rain and the dark, yes, but mostly Hi Man and each
> other. (*ibid*.: 110)

Morrison emphasizes the importance of collective discipline, trusting each
other and the leader Hi Man, following his call, while looking after those
closest to you and, most importantly, communicating effectively despite the
limited equipment and means available. Their improvised response is only
possible because of the hours of practice they have put in to become an efficient unit; this is, of course, paradigmatic of the role of improvisation in the
community, mirrored later in the jazz subculture by such important performers as Louis Armstrong, Charlie Parker and John Coltrane, as Morrison
herself discussed in interview:

> Black people are very interested in making it look as though no
> thought went into it. And the jazz musician's the classic person.
> I mean the hours and hours of work so that you can be so
> imbued with it, so you can actually stand on stage and make it
> up. (Morrison, 1989b)

In the chain-gang passage, discipline and mastery of communication,
despite all attempts by oppressive forces to undermine the former and restrict
the latter, mean that the men are able to release themselves. Their improvisational leap comes not from individual effort but from a collective will that
has emerged as a central facet of African-American culture; as Julian Cowley
points out:

> The improvisatory skills of jazz musicians reflect the need for
> flexibility and immediacy of response in strategies for survival
> necessarily adopted by black Americans given the large part
> played by accidents and the unknown in their lives personally
> and communally. (Cowley, 1988: 196)

What we might call a 'musicking aesthetic' is such an effective mode,
because its key techniques of improvisation and antiphony are a learnt
response to actual historical conditions. Here, the aesthetic provides a methodology which helps Paul D. and his compatriots to liberation. The chain
which had imprisoned them is literally their liberating tool, as it provides them
with a method of communication that allows them to improvise their way to
freedom. 'The best hand-forged iron in Georgia' (Morrison, 1988a: 109),
which is meant to restrain them, becomes, by a bewildering piece of improvisational brilliance, instrumental to their escape as their months of practice
enables them to talk like 'Sam Morse' through it. Or, as Laura Doyle comments on the relationship of the individual Paul D., his fellow prisoners and
the chain:

> the materiality of his chains simultaneously puts him and them
> within the grip of a master and yet constitutes a means of
> resistance to the master. By tugging rhythmically on their chains
> one morning, the men in the ditch signal to one another and so
> effect their escape: the very phenomenality that serves the will to
> power thus also frees Paul D. of tyranny's grasp. Chains may
> both imprison and liberate ... (Doyle, 1994: 233)

Other literary artists in the diaspora have emphasized this duality of chains,
the fact that they imprison but also enable linkage with other slaves. For
instance, Kamau Brathwaite in 'New World A-Comin' from *Rights of Passage*
writes:

> [...] Fire
> falls walls, fashions
> these fire–
> locks darker than iron,
> and we filed down the path
> linked in a new
> clinked silence of iron. (Brathwaite, 1973: 10–11)

Furthermore, although Susan Willis does not allude to these passages specifically when talking about the ambivalent nature of chains in African-
American culture, her comments provide a dynamic gloss which highlights
how instruments meant to be key to the enslaving process were transformed
within vernacular African-American culture:

> the meanings associated with chains are already historically

complex because the chains of slavery were worked upon and
redefined in the African American system of signification
whereby the chains as a means of enforcing enslavement were
also the basis for making connection with Africa and the idea of
release. Shango, the African god who presided over lightning –
thus fire, thus the forge, thus iron – was present in the chains,
carried over the ocean as a hard and fast desire for freedom.
Chains are the simultaneous embodiment of slavery and
freedom. (Willis, 1994: 183)

In this context, Morrison, in reflecting a mythology to structure her passage,
foregrounds an allusion to an African cosmology (Shango is the Yoruba god of
thunder) rather than a Western mythological figure such as Orpheus. This
shows how Morrison is not beholden merely to the Western mythological
tradition. The use of an African cosmology should guard critics against the
slavish adoption of Greek mythical allusions which, though relevant, are not a
dominating factor in Morrison's fiction. As music is key to the transformation
from slavery to freedom, the Orphic mode might seem to provide an apt
framework in which to disuss this emancipation. However, in the original
story of Shango, he escapes into thin air leaving behind an iron chain, the
relevance of which to Paul D.'s liberation is I believe a more convincing
allusive framework for discussing such a dynamic African-inspired rebellion.

Music is central to the transformational and liberational moment Morrison
describes. In her interview with Paul Gilroy, she specifically invokes this
vernacular mode: 'The major things black art has to have are these. It must
have the ability to use found objects [and] the appearance of using found
things' (Gilroy, 1988: 11). For Paul D. and his fellow inmates, the found
object was the chain that had enslaved him, which he now transforms through
vernacular mediation into the means of his liberation; while the principal
found object for the writer is the language of Anglo-America, which had
similarly limited the means of expression, but once transformed by the black
vernacular has the potential to be liberational. As another African-American
novelist, Gayl Jones, succinctly puts it, 'the oral tradition is a laboratory for
making experiments with Western literary tradition' (Jones, 1991: 86). Morrison's use of Signifying, and her knowledge of the centrality of musicking to
the radical traditions of her people, is used to wonderful effect in all her books
to subvert and embellish the literary form of the novel.

As I hope I have shown in examples from these different Morrison texts, the
oral/musical mode is most successfully employed, not at the expense of or as a
diversion from her political agenda, but as integral to her radical project and
at its service. As George Lipsitz has said, such literature 'combines the subjectivity and objectivity, that employs the insights and passions of myth and
folklore in the service of revising history' (quoted in Coser, 1994: 15). Or to be
more specific, Morrison's radical jazz-inflected style originating from African
diasporan culture is integral to her theme of the importance of achieving
African-American autonomy from Anglo-American hegemony and to the
revisioning of majority narratives that seek to deny such autonomy. Such

aesthetic autonomy has been a feature of radical black cultures throughout the history of the black Atlantic, and Morrison's depiction of its relevance to the slave communities of *Beloved*, on the Caribbean islands in *Tar Baby* and in the modern American landscape in such novels as *The Bluest Eye* illustrates the far-reaching nature of a radical chain-dancing mode in opposition to colonial and postcolonial oppression.

7

'THE DOGS OF OLD ENGLAND MEET THE LIONS OF THE NEW WORLD'

THE TRAVELS OF FREDERICK DOUGLASS AND PAUL ROBESON IN THE BLACK ATLANTIC AND THE DEVELOPMENT OF A 'STRATEGIC ANGLOPHILIA'

> I had my suspicions of English
> ladies, actresses, ghosts of the Thames,
> concubines, as we had been into the next
> century. And they had their wiles with him.
>
> (from 'The Love Letters of Helen Pitts Douglass', quoted in Harper, 2000: 295)

If literary figures have chain-danced to freedom through the imagination of such stellar figures as Toni Morrison, so certain historical figures have intervened dynamically in the black Atlantic, undertaking path-breaking sojourns that have inscribed the Atlantic space as liberational as well as enslaving. Arguably, the two most important transatlantic African-American figures of the last 150 years have been Frederick Douglass and Paul Robeson. Douglass's 'consciousness of "race", self and society were profoundly changed by the experience of being outside America' (Gilroy, 1993a: 132), and the same could surely be said of Robeson.

Let us look first at the career of Frederick Douglass. It is impossible to overestimate the importance of Douglass's liberating sojourn for his development as an independent mind in the abolitionist movement. Many contemporary commentators noticed that Douglass emerged from the shadow of his former mentors during this visit. Richard Webb, the publisher of Douglass's *Narrative*, eulogized the leading American abolitionist William Garrison and had a troubled relationship with Douglass; however, he figured accurately (though perhaps unconsciously) a changing dynamic in their relationship when they were together in Britain in October 1846:

> I forgot among the droppers in last night to mention Frederick
> Douglass who looks stately and majestic – with an air that
> makes Garrison a mere baby beside him'. In the same letter he

describes how people 'of the highest rank' in Edinburgh contend for his company and make him quite a lion'. (Taylor, 1974: 294)

Such veneration was due to his wonderful oratorical skills and his galvinizing of the 'Send Back the Money Campaign'. Douglass relates how street urchins shouted the phrase to him as he passed them by and it was not long before it became immortalized in a street ballad. Fortunately, Professor George Shepperson's 1950s scholarship and the good offices of Radio Scotland, whose 1996 documentary featured this ballad, have rescued it from obscurity:

Shall I, as free as ocean's waves,
Shake hands with wi' women whipping slaves,
An' build Kirks wi' the bluid o' slaves?
Send back – SEND BACK THE MONEY! (*Send Back the Money*, 1996)

Douglass's name was also prominent in these ballads, showing that despite the presence of other abolitionists at meetings denouncing the church, it was Douglass whose interventions received attention. For instance, another ballad sung to the tune of 'Ballenomoro Oro' encapsulated Douglass's stellar contribution to the debate:

Nae Douglas has blawn sic' a flame,
That we winna hae peace till the siller's sent hame. (*ibid.*)

Apart from being immortalized in these ballads and in most of the Scottish press, he was also lionized by many ordinary Scots folk, as one anonymous witness reported:

On Munonday nicht our Jock gat me to gang doun an' hear that chiel, Douglass. I had come away wanting ma specks: but frae the luik I gat o' him, he seemed a buirly fellow, ane I shouldna like to hae a tussle wi him either feeseecally or intellecktually. (Shepperson, 1953: 314)

His rhetorical flourishes undermined the hegemony of money-taking members of the Scots clergy, such as Thomas Chalmers, whom he figured as slaveholders' stooges. We have numerous examples of his reception in Scotland which testify to the carnivalesque character of this rhetorical perfomance. One woman commented that:

When the collar and whip were produced, it was remarked that the application of them to you [Chalmers] and your daughter would make you change your views on slavery. This caused laughter ... Oh it is too serious a thing to make a matter of [but] Fred Douglass did make me laught when he preached [to] the boys in Dundee to send back the money. (*ibid.*)

Alasdair Pettinger, despite figuring the position of the Free Church as more complex than such ridiculing might deserve, refers to Douglass's imaginative storytelling rhetoric to show how he spanned the Atlantic to link the Free Church to his own enslavement as its money is collected at the expense of blacks like him (Pettinger, 1999). As we can see from these examples, the consummate rhetorician knew the value of entertainment to get his message across.

During his visit to Britain, he was prepared to speak at any forum against the scourge of slavery. When in 1846 he spoke at a meeting of the British and Foreign Anti-Slavery Society in London, he incurred the wrath of the Garrisonians, but stood his ground. In a letter to Maria Weston Chapman he declared, 'I will speak in any meeting when freedom of speech is allowed and where I may do anything towards exposing the bloody system of slavery' (Taylor, 1974: 277). Douglass was not prepared to act as second fiddle in an ensemble orchestrated by others, and his visit to Britain convinced him of the limitations of the absolutist Garrisonian mindset which precluded alliances with certain other abolitionist groups. As a result, Douglass developed his own strategies and alliances, much to the chagrin of the Garrisonians. Looking back on this period, Douglass felt the visit was key to his development of an independent voice, distancing him from his erstwhile allies and allowing him to see the limitations of their vision. As David Turley puts it, 'while in Britain, he had changed and grown through being able to live his life without fear of threat to his freedom' (Turley, 1999: 59). The language he later employed to describe his previous subjugation to the hegemony of the Garrisonians is telling: 'I am not sure that I was not under the influence of something like a slavish adoration of my Boston friends ... ' (Douglass, 1969: 394). This 'slavish adoration' is something that the mature Douglass has moved beyond, a process that he fervently believed was in part due to the free air of Europe.

This supposed absence of prejudice in Europe and its liberating effect on African-American travellers is a theme echoed by visiters to Europe, from early travellers like Phillis Wheatley to Douglass's contemporaries Harriet Jacobs and William Wells Brown, through James Weldon Johnson at the beginning of the twentieth century to Paul Robeson in the inter- and immediate post-war years. One of the only dissenters was Booker T. Washington, who typically uses his 1899 trip to eulogize the improvement in race relations in America, contrasting the difficulties Douglass encountered with American passengers on the *Cambria* (detailed in Pettinger, 1999) with his own invitation shipboard to address a meeting. Washington's wilful misreading of the incident as proof of improved race relations, when it merely proves the need for radical action to gain your speaking rights, reveals how Douglass's liberating sojourn is open to multiple interpretations. As James Olney notes: 'Washington often adopts the strategy of appropriating Douglass's life to his own and of incorporating and revising Douglass's text in the text of his own life' (Olney, 1989: 17).

Paul Robeson's frequent journeys to Europe were often pleasant escapes from the realities of racism at home. Robeson himself made the link between his visits and those of Douglass a century earlier. After invoking one of Douglass's speeches on the historic links between Manchester and the

Southern states of America he continued, 'my own heart echoes these words of Frederick Douglass' (Robeson, 1978: 410). As Paul Gilroy contends in *The Black Atlantic*, Douglass's 'writings continue to be a rich resource in the cultural and political analysis of the black Atlantic' (Gilroy, 1993a: 58). Such echoing across the centuries testifies to an immensely self-aware transatlantic radical black political tradition which transcends a narrow nationalism that both figures were concerned to eschew. Their lives spent criss-crossing the Atlantic both physically and through their developing ideas are paradigmatic for Gilroy's key idea that 'different nationalist paradigms for discussing cultural history fail when confronted by the intercultural and transnational formation that I call the black Atlantic' (*ibid.*: ix).

As citizens of the world, Douglass and Robeson made liberational fissures for themselves during their European sojourns and developed novel ideas in their correspondence and their political writings. Thus, after visiting Dachau concentration camp in 1945, Robeson was moved to link the Holocaust to the abuses of slavery and its aftermath, racism:

> There I saw the death chambers and the ashes of some of the victims. I remember the ashes of my people, not only in Africa, but in the states of Mississippi, in Alabama and Georgia, in the whole slave South. (Robeson, 1978: 466)

This comparison of Nazi genocide to chattel slavery is calculated to offend complacent American conceptions of the European nature of race hate and link its impetus directly to ideas of racial superiority that underpinned slavery. Robeson's internationalist vision offends against an American liberal elite that promotes American democracy as unproblematic in the post-war imperium. He went further, linking American praxis with that of the Nazis in a later speech: 'It is important for the people of England to know that those basic rights which are part of English civilization are under as sharp a fire today in America as they would have been in Nazi Germany' (*ibid.*: 192). Here, Robeson promotes Britain uncompromisingly as the home of freedom despite its role as a colonial power, exhibiting a strategic Anglophilia in order to attack American racism – a pattern we will see repeated elsewhere in Robeson's political expression. Overall, Douglass and Robeson are linked by a similar transatlantic trajectory. Their developing ideologies and relationships with radicals across the Atlantic meant they were not hidebound to their roots but centrally concerned with what Gilroy would term a 'routedness' that extended way beyond limited and limiting American racial realities. The most important route for them both was across the Atlantic to Britain, as they became pivotal figures in a black Atlantic radical tradition. Thus, Professor George Shepperson, in introducing Robeson at an Edinburgh concert of 1949, also made the specific comparison between his visit and that of Douglass in the previous century (Shepperson, 1998: 233–8). Both men felt at home in Scotland despite their contradictory genealogies and were apt to quote from the national poet Burns whenever the occasion demanded. Like Douglass, who would speechify about how his very name is shot through with Scottish resonance through its summoning of the Black Douglass in Sir Walter Scott's *Lady of the Lake*, so Robeson would frequently refer to the Scottish significance of his name, which unlike Douglass was not chosen but foisted upon his family because of their slave upbringing on the Roberson plantation in North Carolina. The transatlantic resonances were hardly innocent where Robeson was concerned, his very name testifying to how Scots, eager to portray themselves as victims of English imperialism, were all too often implicated in nefarious slaveholding practices themselves. Despite this knowledge, Robeson often stressed the warm welcome he always received in Britain. He had always been made especially welcome in that other Celtic nation, Wales: 'I feel as much at home in the Welsh valleys as in my own Negro section in any city in the United States' (*ibid.*: 453).

Robeson also received a warm welcome in England. As Amiri Baraka contends, 'England for Robeson, was always a more productive venue than the US' (Baraka, n.d.: 15). When invited to play Othello in Britain in 1959, he summed up the hospitality he and his family had enjoyed over nearly forty years in glowing terms: 'I have never met with more warmth than here in Britain. I felt it at Stratford when young people who had never seen me before came to the theatre. I felt it out on the streets, in the trains' (Robeson, 1978: 461). Especially important to Robeson had been the British support he had received when his right to travel was withheld for much of the 1950s by the American authorities. Large petitions were organized throughout the country urging the American government to restore his right to travel, and when these were denied, ingenious methods were devised to circumvent the ban. Thus, on 11 March 1956, Robeson's sonorous tones were broadcast at a meeting in Manchester, and in May a live transatlantic broadcast in front of a sell-out audience meant that Robeson felt 'as though I was on the stage in London myself' (*ibid.*: 442). The use of technology meant that Robeson was able to transcend restrictions imposed by governmental attempts at the suppression of his human rights, so that across the airwaves of the Atlantic he was able to forge liberational alliances with radicals in a transatlantic community of anti-imperialists. Just as the ship had functioned as a liberational mode for Douglass and his contemporaries, so new technologies now helped to span the ocean and undermine the hegemony of imperial conservative ideologies.

Both men made their mark in domestic British politics as well as internationally. While in 1845 Douglass had thrown himself into the domestic debate about the Free Church's morality, Robeson attended May Day galas for the miners, where he sang and spoke. In 1960 in Holyrood Park, Edinburgh, Robeson addressed over 20,000, and 'his fine voice booming across the park stilled [the] crowd' (Shepperson, 1998: 238), while visits to Wales established other links to a radical working-class politics: 'though I was famous and wealthy, the fact was that I came from a working-class people like themselves and therefore they said, my place was with them in the ranks of labour' (Robeson, 1978: 14). Shepperson's remarks on the two African-American trojans noted how their leadership roles in the African-American community were enhanced by their European sojourn. Robeson developed an internationalist vision in London, as he acknowledged later: 'I discovered

Africa in London' (Eschen, 1996: 17). As Penny Von Eschen has commented, 'The world of the black left in Britain shaped the development of African American politics by attracting and influencing black American intellectuals like Paul Robeson and Ralph Bunche' (*ibid.*: 16). While different circumstances a century before meant that the nascent African diasporan community which African-Americans would find so energizing in London in the 1930s and 1940s did not exist, the radical abolitionist community performed a similar function in galvinizing Douglass the internationalist. Robeson also admitted the formative nature of British politics to his development as a radical intellectual, admitting to *Reynolds News* in February 1949 that 'I learned my militancy and my politics from your labour movement here in Britain' (Robeson, 1978: 191). There is a remarkable similarity, too, in both men's perceptions of a welcoming, less racist Europe. In 1935 in Russia, Robeson writes:

> I was rested and buoyed up by the lovely, honest, wondering looks which did not see a Negro. When these people looked at me, they were just happy and interested. There were no double looks, no venom, no superiority. (*ibid.*: 101)

In 1846 in a similar vein, Douglass had written to Garrison:

> the entire absence of anything that looked like racial prejudice against me on account of the color of my skin – contrasted so strongly with my long and bitter experience in the United States that I look with wonder and amazement at the transition ... The truth is, the people here know nothing of the republican negro hate prevalent in our glorious land. They measure and esteem men according to their moral and intellectual worth, and not according to the color of their skin. (Douglass, 1969: 370)

Such veneration of Britain and its freedom-loving propensities is a constant theme of African diasporan discourse and can be traced back to the eighteenth century and such figures as Phyllis Wheatley, whose trip across the Atlantic in 1773 begets a miracle of racial toleration: 'The friends I found here among the nobility and gentry, their benevolent conduct towards me, the unexpected and unmerited civility and complaisance with which I was treated by all, fills me with astonishment. I can scarcely realise it' (quoted in Ferguson, 1992: 126).

We only need compare Wheatley's paean to the treatment accorded Robert Wedderburn shortly afterwards to show that such enlightened reactions were probably more to do with her rich patrons than a general British racial toleration. Moreover, there is some evidence in the testimony of less well-known nineteenth-century black travellers, such as James Watkins, that racism was a harsh reality for many blacks in Britain. Watkins's narrative reveals how he encountered a deep-seated racism in Britain when he first arrived in 1851:

> I could not obtain employment, and not only was I refused

work, but was treated by some people from whom I asked it, with contumely and contempt. I applied to some large Liverpool merchants who, after asking me a great many questions, declared that they would not think of employing 'a nigger who would steal.' Upon expressing my entire innocence of ever acting dishonestly towards my master, I was informed that having escaped from slavery was looked upon as a heinous offence by these gentlemen, who considered that by obtaining my freedom I had robbed my master of the amount at which I was valued in the slave market. (Watkins, 1860: 42–3)

Watkins's treatment reveals a racism that many more privileged black visitors were blind to. The contrastive narrative of Wheatley's sojourn is usually held up as typical of the experience of African-American visitors to Britain in the eighteenth century, and its redolence for visitors in the nine-teenth century was great enough for it to feature in the anonymous novel, *Uncle Tom in England* (1852). Tom is told:

Phillis Wheatley was a poor Negress ... she went to England, a beautiful country, where there are people of great minds and noble hearts, and where men and women are not bought and sold, and there she was treated as a child of God without reference to the color of her skin. (quoted in Fisch, 2000: 50)

Wheatley's example is held up to Tom to encourage him to visit an enlightened Britain and to get away from an America whose vaunted freedoms are debased by the institution of slavery. This novel caters to a British sense of superiority which pervades abolitionist discourse in the mid-nineteenth century, as Audrey Fisch's persuasive *American Slaves in Victorian England* illustrates. It is not just the white abolitionists who create such a discourse, for Wheatley set a trend in what I will coin 'strategic Anglophilia' that later African-Americans travellers followed. For instance, when Harriet Jacobs writes of her time in Britain in 1845 (as maid to a white girl), it is in similarly glowing terms, as she portrays a colour-blind and welcoming Britain. Her description shows how her full emancipation requires a transatlantic journey rather than just a journey Northward:

For the first time in my life I was in a place where I was treated according to my deportment, without reference to my complexion. I felt as if a great millstone had been lifted from my breast. Ensconced in a pleasant room, with my dear little charge, I laid my head on my pillow, for the first time, with the delightful consciousness of pure, unadulterated freedom. (Jacobs, 1987: 183)

A few years later, the abolitionist speakers Ellen Craft and Sarah Parker Remond described Britain as a utopian space for black women. In 1853, Craft declared she would 'much rather starve in England, a free woman, than be a slave for the best man that ever breathed upon the continent of America' (quoted in Midgely, 1992: 142), while Remond, during her speaking tour of 1860, declared how

> I have been received here as a sister by white women for the first time in my life ... I have felt most deeply that since I have been in Warrington and in England that I have received a sympathy I was never offered before. (quoted in *ibid*.: 144)

Despite varying degrees of blindness to the reality of Europe's racial iniquities, through their travelling Wheatley, Jacobs, Craft, Remond, Douglass's and Robeson helped to internationalize the African-American struggle for full human rights, showing how it had implications far beyond the community itself in a relationship with other continents forged within what Paul Gilroy has termed a black Atlantic discourse. The very public and political nature of Douglass's and Robeson's sojourns meant they had the most far-reaching effects. The resonances of Douglass's visit, like Robeson's a century later, were central in a transatlantic trade in ideas which helped to internationalize the struggle, and both men were keenly aware of this. Douglass probably expressed it most succinctly, noting that 'the denunciations against slavery, uttered in London this week may be heard in a fortnight in the streets of Boston' (Douglass, 1969: 417).

However, Douglass's presence in Britain exposed a darker reality beneath the seemingly benign face of white abolitionists, whose forced encounter with an actual black man showed up as many deficiencies as positive qualities. John Estlin illustrates the former in an 1847 letter to Samuel May, in which he says of Douglass:

> You can hardly imagine how he is noticed, – petted I may say by ladies. Some of them really a little exceed the bounds of propriety, or delicacy, as far as appearances are concerned; yet F. D.'s conduct is most guardedly correct, judicious and decorous ... My fear is that after associating so much with white women of education & refined taste & manners, he will feel a craving void when he returns to his own family. (quoted in Taylor, 1974: 305)

Claire Midgely comments astutely on Estlin's coded racism here, ascribing it to a deep-rooted fear of change. Estlin feared the disruption the new relations across race and gender would have on established social relationships. Midgely describes how Estlin 'clearly saw bonds between black men and white women formed through the anti-slavery movement as threatening to disrupt proper relations of gender, race and class' (Midgely, 1992: 141). Such sentiments were not confined to England. In Ireland, Richard Webb used very similar language to report to Maria Chapman his disquiet at Douglass's reception by women in the abolitionist movement: 'From what I hear of her, I wonder how he will bear the sight of his wife – after all the petting he gets from beautiful, elegant and accomplished women in a country where prejudice against color is laughed at' (Blackett, 1983: 112).

Estlin's depiction of an African-American culture devoid of the nourishments of white civilization and Webb's general uneasiness with mixed-race relationships, particularly across the sexual divide, exemplify a racist ideology which unfortunately transcended, and continues to transcend, differences between America and Europe, undermining Douglass's fond hope of a Britain 'where no delicate nose grows deformed in my presence' (Douglass, 1969: 371). The delicate noses were just more discreet. Douglass seemed keen to give the British and Irish the benefit of the doubt when it came to their racialized descriptions of him. He accomplished this by using his trip to berate those at home, comparing them unfavourably with the enlightened Europeans, rather than muddy the waters with accusations which might give succour to his enemies in the slave polity. There are parallels with Robeson's twentieth-century visits, in which he uses similar tactics – what we might call varieties of strategic Anglophilia. For instance, in 1929 when Robeson was barred from the prestigious Savoy Grill in London, he chose not to make a fuss by publicizing the issue, and when the matter became public he was swift to blame the growing prevalence of an 'American Negrophobia' in London for the incident rather than foregrounding native British prejudice (Duberman, 1989: 123–4). This tone of surprise at any racialized incident in a hallowed Britain is reflected in remarks he made to *The New York Times* in May 1930 about the British stage:

> I was a little disturbed when we started rehearsals and rumours
> of an objection to a colored actor playing with white girls came
> to my notice. I felt that in London trouble couldn't possibly arise
> on racial grounds. People here are too broadminded for that
> (Robeson, 1978: 523).

Like Douglass before him, Robeson's espousal of a utopian racial environment in Britain came up against realities which made his stated position anomalous, to say the least. However, Robeson, again like Douglass before him, was more intent on drawing attention to the more deeply invidious and personally debilitating racial realities at home, and felt that the best way to embarrass the American government was to provide them with no ideological ammunition about the situation in Britain. We can detect a similar reluctance to criticize and an inclination to romanticize in turn-of-the-century visits by black Americans to the Caribbean. In his seminal account *Holding Aloft the Banner of Ethiopia*, Winston James describes how Langston Hughes, W. E. B. Du Bois and Paul Robeson were thrilled at the 'absence' of racism there. However, their analysis is comparative and again relates more to racial realities at home in America than to Caribbean realities. As James comments:

> Their response to the racial situation in the Caribbean is of more
> help in understanding the America they left behind than in

understanding the Caribbean societies that they testify about. And so Du Bois's rhapsody about his visit to Jamaica in 1915 tells one more about race in America and more about Du Bois than it does about Jamaica itself, the ostensible object of his report. (James, 1998: 98)

A similar comment could be made in relation to Douglass's and Robeson's reactions to Britain. As I have related, there were anomalous reactions to Douglass's visit: the Dublin Quaker, Webb, used the term 'petting' with reference to Douglass in two other correspondences with American abolitionists, a word that hints at the indulgence given to a domestic animals and is disturbingly similar to the language used by slaveholders about their favourite slaves. He formed this view early, for in November 1845, a mere two months after meeting Douglass, he wrote to Maria Weston Chapman: 'He is very proud and can't bear anything half so sweetly as praise and petting. I dont mean to give him any more advice – but I think he is foolish to resent it' (Taylor, 1974: 243). The theme was continued in later correspondence; when in February 1846 he wrote:

> I have met with some insolence with him such as I was not prepared to meet with from any abolitionist. I think he had no provocation to it except in the headiness induced by the flattery and petting he met with in his travels in Ireland, and which he will not be likely to meet with to anything like the same effect in England and Scotland. (*ibid.*: 254)

Hersh locates the origin of such patronizing views in the Puritan upbringing of the Garrisonians, 'which helped make them the conscience of the nation, but it also inclined them to conservative economic views and limited their social vision' (Hersh, 1978: 129). When Douglass was a central figure for the Garrisonians, the discourse surrounding his relations with white women was confined to private correspondence; however, after his acrimonious break with the movement, they used his relationship with white women such as Julia Griffiths to pillory him, betraying what Maria Diedrich has called 'a deep-seated racism' displayed through their 'inability to perceive an African-American as a free agent, a definer of his life' (Diedrich, 1999: 183). The seeds of this patronizing racism were sown during his visit to Britain, as were a number of increasingly close relations with a range of white European women.

As Diedrich has discussed in her seminal *Love across Color Lines* (1999), Douglass did enjoy close physical relations with a white European woman, Ottilie Assing, in a mutually satisfying intellectual and emotional relationship that carried on over two decades. Robeson, too, had relations with white European women, most famously with his co-star from his stellar 1930 London performance of *Othello*, Peggy Ashcroft. His wife Essie regarded the relationship as demeaning to Robeson, describing in her diary how the incident made her 'feel now he is just one more Negro musician pursuing white meat' (quoted in Duberman, 1989: 142). Despite such justified criticism,

Robeson's infidelity has wider ramifications in a transatlantic context. Both he and Douglass were able more easily to breach the norms of middle-class American morality and to indulge in mixed-race relations that countered rigid ideas of racial separation because of their travels beyond the boundaries of the United States.

The patronizing discourse of petting was not confined to the Garrisonians during Douglass's visit to Britain; opponents also saw him as the pet not merely of the women in the Garrisonian wing of the movement but a lapdog of that whole tendency. According to this view, best espoused by S. H. Cox, Douglass was 'petted and flattered and used and paid by certain abolitionists of the ne plus ultra strain' (Blackett, 1983: 105). One has to ask if a white orator would be so accused? Of course, the question is academic.

Criticism of the naiveté of British responses to visits from black Americans reached their apogee at the end of Douglass's trip. Its stellar success almost certainly contributed to the virulence of the parody of the *New York Express* article, 'English Negrophilism'. After worrying about the depopulation of blacks to Britain in the wake of their new-found popularity on the island, the article describes the Anglophilia of the black abolitionists, who in their speeches exult in the 'British love of liberty'. Such an Anglophiliac black is feted by the gulled British public, so that

> All his movements are chronicled, all his sayings reported, his
> profile is done in mezzotint and circulated, the old ladies invite
> him to their tea drinkings and the young ones exclaim 'what a
> dear!' Such was the excitement, (not a whit exaggerated,)
> created by the arrival of Fred [sic] Douglass in the British
> metropolis, and such ... is likely to continue (till the fashion
> fades out) to be the case, at every new importation of blacks
> from this to the mother-country. (quoted in Fisch, 2000: 71)

The writer interprets Douglass's Anglophilia as flattering to a British public who are deflected from having to examine their own racism or the inequality in their own society by the concentration on American faults. Such an attack is obviously exaggerated, but British abolitionists' own correspondence, as detailed above, points to a kernel of truth in the parody. Abolitionist concern for the 'dear blacks' could turn into a sentimentalized Negrophilia which concentrated more on the black as a strange, childlike, alien other to be unquestioningly lionized than on his/her message of the need for radical change. Audrey Fisch describes how black abolitionist discourse provided the English in mid-century with a convenient anti-Americanism that in its turn served to aggrandize Victorian England: 'The Victorian reader's or spectator's voyeuristic interest in American slavery could, for example, be recuperated: re-defined as the philanthropic and noble interest of a superior nation called to witness the degradation of American society' (*ibid.*: 8).

Among other black abolitionists, Douglass, with his anti-American rhetoric and sustained Anglophilia, strategically contributed to this savage/civilized binary. Despite such apparent confluence between him and the British abolitionists, there were serious fissures which serve to undermine a simplistic reading of this relationship. The language of 'petting' is, of course, just one instance where a patronizing element in the relations between black and white abolitionists is exposed. Such language is prevalent in other important abolitionist–ex-slave relationships on both sides of the Atlantic. Most interestingly, it occurs in the correspondence between and surrounding the relationship between Harriet Beecher Stowe and Harriet Jacobs. Jacobs wanted Stowe to take her daughter Louisa with her to Britain to improve her prospects. Stowe thought such a visit would spoil Louisa and

> was afraid that if her [Louisa's] situation as a slave would be known it would subject her to much petting and patronizing which would be more pleasing to a young girl than useful, and the English was very apt to do it and she was very much opposed to it with this class of people. (Jacobs, 1987: 235)

It is interesting to note that Stowe particularly berates the English for their petting, whereas Webb had identified the Irish as the major culprits in this respect because of their unsophistication, and hoped for better in England and Scotland. I would contend that the problem is not located with the African Americans and their apparent propensity to have their heads turned by too much attention but in the hearts and minds of the abolitionists, who are unable to fight free of a patronizing idea of the limited role of African Americans in their own struggle. It seems that Stowe's aversion to the petting of blacks extended to the mother too, as Jacobs's bitter remark in a letter written to Amy Post in spring 1853 makes clear: 'think dear Amy that a visit to Stafford House would spoil me as Mrs Stowe thinks petting is more than my race can bear well. What a pity we poor blacks can't have the firmness and stability of character that you white people have' (*ibid.*: xix). As Jean Fagan Yellin comments, 'Jacobs distrusted Stowe not because of Stowe's attitudes toward slavery but because of her ideas about race' (*ibid.*: xviii).

Like Douglass before her, Jacobs chafed against the patronizing attitudes of some white abolitionists who encoded their deep distrust of blacks rising above their station and moving to centre-stage through a discourse of indulgence with the fear of the deadly influence of 'petting' at its centre. Moira Ferguson indicts this patronizing attitude which permeated the reform movements of the mid-nineteenth century, describing how 'anti-slavery colonial discourse, in other words, played a significant role in generating and consolidating nineteenth-century British imperialist and "domestic-racist" ideology' (Ferguson 1992: 6).

The whole discourse around 'petting' is illustrative of such a 'colonial discourse'. Intriguingly, Anne Goodwyn Jones offers a possible explanation for Jacobs's and Douglass's disavowal of the patronizing attitudes of some abolitionists – namely, that they actually felt superior to them: 'Because of their class identification, both Douglass and Jacobs may have grown up feeling themselves to be more like than unlike their white privileged families' (Jones, 1999: 98). Webb's comments on Douglass, in particular, hint at a haughtiness in Douglass's demeanour which comes from an assumed superiority more in keeping (in Jones's distinctions) with a Southern class identification (concerning such learnt traits as 'deportment') than with cerebral assumptions of equality.

These descriptions of the 'petting' of blacks became a staple of imperial discourse in the Victorian period, so that when in 1895 King Khama and the other African chiefs came to Britain to lobby for help in fending off the designs of Cecil Rhodes on their territories, their progress through London's radical and missionary circles is described in patronizing terms. In the *South Africa* magazine a final social event and political meeting arranged by the London Missionary Society is the occasion for a thinly veiled racist piece:

> it was amusing, but not a little nauseating, to witness the fuss that everyone made of them. Each was shaken by the hand with something bordering on ecstatic fervour. Ladies of apparently high degree wasted their sweetness on these men.
> Why? In the name of common sense, why? What have they done that they should be petted and caressed in a manner that would strike many a colonist I wot of dumb with astonishment and indignation. (Quoted in Parsons, 1998: 232)

Like Douglass, the chiefs were accused of letting such 'petting' go to their heads, and on their return to Africa they were indicted for their uppity attitude. Again, it is interesting that the expression ('lionising') used to characterize this 'arrogance' is similar to the one used to describe the African-American traveller fifty years before. In 1896, the *Bulawayo Chronicle* reported on King Khama's change since his sojourn:

> As was sometimes feared ... Khama's temper and manner do not seem to have been improved by his lionising in England ... There are very few men able to keep their heads much through a London season when they have been the centre of attention, and it would have been more than wonderful if Khama had returned as sensible and plain a man as when he went away. (Quoted in Palmer, 1997: 247)

While the journey to Britain had undoubtedly changed Khama, it had not made him arrrogant as such testimonies implied. Like Douglass before him and Robeson after him, he was characterized as mere putty in the hands of sophisticated and manipulative white folk; the reality, as shown by his successful negotiations for government protection from the imperialist Rhodes, is not so clearcut.

The petting of Africans and African Americans and its dangers to their integrity is a hyperbole which enables the stereotype of childlike blacks to be propagated even when sophisticated political figures are being discussed, a tendency that is best illustrated by returning to the rhetoric of Frederick Douglass and its multi-layered critique of American mores whose sophistication belies such narrow racism. Douglass had described the difference between his reception in Britain and that in America in his farewell speech at the London Tavern on 30 March 1847:

'Why, sir, the Americans do not know that I am a man. They talk of me as a box of goods; they speak of me in connexion with sheep, horses and cattle. But here, how different! Why, sir, the very dogs of old England know that I am a man!' (Blessinghame, 1979: 50)

As usual, Douglass is not content with this simple and effective oratorical flourish but elaborates on the image to make a joke out of the ridiculous racism of his fellow countrymen. He continues:

I was in Beckenham for a few days and while at a meeting there a dog actually came up to the platform, put his paws on the front of it, and gave me a smile of recognition as a man. The Americans would do well to learn wisdom on this matter from the very dogs of old England. (*ibid.*)

To an extent, such an exaggeration turns on its head the whole discourse of petting, interpreting the fawning British response as a mere politeness entirely absent in the harsher American environment. The world is truly turned upside down by Douglass's trip across the Atlantic as it was to be later for William Wells Brown, who used remarkably similar language to express his own Anglophilia:

No person of my complexion can visit this country without being struck with the marked difference between the English and the Americans. The prejudice which I have experienced on all and every occasion in the United States, and to some extent on board the *Canada* vanished as soon as I set foot on the soil of Britain ... In America I had been bought and sold as a slave in the Southern States. In the so-called Free States, I had been treated as one born to occupy an inferior position – in steamers, compelled to take my fare on deck; in hotels, to take my meals in the kitchen; in coaches, to ride on the outside; in railways to ride in the 'negro-car;' and in churches, to sit in the 'negro-pew.' But no sooner was I on British soil, then I was recognized as a man, and an equal. The very dogs in the streets appeared conscious of my manhood. Such is the difference, and such is the change that is brought about by a trip of nine days in an Atlantic steamer. (Brown, 1991: 98)

There is a profound irony in Brown and Douglass's use of dog imagery to describe the English reaction to their African-American presences in the nineteenth century. Partly, of course, in relation to the discourse of petting I have outlined above, which would seem to figure black abolitionist travellers as akin to these selfsame domestic animals being patronized and fawned over by transatlantic reformers, but even more pointed is the discourse's historical amnesia of a British domestic slavery which in the eighteenth century had turned men into canines by providing domestic slaves with dog collars. Granville Sharp discussed one case where a fugitive fourteen-year-old black boy is described as wearing 'a Brass Collar round his Neck with a Direction upon it to a House in Charlotte Street, Bloomsbury Square' (quoted in Gerzina, 1995: 115). As Sharp himself comments, 'thus the *Black Indian Pompey* was publickly treated with as little ceremony as *a Black Dog* of the *same Name would be*' (*ibid.*). A cynical commentary might agree with Douglass about how things have changed, but instead of positing a transatlantic difference it would describe a chronological change. Black men in Britain have moved from being treated like dogs to being fawned on by them. Douglass and Brown are careful not to mention such complicating narratives, at least not publicly, as they do not want to alienate a British audience proud of their superiority to a backward America in matters of race relations.

Douglass's sojourn has changed his status from beast of burden to man of words, or, as he put it himself later in the same speech, 'I came here a thing – I go back a human being' (Blessinghame, 1979: 50). However, the presence of a discourse of indulgence, a prevalent worry about how too much petting might be his undoing, unfortunately reveals how Douglass cannot escape the racial dynamics that infect and affect many relationships in the transatlantic reform movement. The 'very dogs of old England' might know that he is a man, but his abolitionist allies, in worrying about his limited ability to deal with a flattery which was his due, tend to replicate a patronizing attitude more suited to a commentary on the bringing up of children or domestic animals than to relations with one of the greatest minds of the mid-century. Frankly, they do not treat him as an equal but as an adolescent in danger of corruption by forces beyond his understanding that are often unleashed by too close relations with white women. Though we should beware of letting a few inopportune phrases by the likes of Estlin, Webb and Stowe undermine our assessment of their enormous contributions to the cause of reform, their use of a discourse of 'petting' reveals an anxiety at the heart of their relationship with African Americans. Black abolitionists had already commented in biblical terms on the prevalence of such attitudes at the heart of the reform movement. Samuel E. Cornish (1838) perhaps put it most eloquently: 'here [in the north] our friends have to grapple with slavery, not at arm's length but with a back-hold, where the slimy servant is among them, coiled up in their own hearts and houses'. Such attitudes were also present in the reform movement in Britain.

Douglass's visit to Britain, thus, should be seen as a liberating sojourn for him and for those women abolitionists with whom he communicated especially well (perhaps because of their equally degraded status). As William McFeely contends: 'Something other than his sexual attractiveness drew these women to Douglass; in some ways his quest for liberation urged them on in their repressed quest for their own' (McFeely, 1991: 142). Estlin's daughter Mary was one of many to fall under Douglass's spell, moving from primary identification with a generalized commitment to abolitionism and reform to an overarching concern with 'the dear blacks', as Mary Howitt was to call them. However, we should beware following Douglass in his Anglophilia, his repeated delight in finding 'Monarchical Freedom' in contrast to 'Republican Slavery'. The British on the whole received him very well, but some were just as capable as his American allies of patronizing him and attempting to limit his freedom of association. As Robeson was to find a century later, though, little good would come from publicizing British faults when his agenda meant that hearts needed changing most in the belly of the beast that is American racism. Thus, both men developed a strategic Anglophilia as a very successful tactic for undermining their home country. The 'very dogs of old England' knew very well that Robeson and Douglass were both men: in fact, they admired them as 'lions' of men. These famous African Americans' deep affection for Britain and especially the British on the Celtic fringes was rewarded by a heroic status which they repaid through romanticized depictions of life in the old country. These might have involved a certain false consciousness and an occasional blindness to British faults; however, crucially, they enabled both Douglass and Robeson to create transatlantic counter-cultures of resistance that helped to radicalize political opinion on both sides of the ocean.

=== 8 ===

BLACK BODIES TRANSPORTED ACROSS THE OCEAN IN CHAINS

THE BLACK ATLANTIC IN CINEMA FROM *KING KONG* TO *AMISTAD*

> Western culture can conceive of itself critically only with
> reference to fictions of the primitive. (James Clifford, 1988: 272)

> All the descendants of a Europe whose political and economic
> dominance was fuelled by the slave trade are bearers of
> unmourned trauma. (Griselda Pollock, 1999: 170)

Popular culture's representation of black Atlantic cultures has often been troubled. Paul Robeson's transatlantic radicalism, as detailed in the previous chapter, was compromised by a film industry that refused to see past their stereotypical views of blacks, so that even a luminary like Robeson was unable to gain control of the way he was portrayed in films like *Sanders of the River* (1935). Assuming the film would deal with Africans as fully-fledged human beings, he was 'alight with enthusiasm' about the project in 1934, describing how the film would 'do a lot towards the better understanding of Negro culture and customs' (Duberman, 1989: 178). However, the final cut revealed an apologia for colonialism that depicted white men saving Africa from savagery. Robert Stebbins's contemporary review describes Robeson's failure accurately: 'Here we have the pathetic spectacle of one of the most gifted and distinguished members of the race placed in a position where in actuality he is forced into a caricature of his people' (quoted in *ibid.*: 181).

Robeson's failure to break free from the industry's stereotypical portrayal of the African is just one more example in a litany that drew much of its visual iconography from D. W. Griffith's work. His savage stereotyping of African Americans in the Civil War and Reconstruction South in *The Birth of a Nation* (1915) provided a template for many of the stock 'Negro' characters which inhabited the films of the first half of the twentieth century. But it was not only in films depicting African American lives that race was central: as James Snead has brilliantly argued in *White Screens, Black Images* (1994), the supremely populist monster film *King Kong* (1933) was essentially acquiescent in the construction and maintenance of a racial ideology which spoke to the realities not only of domestic American politics but also to America's global role in racial exploitation and imperialism. The film provides a symbolic referent to the past history of slavery and colonialism and the way they have combined to construct an international transatlantic racialized polity with an imperial America at its centre. The touchstones are not all historical: by the early 1930s, when the film was made, American marines had been involved in an imperial adventure in the black republic of Haiti for nearly twenty years (since 1913), an island across the sea with a majority black population, a situation the film surely refers to obliquely.

This fear of an overwhelming black (or at least on a global scale, non-white) mass that must be tamed is the prerequisite to *King Kong*'s genesis. Carl Denham's expedition to Skull Island is an exemplary plundering, imperial adventure, as can be elucidated from his justifications for their efforts: 'You always bring back a picture, something that nobody's ever seen or heard of.' This searching for something new with an enhanced pecuniary value, an absolute other, an object that will prove you have visited alien parts, is, as Snead describes, like 'any one of a number of forays by Europeans to non-European nations in search of animals, minerals, artifacts, photographs and even human beings' (Snead, 1994: 17). Snead's description of how the Americans carry guns on the way out to bring back a tamed cargo 'is the very definition of "trade" and no less of the slave trade' (*ibid.*); this is emphasized by 'the establishing shots of New York harbour' (*ibid.*) that speak to the central role of American capitalism in the ventures that made the slave trade so financially successful and were to extend colonialism in the twentieth century. The capture of Kong displays the dominance of Western technology, as gas bombs are used to tame him. The prominence of such technology in the final destruction of native resistance to imperialism highlights the film as exemplary in its depiction of colonial realities in the late nineteenth and early twentieth centuries.

In his book *Exterminate All the Brutes*, Sven Lindqvist details the technological advances that accompanied the advance of the colonial powers, which replaced the musket with the more reliable rifle and reached their apotheosis in the patenting in 1897 of the dumdum bullet, which exploded on impact and was only licensed for use in colonial wars. He describes the success of such weaponry at Omdurman in 1898, where 'the whole new European arsenal was tested – gunboats, automatic weapons, repeater rifles, and dum dum bullets'; such an arsenal was essential 'against a numerically superior and very determined enemy' (Lindqvist, 1993: 53). The gargantuan King Kong symbolically represents such a monstrous rampaging other, whose physical strength can only be harnessed by the utilization of Western knowhow and weapons technology. The ideological justification for such genocidal impulses against non-white civilizations was supplied by ultra-rationalist thinkers like Herbert Spencer, who declared in 1850:

> The forces which are working out the great scheme of perfect happiness, taking no account of incidental suffering, exterminate such sections of mankind as stand in their way ... Be he human or be he brute – the hindrance must be got rid of. (quoted in *ibid.*: 8)

As Lindqvist has shown, such ideas of extermination were particularly prevalent in the later nineteenth century and contributed to such concepts as eugenics and to the spread of and justification for the most brutal of colonizing ventures and polities. King Kong's final destruction is the logical conclusion of such imperial discourse. However, there is much to learn before that final denouement. When Denham displays Kong in New York he is manacled on an auction block, an image of domestic impressment which positions the monster as a symbol of American slavery. However, Snead highlights how the middle passage – the seaborne transportation of Kong from his home – is omitted in the film. This, of course, mirrors its elision in the wider culture, where there is a wanton amnesia about the trade: 'The film leaves out, as it were, the entire slave trade, the voyage, and the 200 years of slavery in the New World. It goes straight from the African "discovery" to the American "insurrection"' (Snead, 1994: 22). While Snead is right that the film omits the 'middle passage' in order to rush to the excitement of Kong's escape, the economic logic of Kong's removal is addressed, and it is in this that the slave trade is allegorized fully. The deliberate amnesia of Americans about the shipping of Africans to America is accompanied by a hard-headed business knowledge about the value of that labour to the American polity. This is reflected in the film by the announcement that Kong's display has made $10,000 at the box office. This money is made at the expense of the transported 'other', just as surplus value was made on the transplanted Africans. So, the film addresses both American amnesia about the transportation of Africans and at the same time owns up to the knowledge of the worth of the other's presence. Ed Guerrero has described how 'cinematic expressions of slavery have become sedimented into a range of contemporary film narratives and genres' (Guerrero, 1993: 42) and *King Kong* exemplifies how the monster film also 'sediments' the slave experience. The image of the auction block conjured up in the theatre also highlights how the black body is at its most luminous when it is displayed. This provides additional comfort for the audience, particularly if they have accepted Kong as analogous to African peoples in America, for as Michael Rogin asserts, they entertain at their most non-threateningly when 'they [are] safely in their chains' (Rogin, 1998: 37). As Denham himself narrates, the primitive other has been tamed by the forces of civilization: 'a king and a god in the world he knew, but now he comes to civilization, merely a captive – a show to gratify your curiosities'.

The attraction/repulsion of Kong's displayed body is illustrated here. Black bodies had been on display earlier in the film when the 'natives' had shown off their all-singing, all-dancing selves to the visiting white folk. The awed response of 'Holy mackerel! What a show!' draws our attention to another theme the film mediates, minstrelsy. In these scenes it is highlighted by the white-painted faces of the African 'natives', whose greasepaint (albeit white rather than black) signals minstrel performance. For, it was not only whites who blacked up to perform, but blacks (especially in the history of the early cinema). In his admirably subtle analysis of minstrelsy in 'Change the Joke and Slip the Yoke' (1958), Ralph Ellison outlined its most salient characteristics:

in the entertainment industry … the Negro is reduced to a
negative sign that usually appears in a comedy of the grotesque
and the unacceptable. As Constance Rourke has made us aware,
the action of the early minstrel show … constituted a ritual of
exorcism … The mask was an inseparable part of the national
iconography … This mask, this wilful stylization and
modification of the natural face and hands, was imperative for
the evocation of that atmosphere in which the fascination of
blackness could be enjoyed, the comic catharsis achieved.
(Ellison, 1972: 48–9)

The savage rituals the natives perform in *King Kong* include the donning of
ape masks so that their humanity is hidden and in the racial economy of the
film they become inseparable from Kong as 'neither beast nor man'; or in
Ellison's terms 'grotesque' and 'unacceptable' – in a word, non-white and
effectively non-human. The 'ritual of exorcism' in the film is to distance the
white viewer from empathy with such non-white humans, which is achieved
through the shorthand of the minstrel encounter. As savage entertainers,
rather than autonomous members of a different and autochthonous culture,
their agency and power is crucially neutralized.

The minstrel encounter is at work too in the portrayal of Kong. He is not
merely a monster, but is shown to have human characteristics. However, they
are mediated through what I would term a minstrel symbolic. Thus, the
viewer's first 'human' encounter with the monster is after he defeats the
dinosaur which has threatened to claim the white woman, Ann Darrow. To
the accompaniment of drums, Kong beats his fists on his chest before breaking
into a delighted minstrel grin. This grin had become a staple of racial iconography in the wake of *The Jazz Singer* (1927), where Al Jolson's blackface grin
had been used to publicize the film, and its role here in *King Kong* is to
highlight Kong as an imaginative construction of white signification. Just as
minstrelsy allies Kong with the natives, so it does with manufactured black-
faces in the white imagination. As Eric Lott reminds us:

Black figures were there to be looked at, shaped to the demands
of desire: they were screens on which the audience fantasy could
rest, and while this purpose might have had lots of different
effects, its fundamental outcome was to secure the position of
white spectators as controlling figures. (Lott, 1993: 141)

King Kong's minstrel grin aligns him with such black figures. The film creates
a stereotyped discourse replete with the dangerous legacies of minstrelsy to
create an exoticized and eroticized encounter with blackness, which the fundamentally white audience are invited voyeuristically to be both repelled by
and enjoy. If, as Rogin says, 'blackface domesticated the primitive' (Rogin,
1998: 114), then this film could be interpreted as using a nuanced manifestation of blackface minstrelsy as an ideological tool to control a white fear of a
rampaging black other. By aligning Kong with a minstrelized blackness, the

film, even at this early narrative stage, reassures its audience that they are ultimately in control. This minstrel image was very familiar to Americans by the early 1930s, not least because of its widespread adoption and adaption within both black and white working-class culture since its development in the early nineteenth century, as studies by Lhamon, Lott and Rogin make plain.

Specifically, the imagined primitive was a stock character in African-American performance throughout the early twentieth century, so that Kong's minstrel characteristics should be seen as part of a modernist continuum rather than a unique cinematic treatment of blackness. For instance, floor shows at the Cotton Club for exclusively white audiences displayed an imagined Africa which can be seen as a precursor of *King Kong*'s excesses. Marshall Stearns describes one such event:

> a light-skinned and magnificently muscled negro burst through a papier mache jungle onto the dance floor, clad in an aviator's helmet goggles and shorts. He had obviously been 'forced down in darkest Africa' and in the center of the floor he came upon a 'white' goddess clad in long golden tresses and being worshipped by a circle of cringing 'blacks'. Producing a bull whip from heaven knows where, the aviator rescued the blonde and they did an erotic dance. In the background, Bubber Miley, Tricky Sam Nanton and other members of the Ellington band growled, wheezed and snorted obscenely. (Stearns, 1956: 184)

While there is clearly a great deal of irony in this African-American performance of primitivism, its narrative thrust of black men enthralled by white female beauty in a jungle landscape is translated almost verbatim into the film's unfolding racial mythopoeia. Just as the aviator is entranced by and rescues the blonde, so Kong is captivated by Darrow, and, after rescuing her from the dinosaur's predatory grip, he enacts a version of 'an erotic dance' on his own palm as he toys with his new plaything. The imagined jungle landscapes created in the Cotton Club and in the film provide spaces where taboos against interracial sex are broken down as the audiences 'slum' either in uptown Manhattan or, through the medium of cinema, in a jungle locale far from the restrictions of uptight American bourgeois mores. Ann Darrow's screams of fear might well mask her complicity in a virtual interracial fantasy, as described by Marina Warner, who imagines that 'Kong might be the monster of her dreams' (Warner, 1994: 62).

This fantasy world of transgressional interracial intimacies is played out against an actual American reality of intolerance towards mixed-race relationships, particularly in the Southern states. Jazz performers like Ellington's band and the Cotton Club dancers performed these acts of taboo to white audiences in the fantasy projection of a segregated nightclub; however, merely whistling at a white woman was still a lynching offence in the South in 1955, as Emmett Till's brutal murder shows. (Till, who had been visiting the South from Chicago, was brutally murdered by white racists for the 'crime' of whistling at a white woman.) As for Kong, his racial intimacy with Ann

Darrow and consequent infatuation with her leads directly to his death. The ideological thrust of the film is clear: the breaking of the taboo, the touching of the white woman, has dire consequences for the primitive other.

If the minstrel depiction of Kong delineates a partial humanity exemplified at its most compelling in his tenderness towards Ann Darrow, this is only ever one aspect of the dualistic delineation of Kong's surrogate blackness. His blackness is also defined through a savagery which is the flip side of this childlike simplicity, by acts which define savagery such as cannibalism. Not content with killing those who try to capture him on the island, he consumes many of the native warriors, while later in New York he engages in another rampaging cannibalistic orgy. Such actions exemplify a stereotyped view of the savage other which I have discussed earlier in this study. As I described, such imagery represents an Anglo-American projection which masks the actual exploitation of blacks by whites. Jerry Phillips describes how cannibalism functions as a marker of the other that distinguishes the primitive from the civilized; however, it does more than this, as it also disguises the actual cannibalistic beast, the white imperialist: 'man-eating in the visceral sense of ingesting human flesh could be made to obscure man-eating as a morally instructive trope, whose real world referent is the colonialist extermination of peoples envisaged as "brutes"' (Phillips, 1998: 194).

The narrative of King Kong's cannibalistic orgy masks and justifies the colonial exploitation that is attendant on the arrival of the civilized whites. More than this, though, cannibalism's monstrous depiction also highlights white fears of the African in their midst and of their own attraction to forbidden acts; it is, in Marina Warner's apposite phrase that combines these two readings, 'evidence of the imperial ethnographic escapade' (Warner, 1998: 167). As Ed Guerrero asserts, 'the monster always constitutes the return of the socially or politically repressed fears of a society, these energies, memories, and issues that a society refuses to deal openly with' (Guerrero, 1993: 42). For Africans in the diaspora, such projections are psychologically disabling, as Frantz Fanon described in his landmark *Black Skin, White Masks* (1952). The hegemonic power of such ideas means that even the gaze of a white child is a defining one, a 'whiteness that burns' (Fanon, 1970: 81), and has as its ultimate fear/fantasy ingestion by the black other. As Fanon elucidates, the encounter makes him into the monster the boy fears:

> My body was given back to me, sprawled out, distorted,
> recolored, clad in mourning in that white winter day. The Negro
> is an animal, the Negro is bad, the Negro is ugly; look a nigger,
> it's cold, the nigger is shivering with cold, that cold that goes
> through your bones, the handsome little boy is trembling
> because he thinks that the nigger is quivering with rage, the little
> white boy throws himself into his mother's arms: Mama, the
> nigger's going to eat me up. (*ibid.*: 80)

The primordial nature of the fears make their translation into a monster movie like King Kong exemplary. Of course, such brutal depictions of blacks and their blackfaced or monster-costumed surrogates were already a staple of cinematic convention, having been firmly established in D. W. Griffith's *Birth of a Nation* in the character of the black 'rapist' Gus. Kong's rampage through the streets of New York City in search of Ann Darrow culminates in his discovery of her in a hotel room. The camera fixes on the gaze he directs at her and on his enlarged rolling eyes. Such an image borrows directly from Griffith's multiple shots of Gus's rolling eyes as he pursues the Southern white woman with rape on his mind. It is a minstrel stereotype, but one that promotes ideas of the bestial. As Ed Guerrero asserts, such demonized sexuality carries 'the threat of a dreaded primordial "blackness"'. He continues: 'Certainly the same principle threatens an innocent white reality in King Kong's fatal, obsessive encounter with pure white womanhood' (Guerrero, 1993: 41). The monster here stands in for the black beast of the white imagination. In such a cinematic mode, the mythic racial dynamics of America can be safely played out:

> the white woman as the essence of whiteness, the most prized
> possession of the white man and the object of desire of all other
> races, is a powerful representational current running through
> Western literature and cinema and is one of the generic sources
> of race imagery in this century. It is the threat of the white
> woman's rape by the monstrous, black other that gives white–
> black contrasts much of the social charge and meaning.
> (*ibid.*: 64)

In discussing the phenomenon of the *Tarzan* stories, Marianna Torgovnick highlights how beasts are often used as surrogates for non-whites in colonial fantasy, so that in attacks by beasts on white women are 'encode[d] the "unnatural", the threat of miscegenation, disguised as species difference' (Torgovnick, 1990: 53). Films like *King Kong* provide a less threatening, fantastic way to talk about white fears of the black other. They describe a comforting Manichean reality for colonial/racist fantasists where

> qualities like lust belong to animals and blacks, not to Euro-
> Americans, except when they are renegade, outcast; flirtations
> with miscegenation are allowed, but miscegenation, especially
> between white females and nonwhite males, must never occur.
> (*ibid.*: 53)

We might expect the fantasy projections of *King Kong* to be at their most extreme on Skull Island; however, there is a sense in which, when the film crosses the Atlantic, there is no let-up in the depiction of an unrealistic worldview, almost in spite of the verisimilitude of the projected cityscape. While the skyscrapers and street scenes of Manhattan form the backdrop to Kong's frenzied progress through New York, there is a significant absence in the portrayal of its population – there are no black people. By 1933, due to the Great Migration, the black population of New York City had risen from around 1.3 per cent in 1890 to at least 11 per cent (Douglas, 1997: 73); yet, throughout *King Kong*, African-Americans are notable by their complete absence: in the theatre where Kong is chained, on the city streets where he rampages and even on the elevated railway which he destroys. In all the crowd scenes, white faces are ubiquitous. Such absence is in complete contrast to majority views of a veritable invasion of blacks onto Northern city streets after the Great War. The film's iconography, though, has no need of actual blacks, as Kong stands in for them all. He is the rampaging black beast incarnate symbolizing the miscegenist fears of the majority population. The omission of actual diasporan Africans and their replacement by a fantasized projection is key to any understanding of *King Kong*, and again James Snead's perceptive criticism provides us with a language to describe such deliberate black absence from Anglo-American film. He describes such a racialized cultural mode as

> white America's traditional form of what might be called
> 'exclusionary emulation', the principle whereby the power and
> trappings of black culture are initiated while at the same time
> their black originators are segregated away and kept at a
> distance. (Snead, 1994: 60)

Such 'exclusionary emulation' is played out through the symbolism of the ape-like monster who performs blackness on the screen even as blackness is expunged from the streets on which he performs. To have shown African-Americans in these scenes would have interpellated them as citizens who experience fear and horror too, thus destroying the binary illusion of white civilization/black savagery the film so carefully constructs. Of course, such distinct binaries were crucial to the definition of the African as animalistic other that provided intellectual justification for the slave trade and for the racial segregation that followed. The African as baboon/ape-like monster is a stereotype as old as the peculiar institution itself, and rogue slaves were often caricatured as bestial. Thus, in 1734 a notice about a runaway slave in the *South Carolina Gazette* included the following crude joke:

> Whereas a stately Baboon hath lately slipped his Collar and run
> away; He is big-bon'd, full in Flesh, and has learn'd to walk very
> erect on his two Hind-Legs, he grins and chatters much, but will
> not bite, he plays Tricks impudently well and is mightily given to
> clambering, whereby he often shews his A —. (quoted in Jordan,
> 1969: 238)

This discourse of racial otherness as species difference continues into the twentieth century. Thus, dialogue between New Yorkers while waiting for Kong's unveiling highlights the uncivilized nature of some of the city's citizens. One says, 'I hear it's a gorilla – Gee have we got enough of this in New York.' Such commentary hints at the racial tensions that existed in New York during this period. Discussions about the 'mongrelization' of New York were widespread in the 1920s and 1930s among conservative social critics, as Ann

Douglas's seminal monograph *Terrible Honesty: Mongrel Manhattan in the 1920s* (1995) shows, and public space was often the territory where such social tensions were played out. So seriously did conservative African-American social commentators take this critique that they appropriated its language to describe their dismay at lower-class black impoliteness. According to the black paper the *Amsterdam News*, black youth should 'deport themselves with greater decorum and decency on street cars [and stop behaving] like so many jungle apes. [They] enter the car in full monkey regalia and strut as though they were the princes of the jungle' (quoted in White and White, 1999: 232). Such intemperate language about black youth uses racist clichés about the bestiality of black people in much the same way that *King Kong* appropriates jungle imagery and transposes it to New York. In the film, Kong is in 'full monkey regalia' as he derails the streetcar and terrorizes its inhabitants, regarding them as mere toys and tasty morsels. There is no need for an actual African-American presence in the film to feed white racial stereotypical notions, as they are symbolically present in Kong's performative savage violence. Kong as roving, destructive black beast is the projection of Anglo-America's worst nightmare, the race riot. James Snead foregrounds these domestic racial tensions as crucial to King Kong's conception, as 'the race riots of the early twenties (many of them in the North) still hovered in the collective memory, their recurrence an ever present possibility' (Snead, 1994: 20). Yet this specific genesis is only one part of the film's continuing appeal to white American audiences, as Snead elucidates:

> for audiences in 1933, and presumably ever since, the image of an amorous black ape running amok in New York City with a white woman he has abducted must indeed have addressed on some profound level the question of how to deal with the 'cargo' that the twin imperatives of trade and greed have caused to be imported into the non-Western world. (*ibid.*: 21)

What comes to the rescue of beleaguered whiteness is modernity. As Kong escapes with Darrow and climbs up the Empire State building, something new happens in the film – Kong is dwarfed in the modern cityscape. The *mise en scène* suddenly captures him against the backdrop of the city rather than lording it on its streets. Camera angles from above replace those that had looked on him with awe from below, and just as technology had proved his undoing on Skull Island, so now aerial power dynamically intervenes. Fighter planes buzz around him like so many flies and some fall victim to his gigantism, but their machine-gun technology finally overhauls him. The planes are essential to his defeat, as they both keep him under surveillance and display a technological supremacy that eventually overwhelms him. As Lindqvist would editorialize, the beast, that threat to Western progress, to white Euro-American hegemony, had finally been exterminated.

Robyn Wiegman has talked of how 'the disciplinary power of race ... must be read as implicated in both specular and panoptic regimes' (Wiegman, 1995: 39). In *King Kong*, such regimes, from the intrusive, colonial camera on Skull

Island to the belittling, modernistic camera in Manhattan, work to inscribe Kong as a surrogate, controlled diasporan African whose threat to white civilization is tamed by their intervention. In this sense, the film is an appropriate symbol for a cinematic history which continues the work of minstrelsy in foregrounding stereotyped black presence while colluding in a fantasy of black absence. Or as Susan Gubar puts it, 'one of the predicaments of white culture has resided in its blindness about its dependency on represented (and thus effaced) black bodies' (Gubar, 1997: 40). King Kong is such a represented body, whose eventual effacement mirrors that of African-Americans in the New York cityscape.

The 1933 film of *King Kong*, then, was complicit in exclusionary racial praxis. Its iconography of an ape-like beast, rolling its eyes in a modernist cityscape, was not, however, confined to 1930s America. Its resonances continue into 1990s Britain, with tabloid journalism employing it in such headlines as the *Sun*'s 1998 construction 'Wide-Eyed Frank Made Me Quake with Terror' concerning the black British boxer Frank Bruno (quoted in Carrington, 2000: 156); and Sky TV invoked it in their title sequence for Mike Tyson's first fight in Britain against Julian Francis, in which 'menacing music and a panorama of New York's skyline, with an instantly recognisable King Kong motif' (Kelner, 2000) is used to evoke the 'monstrous' Tyson. King Kong might be long dead, but the means and modes of representing blackness remain depressingly familiar. As Kobena Mercer appositely summarizes, 'through slavery and imperialism the black body is opened up for power, primarily through the gaze by being constituted as a specular object for the other who is also the master' (quoted in Read, 1996: 147).

This objectification of diasporan Africans is even present in films which supposedly champion their agency, like Steven Spielberg's *Amistad* (1997). Paul Gilroy highlights how the Africans in the film 'arrive at their Cuban auction block fresh from the horrors of the Middle Passage', yet are displayed in a mode that undermines the horror of that experience:

> They are buffed: apparently fit and gleaming with robust good
> health. They enjoy the worked-out and pumped-up musculature
> that can only be acquired through the happy rigors of a
> postmodern gym routine. Against the grain of white
> supremacy's indifference and denial, the middle passage has
> been deliberately and provocatively recovered, but it is rendered
> in an impossible and deeply contentious manner that offers only
> the consolation of tears in place of more challenging and
> imaginative connections. (Gilroy, 2000: 25–6)

The slaves are reduced to mere bodies subjected to the gaze of the predominantly white cinema audience. Verisimilitude, which Spielberg's film elsewhere appears intent to foreground as a virtue (even going so far as to distribute a teaching pack through his company DreamWorks which 'repackages the movie as an apparatus of documentary truth, as history' [Osagie, 2000: 130]), is not in this scene warranted important enough to disrupt the camera's lingering gaze on a strangely healthy black flesh. Having depicted the myriad horrors of the middle passage in probably the most effective scenes in the film, Spielberg is unable to show the sickly bodies that such horrors produced. The horror of calloused and deformed bodies is, however, not the only flagrant omission in the film's depiction of the background to the shipboard revolt. In my chapter on cannibalism, I highlighted how rumours of white cannibalism contributed to the decision of the Africans on board the *Amistad* to revolt. Such fears were activated by the mulatto cook, Celestino, who had indicated to the rebellion's eventual leader, Cinque, that when they landed they would be made into meat. The centrality of these fears to the rebellion are confirmed by the testimony of fellow rebels Kale and Kinna, both of whom wrote in 1841 to John Quincy Adams about how the cook's discourse about cannibalism had inflamed them to revolt (quoted in Lemisch, 1999: 64). As Spielberg omits this prime precursor to the revolt in the film the uprising is given no specific spark but appears to be a spontaneous reaction to the loss of liberty. As Lemisch points out: 'The Africans attached great significance to this event [cannibalism], and its omission from the film falsely exaggerates the spontaneity of the uprising, while undermining the rationality and underlying principles of the act (*ibid.*). The Africans' pragmatic and carefully planned communal act of putting their bodies beyond incorporation by rebelling is reinterpreted by Spielberg as the wilful act of a black individualistic hero figure spontaneously rising up against the oppressors.

Spielberg is not the first to be uncomfortable with the cannibalistic sub-plot to the uprising. Lydia Maria Child reports how in 1841 she had taken exception to the way her discovery of this aspects of the episode had ruined the moral certainties of the rebellion's narrative, reporting how it 'knocked on the head all of my romantic associations with Cinque as a brave soul preferring death to slavery' (quoted in Sale, 1997: 210). Child resents the way a realistic rendition of the uprising and its causes disrupts a liberal humanist reading of the rebellion. The spectre of cannibalism and the Africans' uprising against its manifestation introduces an element of superstition that works in contradistinction to the creation of a Westernized civilized hero. *Amistad*'s avoidance of this key precursor to the rebellion illustrates how a discourse of cannibalism continues to upset a liberal reading of the historical event enough for it to be elided.

Spielberg omits such a significant dynamic as cannibalism because it would complicate his narrative. First, it would foreground communal enterprise rather than the heroic individual endeavour of Cinque he prefers to emphasize. Furthermore, the mulatto cook's mixed-race status means that his taunting of the slaves would problematize Spielberg's binary narrative of white venality and black victimhood. Spielberg's reductive account of the uprising is further enhanced by decisions made about the depiction of the African rebels. The rebels speak in Mende and are given no subtitles (unlike the Spanish); thus throughout the early part of the film, they are effectively muted or their words interpreted by their Spanish enemies. Their actions are thus accompanied by grunts and an incomprehensible babble (this is compounded by Cinque's 'animal-like breathing' [Osagie, 2000: 128] which opens the film). In those early scenes, the rebels are portrayed as animalistic and engaging in an almost nihilistic, violent attack on their white oppressors. Their language and actions during the revolt are as incomprehensible and seemingly random as the ragings and babble of Kong. As Lemisch comments:

> As part of the process of reducing rebellion ... Spielberg makes it into an unpremeditated outburst without planning or prior root in events on shipboard ... the effect of this is to ignore the intelligence behind the uprising and to focus instead on what thus appears to be instinctual and stereotypically animalistic behaviour. (Lemisch, 1999: 60)

This is accentuated by the slow-motion technique used to portray the killing of the whites and the repeated stabbing of already fatally wounded victims. This amounts to a fetishization of slaughter, as Spielberg portrays the Africans as so demonized by slavery that they have abandoned rationality. If so, then surely all their oppressors would have been murdered. But Cinque and his co-conspirators were conscious enough of their need to gain effective liberty to spare the lives of those Spaniards who can help them navigate their boat to freedom. By his choice of emphasis in these scenes (on violent and alienated Africans) Spielberg has, however unwittingly, foregrounded nihilistic black violence in slavery rather than emphasizing the violence of the institution itself. In Iyunolu Folayan Osagie's apt phrase, he 'succeeded in consolidating ideological representations of blackness as absence and as violent nihilism' (Osagie, 2000: 127). She continues:

> The tie between blackness and violence in the movie reinforces rather than disentangles the mainstream American image of the black male body as violent. The full-bodied presence of the actor Djimon Hounsou, coupled with the seemingly endless rage with which he infuses his character, confirms rather than negates the typical American impression of black male violence – uncontrollable anger that is unsupported by a rational response to circumstances. (*ibid.*)

This stereotypical depiction of the black other is, to some extent, countered as the film develops and constructs a sympathy with the rebelling slaves and their cause of freedom through the portrayal of the various legal battles which ultimately led to the freeing of the *Amistad* blacks. In particular, the character of John Quincy Adams is shown to identify with Cinque's plight. This identification is achieved in the film through the characters' parallel summoning of their ancestors. Adams 'call[s] on the founding fathers as witnesses to the deliberation in the Supreme Court', while Cinque believes 'his ancestors also have a stake in the outcome of the trial' (*ibid.*: 123). As the camera pans round the portraits of America's illustrious founders and Adams glories in the American freedoms they promoted, to the accompaniment of patriotic strings, it is all too easy to get carried away. The easy identification of African and

Euro-American ancestors that the film promotes elides a crucial difference: namely, that some of the white ancestors (evoked so eloquently by Adams) were slaveholders themselves (Jefferson, Washington, etc.), and all acquiesced to a constitution that enshrined slavery as part of American life. Osagie is right when she claims that 'Spielberg's movie as whole challenges Americans of all races to ponder the implications of the past in the present' (*ibid.*: 131). Unfortunately, its narrative of historical American freedom is merely a rhetorical one which cannot be sustained when juxtaposed with the facts of contemporaneous American slavery. The film wants the viewer to 'ponder the implications of the past in the present' through the lens of a contemporary American liberal humanism that obscures the troubled complexity of a freedom for whites built on the simultaneous enslavement of blacks.

Spielberg is keen to portray the *Amistad* case as a crucial historical moment in the ending of slavery in America – hence his juxtaposition of the ending of the trial with scenes from the Civil War. However, the only reason the Africans are allowed their freedom is, paradoxically, that they are not domiciled on the American side of the Atlantic. The court case hinged on it being shown that the *Amistad* captives were newly enslaved. Had the human consignment on the *Amistad* been part of an internal slave trade, the Spanish owners would have won their claim for their retrieval. Hence, the 'specific Amistad court victory did not affect the condition of slaves in the South' (*ibid.*: 117). Despite Adams's eloquent words, the bastions of slavery remained intact long after the case. The ideology of Spielberg's film promotes American mores as key to the ending of slavery and makes this jurisdictional framework the means of achieving it. However, American jurisdiction was at this moment defending American slavery and would continue to do so for the next twenty years.

Spielberg's historical amnesia here is bolstered by his stereotyped portrayal of the abolitionists as 'zealots, fanatics and True Believers' (Lemisch, 1999: 67), and his rewriting of an abolitionist who defends the Africans, Roger Baldwin, as 'earthy, practical and non-ideological' (*ibid.*). In doing this, he marginalizes abolitionist involvement, prioritizing the ex-President John Quincy Adams's intervention over theirs. Thus, a tale of black political collusion, interracial cooperation and politically effective abolitionist action is reduced to a narrative of anodyne, individualistic American heroism within the conceptual framework of American liberalism. The *Amistad* rebels chain-danced their way to freedom by a collective act of rebellion that serves as a beacon to radicals that follow. Spielberg's narrative not only marginalizes this dynamic act of self-expression gained through a conscious violent strike for freedom, but substitutes such agency with a counter-narrative of white American benevolence, or 'whites freeing blacks' (*ibid.*: 66). As a film which claims to show the realities of the black Atlantic, *Amistad* is in this way at least nearly as fantastically absurd as *King Kong*.

═ 9 ═

FROM SHIPS ON THE HEAD TO STONE-MARKERS ON THE SHORE

THE CONSERVATION OF BLACK ATLANTIC MEMORY

There is no place you or I can go, to think about, or not think about, to summon the presences of, or recollect the absences of slaves; nothing that reminds us of the ones who made the journey and of those who did not make it. There is no suitable memorial or plaque or wreath or wall or park or skyscraper lobby. There's no 300-foot tower. There's no small bench by the road. There is not even a tree scored, an initial I can visit, or you can visit in Charleston or Savannah or New York or Providence, or better still on the banks of the Mississippi. (Toni Morrison, 1989: 4)

My mother kept a basket of shells from Zanzibar as an ornament for many years, for some reason I can't remember if she still has them even though I was in her house only two weeks ago. One shell was very smooth and round, it was beige and had brown spots, the basket was shallow and thin, pale and brittle. There was a white shell, also quite round, but ridged, it was thin and light and almost translucent. Coral, white and pink, good to look at but horrible and rough to touch. There were small, smooth shells with ridged openings which I longed to pop into my mouth like a delicious sweetie. (Lubaina Himid, 1999b: n.p.)

On 23 August 1999, at a ceremony to commemorate those who suffered or died as a result of the Atlantic slave trade at the dockside in Liverpool, the black British Member of Parliament Bernie Grant (1994–2000) talked movingly about the occasion in the early 1990s when he visited a slave fort on the west coast of Africa with the Reverend Jesse Jackson. Like all visitors to the fort, he and Jackson were locked in the cellar dungeon for a few minutes so they could 'experience' the extremity of the conditions the slaves endured while waiting to be sold to the slave captains from Europe trading down the coast. This primal historical moment links the two in ways that transcend their different national backgrounds. Thinking of their common ancestors who had undertaken such horrific journeys, the British MP and the American Congressman wept together. The criss-crossing of the Atlantic by Grant's ancestors from Africa to the Caribbean, then onwards to Britain and finally this contemporary journey homeward to Africa approximates the development of the triangular trade in the eighteenth century that made slavery an efficient system. Jackson's return to Africa is a journey undertaken by many African-Americans at the end of the millennium as they seek the 'Roots' popularized by Alex Haley and eulogized by a range of artists from Duke Ellington to John Coltrane, Langston Hughes to Toni Morrison, The Last Poets to Public Enemy. Caryl Phillips interrogates this phenomenon in *The Atlantic Sound* (2000), describing the excesses of certain sentimentalized appropriations of the African locale by diasporan Africans, which have far more to do with bogus emotionalism than a proper coming to terms with the past. He comments acerbically on one particularly anodyne ceremony that took place at Elmina Castle during the Panfest festival, which was undertaken by 'people of the diaspora who expect the continent to solve whatever psychological problems they possess' (Phillips, 2000: 173). Phillips's reservations about the appropriation of African memorial space by narrow Western-educated interest groups is well made. It illustrates the malleability of meaning for such a locale in a black Atlantic replete with varied interest groups. For, in a global economy, where the marketing of black memory provides mercantile opportunities for some, there is also ideological payback for others who want to interpret sites like Elmina through a narrow nationalistic gaze. Those left out in such a marketplace of ideologies are usually the local disenfranchised Africans who do not have the economic power of the diasporan tourists. This is exemplified by the restrictions imposed around Elmina Castle that ban all people 'except tourists' (Singleton, 1999: 158). Bearing such contestation in mind, I would like to return to Grant and Jackson's rendezvous on the west coast of Africa, with all its emotional valencies, as it exemplifies the importance of roots for diasporan cultures.

As I have discussed before, though, Paul Gilroy encourages us not to focus on 'roots' alone, for what is just as, if not more, important is its homonym 'routes'. For, as we have seen throughout this study, the creation of different black cultures on all sides of the Atlantic seaboard is pivotally dependent on marine rather than land-based exigencies, on cultural exchange rather than national homogeneity and the ideologies that flow from a controlling nation-state. As Gilroy himself succinctly put it: 'Nationalist paradigms for thinking about cultural history fail when confronted by the intercultural and trans-national formation of the Black Atlantic' (Gilroy, 1993a: ix). Nowhere is this more apparent than in the attempts by arbiters of national cultures (both European and African) to narrativize or memorialize the history of the middle passage.

The multiple valencies of potential memorials to slavery such as that imagined by Lubaina Himid in her *Memorial to Zong* (discussed in Chapter 3) can be contrasted to the lack of a sufficient memorial to the trade and its victims in Britain's largest slave port, Liverpool. Building after building proudly displays its slave lineage on its richly frescoed outer walls. For instance, the entrance to the Martin's Bank building is guarded by frescos depicting African boys manacled at the feet and neck. However, the only memorial that consciously seems to portray slavery as anything but benign and natural is the homage to Nelson's victories which has manacled and chained figures at its base. But these are of no direct relevance to the transatlantic slave trade as they depict French prisoners of war. Caryl Phillips describes how 'it is impossible to look at this fountain and its sculpture and not think of the slave trade' (Phillips, 2000: 82), but such memorialization is merely accidental. The Merseyside Maritime Museum did seek to rectify this amnesia in the city by inaugurating a small plaque at Albert Dock, which was unveiled by Bernie Grant in 1999. It depicts a ship and an African sculpture from the Slavery Gallery exhibit, but it is dwarfed by the memorials to British imperial endeavour elsewhere on the waterfront. (Even though I know it is there, I frequently walk past it una- wares.) Tony Tibbles, curator of the Slavery Gallery at the museum, describes it as merely an 'information plaque' and maintains that it is not meant to have a memorial function (Tibbles, 2001). However, with no other specific record to the trade on the Liverpool waterfront, it is forced to do the work of a memorial. Thus, the area around it has become a focus for the annual slavery memorial day in August. Overall, the plaque seems inadequate and tokenistic, particularly in contrast to the grandiloquent *Titanic* memorial further along the dock, which commemorates the hundreds of merchant marines killed in the disaster and in the subsequent world war. Surely the deaths of thousands of white seamen in the slave trade as well as the deaths and displacement of millions of slaves demand recognition on a par with the loss of one (albeit legendary) ocean liner. Liverpool's desire to forget its part in the trade is confirmed by an act of vandalism that occurred soon after the plaque was unveiled in which the word 'slave' in 'slave ship' was erased, a graphic example of how the city is still unable to come to terms fully with its asso- ciation to slavery.

It might be thought that the opening of the Slavery Gallery in 1992 at the Merseyside Maritime Museum went some way to expunging amnesia about the trade. Marcus Wood, however, indicts it for its inadequacy as an exhibi- tion on the middle passage. In a carping coda to his book *Blind Memory*, he indicts the museum for failing to to 'occupy a central space in our cultural memory' (Wood, 2000: 296). Wood apparently believes that museum exhi- bitions should perform a memorial function; however, their primary need to narrate a history and to purvey information vitiates against such a function. Museums play a large part in fighting amnesia, but this does not mean they are prime sites for memorialization. They are fixed, mainly non-interactive sites that can never rival the best of memorial sites that I describe later in this chapter.

Wood critiques the title of the exhibition *Against Human Dignity* as woeful and typical of an English obsession with civilized values and a simultaneous evasion of the economic imperative that actually spurred the trade (*ibid.*). Yet the title is not an English phrase but was translated from the French. Adapted by Tony Tibbles, curator of the gallery, as an attempt to internationalize the portrayal of the slave trade, it was not merely coined to domesticate the trade, as Wood implies (Tibbles, 2000). Wood is on more solid ground in his critique of the African section of the exhibit, which he indicts for exoticizing Africans, in contrast to the rooms depicting Europeans whose 'foreignness is mediated by the familiarity of historical displays in museums' (*ibid.*: 299). Just as lamentable in the African section is the lack of a sustained discussion of how the displayed objects were plundered during colonialism. There is mention made of the sacking of Benin, but overall, a chance to link the slave trade and its aftermath to museumology is missed and the exhibit is depoliticized as a result. What Wood detects in the exhibit (albeit tendentiously) is a lack of municipal self-consciousness, which would have increased its political acuteness and strengthened its ability to shed light on the trade as a whole.

But what of the memorialization Wood demands of the museum? Surely that is better placed elsewhere in the city. Eric Lynch, a Liverpool slave sites tour guide, and other Liverpudlians want a permanent memorial to slavery in their city (specifically to those who died in the struggle to end the trade), but the city burghers have so far turned a deaf ear to calls for a small memorial garden in Mount Royal – an especially pertinent site, because it contains the remains of an anti-slave trade Liverpudlian, William Roscoe (Lynch, 2001).

The depiction of slavery is rarely without controversy, a fact that was illustrated most appositely when the National Maritime Museum in Greenwich sought to highlight the central role it played in the success of the British Empire when the new Empire and Trade galleries were inaugurated in 1999. At the centre of the exhibit was a tableau of a manacled black hand emerging from a hatch beneath an English lady drinking tea. Its intention was to illustrate how British refinement was bought at the cost of human degradation and exploitation. It proved too difficult for many British commentators to stomach, and after a series of splenetic letters to national newspapers and to the gallery itself, it was finally withdrawn. Robert Blyth, a curator at the museum, said that, although regrettable, the climb-down in the face of such pressure was not disastrous, as 'the tableau had done its job by the controversy it had generated' (Blyth, 2001). However, the effective censorship of the tableau meant that a crucial aspect of the narrative of Empire had been elided, so that the galleries effectively moved from being a potential *lieu de mémoire* (however limited) to an actual *lieu d'oubli*.

Unlike Liverpool and London, Bristol has at last constructed an appropriate memorial to the trade to accompany its belated exhibit *A Respectable Trade? Bristol and Transatlantic Slavery* (1999) – a bridge across the harbour named after Pero, an African servant of the Pinney family who lived in the city's Georgian House museum in the late eighteenth century, having come from the Pinney estate in Nevis in 1784. Its central double arch of horns reflects both the musical heritage Pero and his compatriots brought with them and, more symbolically, the way their history resonates today, while the ladders in the middle of the bridge are a reminder of the ladders on the riggings of the ships

Figure 9   Frederick Douglass IV at the Wye plantation.

that brought Africans across the Atlantic and back again. Such a memorial shows what is possible and how even the most pragmatic of architecture can be used to commemorate and celebrate a black presence. Such architectural remembrance is particularly crucial to Bristol where, an anonymous commentator opined, 'There is not a brick in the city but what is cemented with the blood of a slave' (quoted in Dresser, 2001: 96).

Collective amnesia is the more general pattern, though, and is not confined to Britain, but remains prevalent throughout North America. For instance, the Wye plantation where Frederick Douglass was brought up has not become a national monument and is in fact still owned and run by descendants of the Lloyds', his former masters (Figure 9). During my visit to the plantation in September 1999, the Lloyd descendant who led the tour was reluctant to talk about Douglass, preferring to concentrate on the architecture and fixtures and fittings that attested to his family's successful stewardship of the estate over three centuries. The Aaron Anthony House next to the main house was being converted into a small retirement cottage for the matriarch of the household, its domestic ordinariness belying a tortured history. It was in this house, in a cupboard off the kitchen, where Douglass slept and from which, through a keyhole, he witnessed the vicious whipping of his Aunt Hester – probably the most famous account of slave punishment in the American literary tradition (Douglass, 1845: 51–2). Far from being an effective memorial site to such harrowing incidents, the estate, in its reluctance to acknowledge either Douglass's life or the presence of slavery, represents an exemplary *lieu d'oubli*. This is confirmed by the grave sites on the estate. For the white scions of the Lloyd family, a mass graveyard close to the house complete with individual markers. For the slaves, a space across a cornfield a long way from the house which has only recently attracted a memorial stone. Inscribed on the stone are the words, 'For those who served', which effectively obscures the slave status of those interred below and replaces it with the more neutral idea that these enslaved peoples were somehow willing servants.

If the absence of an appropriate memorial for slaves on a plantation still in the hands of Southern scions is relatively unsurprising, Caryl Phillips describes a far more weighty omission. Sullivan's Island, close to Charleston, has been called the black Ellis Island, as over 30 per cent of all the slaves who first landed in North America were processed there. Yet there is no memorial to their presence. The pest houses where they were processed are no longer standing, and the amnesia is so extreme that Phillips can find no record of their original sites. As he says, 'nobody has thought it necessary at least to speculate and mark a place with a monument or plaque' (Phillips, 2000: 207). Such amnesia is made more marked by the profusion of elite leisure activities that occur there now. The island that was the entrepôt for the most significant creator of Southern wealth, black slave labour, is now, in a rich irony, home to the inheritors of that wealth, the present-day Southern elite of Charleston. This connection is elided by the lack of public (or indeed private) memorials to the slave presence. American mourning rarely has included its African population.

Such omissions are compounded by the cultural realities of a diasporic population. Part of the problem with constructing permanent memorials is that the diasporic history of Africans militates against their being adequately remembered by stone memorials. As I have demonstrated earlier in this study, because of the particular valencies of the slave trade and its aftermath, cultures developed literally on the move: art forms which were easily transportable, such as chanted songs and performed folktales, were crucial means of cultural transmission throughout the period of the slave trade and beyond. Remembering how they reached their scattered destinations became central to African diasporan people's sense of themselves, to the development of what we might call a diasporic memory. Thus, traces of African routedness can be discovered in the most banal of examples.

For instance, Joseph Johnson, a black London beggar of the early nineteenth century, famously wore his diasporic signature on his hat in the form of 'a fairly sizeable replica of a ship, complete with masts and sails with all their meticulous riggings' (Dawes, 1999: 18) (Figure 10). He was reduced to beggary because he received no pension despite many years as a sailor in the merchant marine. Kwame Dawes incisively interprets 'the wearing of such a hat as a profoundly symbolic gesture', as the headdress connected him 'to West Africa where similar headdresses were and are still quite common' (*ibid.*). For instance, the remodelled Sainsbury Gallery at the British Museum includes an ancestral screen made by the Kalabari people of the Eastern Niger Delta in the nineteenth century that depicts a figure with a European ship as a headdress (Figure 11). It would have been used as the backdrop to masquerade ceremonials that reflected the Kalabari involvement in the slave trade and the doleful impact of European mores on the culture. Contemporary Kalabari

Figure 10   Illustration of Joseph Johnson in J. T. Smith, *Vagabondiana*, 1815, reprinted 1874. Reproduced by permission of the Bodleian Library, Oxford.

culture continues to celebrate the ship in masquerades wherein men wear ships on their heads. These ceremonials use the human body as a 'base upon which to erect different kind of extensions which result in a great range of overall forms' that interact with 'drum rhythms to generate a cornucopia of different balletic patterns' (Robin Horton, quoted in Camp, 1995b: n.p.). The 'ship on the head' as a motif is dramatically used by the contemporary female sculptor Sokari Douglas Camp, whose *Big Masquerade with Boat and Household on His Head* (1995a) (Figure 12) illustrates the continuing importance of routes taken and denied for Africans in the diaspora. The piece is poignantly inscribed 'to the artist's niece who was not allowed to join her for a holiday by the immigration authorities' (Sue Hubbard, quoted in *ibid*: n.p.). The metallic figure wielding cutlasses and wearing a blood-spattered apron is a stark contrast to the ultramarine blue ship sailing atop the masquerader's headdress.

Joseph Johnson's masquerade, though linked to these West African practices, has its own routed logic. The ship here is a literal sign of Johnson's

Figure 11   *Ancestral Screen. Duein Fubara.* Kalabari, Nigeria, eighteenth to nineteenth century. British Museum Collection. Af 45.334. © The British Museum.

routedness and rootedness, a picturesque memorial sign of the sea voyages which have led him to the metropolis and a reminder of the African culture he has physically left far behind. The ship (a model of the *Nelson*), 'his instantaneous narrative of journey' (Dawes, 1999: 18), remembers the ocean as key to his identity, in a colourful gesture that distinguishes him from the numerous other beggars on London's streets. Such a gesture contains both an economic and a poetic motive. The former is shown in the way his carved headpiece adds to the pecuniary value he can extract from his mendicant status. The performative excess of his attire makes him a more attractive recipient, as does the connection through the model ship to his involvement (along with many other black sailors) in a British marine tradition that in the aftermath of Nelson's victory at Trafalgar in 1805 was a repository for British ideas of imperial superiority. Like his contemporary Robert Wedderburn, whose lesson of communal solidarity came (in part at least) from his marine experience, Johnson abrogates British naval triumphalism for his own purposes. In a

Figure 12 Sokari Douglas Camp, *Big Masquerade with Boat and Household on His Head*, 1995. Af8.2. © The British Museum. Reproduced by permission of the artist.

gesture of trickster reversal, he uses the ship, sign of British imperial might, to fashion an alternative reading – namely, the ship as sign of admixture, hybridity and black presence that undermines cosy notions of British racial superiority. He reinforced this by the singing of quintessentially British songs such as 'The British Seaman's Praise' and 'The Wooden Walls of Old England' (Smith, 1874: 33), which promoted his rights as an Englishman, though many would deny him this identity because of the colour of his skin. The headpiece is ultimately only in part a memorial of Johnson's past; it is also a performative shortcut to an understanding of him for his white clients, 'a rationale for his presence, his existence and his condition' (Dawes, 1999: 18), that in the end makes him unique in the crowded territory of London beggary.

Such memorialization images a black Atlantic even while Johnson walks on land. It is, in Pierre Nora's apt phrase, one of many *lieux de mémoire* which encompass the black Atlantic experience. Such *lieux de mémoire* foreground memory less 'as a narrativized representation of the past' and locate memory more in 'specific sites or realms that individuals and groups have invested with effective ties of longing and belonging' (Wood, 1999: 3). Johnson's ship is literally where he belongs and is a memory trace of his life as a black sailor. It tells the story of his past more effectively than written narrative. The ship is all the more pertinent for being an integral part of his attire. Johnson's performative progress inscribes the ship as vitally important in constructing identity for African diasporan people. As Gilroy (1993a: 17) notes and Equiano's *Narrative* exemplifies, ships were crucial vessels of European modernity, which forced Africans to reinterpret their perceptions of the world. Thus, it is an obvious symbol for Johnson to manipulate for his own uses. As Smith describes, the ship is given added presence by Johnson's 'kinesthetic imagination' (Roach, 1996: 27). He manipulates the *Nelson*, consciously invoking the ocean, as 'when placed on his cap he can, by a bow of thanks, or a supplicating inclination to a drawing-room window, give the appearance of sea-motion' (Smith, 1874: 33). Rooted on land by 'his wounds rendering him incapable of doing further duty on the ocean, and having no claim to relief in any parish' (*ibid.*), Johnson invoked his routedness to stake his claim to a diasporan black British identity that he hoped would make him a sympathetic case among those able to help him. In a predominantly white public space, and by employing an imaginative kinaesthetics, Johnson becomes more than an ordinary beggar and memorializes his African background. As Gilroy says of such performative acts, they illustrate the 'concept of the body in motion which is the residue of our African cultures' (Gilroy, 1993b: 246). Johnson's memorial of his past is a dynamic and creolized example that is illustrative of many diasporan African lives in the eighteenth and nineteenth centuries. His biography destabilizes classic ideas of discrete homogenized cultures and promotes the hybrid and the heterogeneous. As Renato Rosaldo asserts:

> In contrast with the classic view which posits culture as a self-contained whole made up of coherent patterns, culture can arguably be conceived as a more porous array of intersections where distinct processes crisscross from within and beyond its borders. (quoted in Roach, 1996: 29)

Like his contemporary Equiano, Johnson accommodates in part to the hegemonic discourse of Britain's imperial might while subtly critiquing it through the use of a competing Africanist discourse. His performance might be more oblique than Equiano's written version, but it is no less important for that. Most pertinently, Johnson's model ship gives him a modicum of self-expression normally denied to mendicants. His performance gives him control of his self-image, so that he can fashion a positive reading from his tragic circumstances.

Johnson's vibrant living memorial can be contrasted to the main memorials to black presence in Britain in the eighteenth and early nineteenth centuries, grave markers. The traces of African routedness can be readily uncovered in these most banal of examples. Recognizably black graves in Britain from the period before the abolition of slavery in the colonies are relatively rare and were usually erected by white owners or masters. As such, their meaning is often as much about the erectors of the memorial as it is about the memorialized. They demonstrate the Christian piety of the owner, who enshrines his own humanity in a gesture of inclusivity to his former slave or servant. Thus, the gravestone of Charles Bacchus (an African) in Culworth churchyard, Northamptonshire, reads:

> Died March 31, 1762. He was belov'd and Lamented by the
> Family he Serv'd was Grateful and Humane and gave hopes of
> Proving a faithful Servant and a Good Man. Aged 16. Here titles
> cease. Ambitions o'er. And Slave or Monarch no more. The
> good alone will find in Heav'n Rewards assign'd and Honours
> giv'n. (Butler, 1999: 22)

Bacchus is posthumously given hope of advancement in an afterlife that might elevate him beyond his earthly role. There he will be judged equally with reference to his soul's virtue rather than his chattel status. His owner's 'generosity of spirit' is a facile gesture, which costs him the price of a stonemason and does not affect master–slave relations in this world. Bacchus's grave site, though, has resonances beyond his master's control, for it shows the trace of a black presence in mid-eighteenth-century rural Britain that problematizes the idea of a homogeneous Anglo-Saxon Britain. This presence is also attested to by country-house family portraits that often contained a black servant as a semiotic signal of the sitters' wealth created far away in the colonies (Dabydeen, 1985). Similarly, the grave of Samuel Ally near Douglas on the Isle of Man marks out the conspicuous imperial wealth of his master Colonel Mark Wilks, who had been governor of St Helena during Napoleon's exile there. Samuel Ally was a slave on the island whom Wilks emancipated and brought back to the Isle of Man as a servant. He did not thrive and was dead by 1822 at the age of 18. The memorial stone traces Ally's early slave life and his transformation into 'a model of TRUTH and PROBITY'. Ally's brief black presence on the Isle of Man foregrounds the island's links with the slave trade, which had been at their height in the mid-eighteenth century when Liverpool and Lancaster slavers stopped off to load illegal duty-free Rotterdam cloths and Manx maritime tradition provided captains and crew members for the trade, including one of its most famous exponents, Captain Hugh Crow. Ally's grave is a physical marker of a history that until Frances Wilkins's (1999) timely work was buried in the footnotes of history.

Another intriguing grave site highlights the lineage of a black family in eighteenth-century Scotland and was erected, not by a white master but by a black son. Located in Kirkoswald churchyard in Ayrshire, the gravestone of Scipio and Douglas Kennedy reads: 'This stone is erected by Douglas Kennedy in Memory of his Father Scipio Kennedy who died June 24 1774 Aged 80 years. Also here lieth the body of said Douglas Kennedy who died July 21 1781 aged 49 years' (Denning, 1997: 26). Scipio's biography, in common with many others in these pages, exemplifies the routedness of African lives during the slave trade. Captured in Guinea as a six-year-old around 1700, he was taken to the West Indies and only saved from a life as a plantation slave through his chance purchase by Captain Andrew Douglas of Mains in Dumbartonshire. Taken back to Scotland in 1702, he was eventually passed on to

Douglas's daughter Jean, who married John Kennedy, the future tenant of Culzean Castle, Ayrshire. It is as a slave to this couple that Scipio became a Christian before eventually being awarded his freedom in 1725. Two years later, revelling in his freedom, he indulged in 'fornication' with Margaret Gray, which eventually led to the birth of a daughter, Sarah, in 1728. He married Margaret later that year and had several other children, all of whom took the name of Kennedy. The family continued to live in the environs of the castle with Scipio, now a paid servant to the Kennedy lairds (*ibid.*: 26). This mixed-race Kennedy family attests to the presence of Scottish diasporan Africans in the very heartland of Burns country. Of course, one should not be surprised by such a presence, as Scots were at the centre of the slave trade, often serving as factors on West Indian estates. Indeed, in 1786, the national poet Burns was himself on the verge of leaving to find his fortune as an overseer in Jamaica when the success of his first book made him 'exchange a future as a poor Negro-driver in the Caribbean ... [to] head for the "new world" of literary Edinburgh' (quoted in Pettinger, 1999: 53). Involved in the intricate network of the transatlantic trade like their neighbours in England, it is hardly surprising that occasionally they brought their African servants back with them, whose settlement problematizes a story of national and racial homogeneity. As Mary Denning speculates on Scipio's descendants:

> And what of his children, half Scottish, half African, and living
> under the name of Kennedy? Did they marry and have children
> of their own? Is Scipio's line in existence today? Perhaps there
> are Kennedys in Ayrshire even now who are not from the noble
> family of Kennedy, descended from Robert the Bruce, but
> instead are a living testament of one small child stolen from his
> home in Africa 300 years ago. (Denning, 1997: 26)

Despite the path-breaking research of writers like Denning and curators like Polly Rewt, whose 1997 exhibition *Africa in Scotland* brought together a wealth of documentary and pictorial evidence of longstanding links, African presences are continually omitted from Scottish national consciousness in the most prestigious museum spaces. Thus, the new galleries of the National Museum of Scotland, which claim to tell the story of Scotland from prehistoric times to the present, inevitably deal with the tobacco and other colonial trades which made the wealth that created a modern industrial Scotland in the nineteenth and early twentieth centuries; however, there is no mention of the mode by which that wealth was created – slave labour in the Americas by imported Africans. Scottish entanglement in the world of slave trading is exemplified best by the grotesque parody of the national game of golf played on a short course on Bunce Island off Sierra Leone in the 1770s by visiting captains and European factors. As David Hancock in his brilliant *Citizens of the World* (1995) relates, 'the caddies were slaves in kilts' (Hancock, 1995: 10).

This collective amnesia, which seeks to glorify a radical Scottish past of racial democracy, obscures the contribution to British slavery of Scottish merchant entrepreneurs, sea captains and crew, planters and overseers, exemplified in these pages by James Irving and his nephew and the cruel Scots-Jamaican planter James Wedderburn. During a visit to Scotland in the 1990s, Maya Angelou, in the tradition of her great forebear Frederick Douglass, praised Scottish contributions to racial democracy encapsulated in Robert Burns's famous expression 'A Man's a Man for all that'; in a panegyric to Burns in a BBC documentary *Angelou on Burns*, she lauded his contribution to a discourse of transatlantic freedom:

> The battle for freedom ... from Birmingham, Alabama, to
> Birmingham, Britain, from Dumfries, Scotland, to Dunbar,
> Ohio ... it is because of my identification with Robert Burns,
> with Wallace, with the people of Scotland for their dignity, for
> their independence, for their humanity, that I can see how we
> sing, 'We Shall Overcome'. (quoted in Taylor, 2001: 189)

Unfortunately, this radical linkage belies a more complex Scottish heritage and exemplifies an African-American 'Celtophilia'; for like Douglass before her, Angelou was reticent to foreground Scottish contributions to the peculiar institution, and Scottish commentators were (and sometimes still are) on the whole content to collude in this elision. Memorials like that to Scipio Kennedy cut across such collective amnesia and as such should be highlighted in general exhibitions of Scottish history, so they are no longer marginalized and posited as peripheral to the national story.

Scipio Kennedy's memorial stone at Culzean attests to a full life despite the debilitating, exploitative practices of the middle passage. A gravestone that perhaps memorializes black Atlantic loss even more poignantly is that of the adolescent Sambo, which can be found at the mouth of the Lune Estuary near Sunderland Point (Figure 13). According to *The Lonsdale Magazine* of 1822, he had arrived in around 1736 from the West Indies in the capacity of a servant to the captain of the ship (to this day unnamed):

> After she had discharged her cargo, he was placed at the
> inn ... with the intention of remaining there on board wages till
> the vessel was ready to sail; but supposing himself to be deserted
> by the master, without being able, probably from his ignorance
> of the language, to ascertain the cause, he fell into a complete
> state of stupefaction, even to such a degree that he secreted
> himself in the loft on the brewhouses and stretching himself out
> at full length on the bare boards refused all sustenance. He
> continued in this state only a few days, when death terminated
> the sufferings of poor Samboo. As soon as Samboo's exit was
> known to the sailors who happened to be there, they excavated
> him a grave in a lonely dell in a rabbit warren behind the village,
> within twenty yards of the sea shore, whither they conveyed his
> remains without either coffin or bier, being covered only with
> the clothes in which he died. (J. T., 1822: 190)

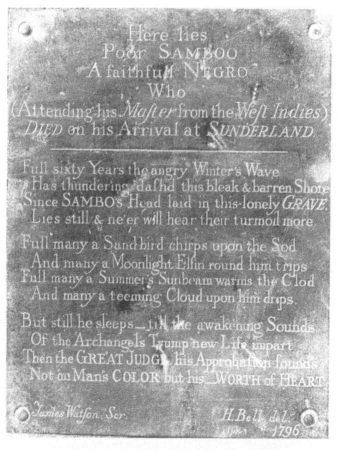

Figure 13 Sambo's grave, Sunderland Point, Lancaster. Photo: Denis Wilkins. Reproduced by permission of Denis Wilkins.

Sambo was buried in such a lonely grave because he had not been baptized, and thus had to be laid to rest in unconsecrated ground. Like most Africans arriving in Britain as 'servants' (usually slaves), he appeared to suffer a profound sense of culture shock once ashore among strangers with whom he could not communicate. There has been much speculation about the cause of his death, ranging from the pragmatic (pneumonia) to the sentimental (profound homesickness). The latter provided the grist for anti-slavery panegyrics such as the Reverend James Watson's 1796 elegy, which was eventually appended to a brass plate on a freestone slab at the site itself. Watson collected the money for the memorial from visitors to the Point. His interest in the slave's grave is not without irony, however, as his brother was a leading light in the Lancaster slave trade. The tone of the memorial is sentimental in the extreme, praising Sambo as a 'faithful Negro' who had died because of his 'service' to his master. The memorial has many implications for the late-eighteenth-century construction of an anti-slavery sentiment that elided Africans as actors in their own struggles precisely at the time of the San Domingo uprising, which exemplified a dynamic revolutionary African diasporan tradition. African agency is downplayed by such a discourse, and a character like Sambo is saved from obliquity by the workings of English sentiment long after it can do him any practical good.

However, it is not its meaning to an eighteenth-century audience which I want to tease out here, but the way in which the memorial has been an important site for remembering the horrors of slavery over two hundred years later. Lancaster has never really come to terms with its status as Britain's fourth largest slave port, from where over 180 voyages were made in the mid-eighteenth century, the consequent slave trade contributing greatly to the wealth of the city and its inhabitants (Elder, 2001). It is not only the direct slave trade which indicates the interweaving of Lancaster with the slave economy but also its trade in goods produced and harvested by slaves, such as rice, cotton, sugar and particularly mahogany, which made the fortune of the Gillows furniture company in the eighteenth century (Sartin, 2001). As in many British slave ports, there is widespread amnesia about the slave trade: in Lancaster, for instance, there is no specific memorial to those who were affected by the trade that originated in the city itself (probably at least 5000 dead and over 30,000 transported). The new Millennium Bridge, recently opened in early 2001, could have been named in commemoration of a Lancaster slave, as is the case with as Pero's Bridge in Bristol; however, such a memorializing of the trade was never even debated, despite reflecting Lancaster's seaborne trade in its spectacular design that evokes a ship's rigging.

To an extent, Sambo's grave provides a memorial touchstone, despite its lonely isolation many miles from the city itself. This is confirmed by a recent phenomenon, in which schoolchildren have been leaving coloured and painted stones inscribed with messages for Sambo to accompany the marker stones and flowers left by adult visitors. The grave has become alive with colour and resembles African and African-American graves with their relics of the dead placed over the body (Figure 14). Sambo is now remembered, but how? There is a sense in which the schoolchildren's bathetic messages – 'I made this for you Sambo, love from Hayley' (with a picture of a ship), 'Rest in Peace Sambo, Margaret and Pauline' (with a picture of a bridge and the Lune) and 'Sambo as promised, Kirsty' (abstract coloured stone) – could be interpreted as just an extension of the Reverend Watson's sentimentality imbued by the infants from an over-enthusiastic liberal schoolteacher. I prefer not to be so cynical. Without memorial sites, memorialization is problematic, especially in such a contested terrain as Britain's slave past, and Sambo's grave gives all Lancastrians an opportunity to remember without being guided by museum curators or politicians on the make. Its very isolation with views across the sea means it serendipitously places visitors at the point of arrival and departure for the ships which had taken part in the trade. Lubaina Himid has talked of such spaces, describing the importance of the beach as a border zone, 'a site of pleasure and absolute conflict and division' (Himid, 2001). Her contention, that the beach cannot be an incontestably utopian space in the context of a transatlantic slave trade that began its horrors on West Africa's golden beaches, points to the presence of conflict and division from the moment of first contact between African and European cultures. The grave negotiates Himid's stark binaries, as a pleasant walk across the tidal bridleway, with its wonderful views back to land and out to sea, is interrupted by the chilling reminder of the more sinister seaborne exigencies that international trade has fostered.

James E. Young, in talking about the open-air memorial to the Holocaust in Lincoln Park, San Francisco, designed by George Segal and installed in 1982, regrets the way the scattered bodies of the victims 'become part of the great outdoors', thus, in his view, undermining its impact as a memorial space by making them 'too much part of the present moment' (Young, 1992: 64). For me, though, the real world intruding on memorial space can sharpen its impact. Life going on in all its banality sharpens the grief of lives cut short by exploitation and genocide.

The appropriateness of the schoolchildren's gestures of memorialization is emphasized by an earlier memorial left at the grave in the mid-1990s. A Ghanaian visitor, struck by the fact that Sambo would have originally come from West Africa, left a carved statuette on the grave to link Sambo to his homeland. Less appropriately, another visitor has left a crucifixion, which is highly ironic in light of the fact that Sambo's body was buried on unconsecrated ground. The landscaping of the grave changes as visitors leave different tokens, making it an extremely dynamic *lieu de mémoire*. I would contend that malleable sites like this make the most effective memorials to those who died in the slave trade. Erected not by civic guilt or sustained by false ideologies of a slave-freeing British imperium, it takes on a life of its own, sustained by what Pierre Nora would call our 'commemorative vigilance' (Nora, 1994: 289) that guards against amnesia. Nora has the perfect symbol for such a coastal site: 'moments of history torn away from the movement of history, then returned; no longer quite life, not yet death, like shells on the shore when the sea of living memory has receded' (*ibid.*).

Watson's eighteenth-century plaque, its vandalism and replacement, the crucifix and African statue, flowers placed, dying and replaced and finally the children's coloured stones all build a bricolage of memory that rescues Sambo from the obliquity traditional historiography had reduced him to. In visiting his grave, we remember and memorialize (as far as we ever can) Sambo and slavery, but, more pertinently, we realize how fragile these memories are, plucked from obscurity by guilt and historical chance. Nancy Wood reminds us that 'analysis must embrace not only memories that achieve public articulation, but those that are denied expression or recognition, as well as those memories that are displaced or merely alluded to' (Wood, 1999: 10). Wood describes how such *lieux d'oubli* (sometimes embodying a literal 'organisation of forgetting' [*ibid.*]) can be transformed by social and political activism into *lieux de mémoire*, and Sambo's grave is a prime example of such a phenomenon (*ibid.*), gaining much of its power as a site because of its minor status and local scale. Enslaved Africans dispersed throughout the Atlantic triangle are most effectively remembered at such local sites that conjure up their thoroughly routed existence.

Sambo's tragic biography and creolized name posit an eighteenth-century reactionary sentimentality which is overlaid by a twenty-first-century pilgrimage that remembers him as representative of the lives wasted in the exchange of bodies for goods. As such, Sambo's grave is atypical, being a physical memory of black British historical presence in an environment where the memories of such bodies are usually hidden. His grave can only perform as a radical narrative of the black Atlantic by the force of our memorializing activity. By performing his memorialization, however, we disavow the silence his grave could be said more properly to bear witness to – a fitting and mute commentary on the sacrifice of bodies to the greed of the slave traders. A mute voice speaks, but only as we ventriloquize it, and surely that makes the memorialization successful mainly for ourselves.

Black figures have chain-danced to freedom throughout this study, from Olaudah Equiano and Mary Prince, who escaped from slavery to literary radicalism, through Shine on the *Titanic* and Lubaina Himid's seaborne African women to Paul D. in Toni Morrison's *Beloved*. Finally, though, we are confronted with the stasis of a grave site located a long way from home which encapsulates the reality of the black Atlantic for all too many diasporan Africans. In praising the radicalism of this study's heroes and heroines – chaindancing to freedom – we must bear witness to the countless thousands whose chains barely danced, most of whom have no memorials. At Sambo's grave, however inadequately, we remember them all.

BIBLIOGRAPHY

Abbot, Lynn and Seroff, Doug (1996). ' "They Certl'y Sounded Good to Me": Sheet Music, Southern Vaudeville and the Commercial Ascendancy of the Blues', *American Music* Winter: 402–53.

Abrahams, Roger D. (1970) *Deep down in the Jungle: Negro Narrative Folklore from the Streets of Philadelphia*. Chicago: Aldine.

Abrahams, Roger and Szwed, John (eds) (1983). *After Africa: Extracts from British Travel Accounts and Journals of the Seventeenth, Eighteenth and Nineteenth Centuries Concerning the Slaves, Their Manners, and Customs in the British West Indies*. New Haven, CT: Yale University Press.

Adams, Robert (1999). *The Narrative of Robert Adams: A Sailor Who Was Wrecked on the Western Coast of Africa, in the Year 1810 ... White Slaves, African Masters: An Anthology of American Barbary Captivity Narratives*, ed. Paul Baepler. Chicago: University of Chicago Press, pp. 208–45.

Alexander, Ziggi (1986). Preface, in Mary Prince, *The History of Mary Prince: A West Indian Slave*. 1831, ed. Moira Ferguson. London: Pandora Press, pp. vii–xiii.

Aravamudan, Srivinas (1999). *Tropicopolitans: Colonialism and Agency, 1688–1804*. Durham NC: Duke University Press.

Archer, Rosemary, Pearson, Colin and Covey, Cecil (1978). *The Crabbet Arabian Stud: Its History and Influence*. Northleach, Gloucestershire: Alexander Heriot and Co.

Arens, W. (1979) *The Man-eating Myth: Anthropology and Anthropophagy*. Oxford: Oxford University Press.

Armstrong, Louis (1983). *Greatest Hits*. LP. CBS.

Ashcraft-Eason, Lillian (2000). ' "She Voluntarily Hath Come": A Gambian Woman Trader in Colonial Georgia in the Eighteenth Century', in Paul E. Lovejoy (ed.), *Identity in the Shadow of Slavery*. London: Continuum, pp. 202–21.

Atkins, John (1735). *A Voyage to Guinea, Brasil and the West Indies in His Majesty's Ships the* Swallow *and the* Weymouth. London: C. Ward and R. Chandler.

Austin, Allan D. (1995) *African Muslims in Antebellum America: Trans-atlantic Stories and Spiritual Struggles*, abridged edn. London: Routledge.

Ayler, Albert (1967). 'Truth Is Marching In', *Albert Ayler in Greenwich Village*. LP. Jasmine.

Baepler, Paul (ed.) (1999). *White Slaves, African Masters: An Anthology of American Barbary Captivity Narratives*. Chicago: University of Chicago Press.

Baker, Houston A., Jr (1987). *Blues, Ideology and Afro-American Literature*. Chicago: University of Chicago Press.

Bakhtin, Mikhail M. (1981) *The Dialogic Imagination: Four Essays by M. M. Bakhtin*, ed. Michael Holquist, trans. Caryl Emerson and Michael Holquist. Austin: University of Texas Press.

Baldwin, James (1985a). *Evidence of Things Not Seen*. New York: Henry Holt and Co.

Baldwin, James (1985b). *The Price of the Ticket: Collected Non-Fiction 1948–1985*. New York: St Martin's.

Bambara, Toni Cade (1992). Preface, in Julie Dash, *Daughters of the Dust: The Making of an American Film*. New York: New Press, pp. xi–xvi.

Baquaqua, Mahommah G. (1998) 'Biography of Mahommah G. Baquaqua, a Native of Zoogoo in the Interior of Africa', in Alasdair Pettinger, *Always Elsewhere: Travels of the Black Atlantic*. London: Cassell, pp. 22–8.

Baraka, Amiri (a.k.a. Leroi Jones) (1963). *Blues People*. New York: Morrow.

Baraka, Amiri (n.d.). *Paul Robeson*, Newark, NJ: self-printed.

Barber, John W. (1840) *A History of the Amistad Captives*. New Haven, CT: E. L. and J. W. Barber.

Bartolovich, Crystal (1998). 'Consumerism, or the Cultural Logic of Late Cannibalism', in Francis Barker, Peter Hulme and Margaret Iverson (eds), *Cannibalism in the Colonial World*. Cambridge: Cambridge University Press, 204–37.

Beckles, Hilary McD. (2000) 'Female Enslavement in the Caribbean and Gender Ideologies', in Paul E. Lovejoy (ed.), *Identity in the Shadow of Slavery*. London: Continuum, pp. 163–82.

Berliner, Paul (1995). *Thinking in Jazz*. Chicago: Chicago University Press.

Bhabha, Homi (1986). 'Signs Taken for Wonders: Questions of Ambivalence and Authority under a Tree Outside Delhi, May 1817', *Critical Inquiry* 12(1): 144–65.

Bhabha, Homi (1991). 'The Post-Colonial Critic', *Arena* 96: 47–63.

Bhabha, Homi (1994). *The Location of Culture*. London: Routledge.

Biel, Steven (1996). *Down with the Old Canoe: A Cultural History of the Titanic*. New York: W. W. Norton.

Birth of a Nation (1915). Dir. D. W. Griffith. Epoch.

Blackburn, Robin (1998). *The Making of New World Slavery: From the Baroque to the Modern 1492–1800*. London: Verso.

Blackett, Richard J. M. (1983) *Building an Anti-Slavery Wall: Black Americans in the Atlantic Abolition Movement, 1830–1860*. Baton Rouge: Louisiana University Press.

Blessinghame, John W. (ed.) (1979) *The Frederick Douglass Papers. Series*

One: Speeches, Debates and Interviews, Vol. 2. New Haven: Yale University Press.

Blunt, Lady Anne (1881). *A Pilgrimage to Nejd.* London: John Murray.

Blunt, Lady Anne (1986). *Journals and Correspondence 1878–1917.* Cheltenham: Alexander Heriot and Co.

Blyth, Robert (2001). 'Tour of Empire and Trade Galleries'. National Maritime Museum, Greenwich, 10 March.

Bobo, Jacqueline (1998). *Black Women Film and Video Artists.* London: Routledge.

Boime, Albert (1990). *The Art of Exclusion: Representing Blacks in the Nineteenth Century.* Washington: Smithsonian Institution Press.

Bolster, Jeffrey (1997). *Black Jacks: African American Seamen in the Age of Sail.* Cambridge, MA: Harvard University Press.

Boucher, Philip P. (1987) *Cannibal Encounters: Europeans and Island Caribs 1492–1763.* Baltimore: The Johns Hopkins University Press.

Brathwaite, Edward (later Kamau) (1973). *The Arrivants: A New World Trilogy.* Oxford: Oxford University Press.

Brathwaite, Kamau (1999). *Conversations with Nathaniel Mackey.* New York: We Press and Xcp: Cross-Cultural Poetics.

Bride, Harold (1999). 'This Kind of a Time', *New York Times*, 19 April 1912, in John Wilson Foster (ed.), *Titanic.* Harmondsworth: Penguin, pp. 127–33.

Brock, Sabine (1999). *White Amnesia – Black Memory? American Women's Writing and History.* Frankfurt: Peter Lang.

Brown, William Wells (1991). *The American Fugitive in Europe: Sketches of Places and People Abroad. 1855. The Travels of William Wells Brown,* ed. Paul Jefferson. Edinburgh: Edinburgh University Press.

Bryant, Sd. J. (1991) 'PRO HO 42/195, Hopkins Street Chapel, [9 August 1819]', in Ian McCalman (ed.), *The Horrors of Slavery and Other Writings.* Edinburgh: Edinburgh University Press, 114–15.

Bulsterbaum, Alison (1984). ' "Sugarman Gone Home": Folksong in Toni Morrison's *Song of Solomon*', *Papers of the Arkansas Philological Association* 10: 15–28.

Butler, Helen (1999). Letter, *Black and Asian Studies Association Newsletter* 25 (September): 22.

Callahan, John F. (1996) Introduction, in Ralph Ellison, *Flying Home and Other Stories.* New York: Vintage, pp. ix–xxxviii.

Camp, Sokari Douglas (1995). *Play and Display: Steel Masquerades from Top to Toe,* exhibition catalogue. London: British Museum.

'A Capitalist Disaster' (1999). Editorial, *Appeal to Reason* (Kansas), 4 May 1912, in John Wilson Foster (ed.), *Titanic.* Harmondsworth: Penguin, pp. 165–7.

Carlyle, Thomas (1964). 'Occasional Discourse on the Nigger Question.' In *English and Other Essays.* London: Dent (first published 1853).

Carretta, Vincent (ed.) (1996). *Unchained Voices: An Anthology of Black Voices in the English-Speaking World of the Eighteenth Century.* Lexington: The University Press of Kentucky.

Carretta, Vincent (1999). 'Olaudah Equiano or Gustavus Vassa? New Light on an Eighteenth-Century Question of Identity', *Slavery and Abolition* 20(3): 96–105.

Carrington, Ben (2000). 'Double-Consciousness and the Black British Athlete', in Kwesi Owusu (ed.), *Black British Culture and Society: A Text Reader*. London: Routledge, pp. 133–56.

Cheyfitz, Eric (1991). *The Poetics of Imperialism: Translation and Colonization from The Tempest to Tarzan of the Apes*. Oxford: Oxford University Press.

Chrisman, Laura (2000). 'Journeying to Death: Gilroy's Black Atlantic', in Kwesi Owusu (ed.), *Black British Culture and Society: A Text Reader*. London: Routledge, pp. 133–56.

Clarke, Deborah L. (1993) ' "What There Was before Language": Preliteracy in Toni Morrison's *Song of Solomon*', in Carol J. Singley and Susan Elizabeth Sweeney (eds), *Anxious Power*. Albany: State University of New York Press, pp. 265–78.

Clifford, James (1988). *The Predicament of Culture: Twentieth-Century Ethnography, Literature and Art*. London: Harvard University Press.

Cohn, Michael and Platzer, Michael K. H. (1978). *Black Men of the Sea*. New York: Dodd, Mead and Company.

Columbus, Christopher (1994). *Journal of the First Voyage to America 1492–1493*. *Heath Anthology of American Literature Volume One*, ed. Paul Lauter and Richard Yarborough *et al*. Lexington, MA: D. C. Heath, pp. 117–25.

Conneau, Theophilus (1976). *A Slaver's Log Book or 20 Years Residence in Africa*. Englewood Cliffs, NJ: Prentice Hall (first published 1853).

Cooke, Michael G (1984). *Afro-American Literature in the Twentieth Century: The Achievement of Intimacy*. New Haven: Yale University Press.

Cornish, Samuel (1838). Editorial, *Colored American*, 9 June, n.p.

Coser, Stelamaris (1994). *Bridging the Americas: The Literature of Paule Marshall, Toni Morrison, and Gayl Jones*. Philadelphia: Temple University Press.

Costanzo, Angelo (1987). *Surprising Narrative: Olaudah Equiano and the Beginning of Black Autobiography*. New York: Greenwood Press.

Cowley, Julian (1988). 'The Art of the Improvisers: Jazz and Fiction in Post-Bebop America', *New Comparison* 6: 194–204.

Cugoano, Quobna Ottobah (1999). *Thoughts and Sentiments on the Evil of Slavery and Other Writings*, ed. Vincent Carretta. Harmondsworth: Penguin (first published 1787).

Dabydeen, David (1985). *Hogarth's Blacks: Images of Blacks in Eighteenth-Century English Art*. Coventry: Dangaroo.

Dabydeen, David (1994). *Turner*. London: Cape.

Dance, Daryl Cumber (1978). *Shuckin' and Jivin': Folklore from Contemporary Black Americans*. Bloomington: Indiana University Press.

Dannatt, Adrian (2001). Obituary of Michael Richards, *Independent*, Monday Review, 24 September, p. 6.

Dash, Julie (1992). *Daughters of the Dust: The Making of an American Film*. New York: New Press.

Daughters of the Dust (1992). Dir. Julie Dash. Screen Actors Guild.

Davidson, Basil (1968). *Black Mother: Africa, the Years of Trial*. London: Victor Gollancz.

Davie, Michael (1999). 'The Starting Point', in John Wilson Foster (ed.), *Titanic*. Harmondsworth: Penguin, pp. 5–9.

Davies, Jude and Smith, Carol (1998). *Gender, Ethnicity and Sexuality in Contemporary American Film*. Edinburgh: Edinburgh University Press, BAAS Paperback.

Dawes, Kwame (1999). 'Negotiating the Ship on the Head: Black British Fiction', *Wasafiri* 29 (Spring): 18–24.

De Weever, Jacqueline (1980). 'Toni Morrison's Use of Fairy Tale, Folk Tale and Myth in *Song of Solomon*', *Southern Folklore Quarterly* 44: 131–44.

Defoe, Daniel (1982). *Robinson Crusoe*. New York: Penguin (first published 1719).

Delgado, Richard and Stefancic, Jean (eds) (1997). *Critical White Studies*. Philadelphia: Temple University Press.

Denning, Mary (1997). 'Culzean's Child of the Sun', *Heritage Scotland* 14(3): 26.

Diedrich, Maria (1999). *Love across Color Lines: Ottilie Assing and Frederick Douglass*. New York: Hill and Wang.

Diedrich, Maria, Gates, Henry Louis Jr and Pedersen, Carl (1999). *Black Imagination and the Middle Passage*. Oxford: Oxford University Press.

Dixon Gottschild, Brenda (1996). *Digging the Africanist Presence in American Performance: Dance and Other Contexts*. Westport, CT: Greenwood Press.

Donnan, Elizabeth (1969). *Documents Illustrative of the History of the Slave Trade to America*, 4 vols. New York: Octagon (first published 1935).

Douglas, Ann (1997). *Terrible Honesty: Mongrel Manhattan in the 1920s*. London: Macmillan.

Douglass, Frederick (1969). *My Bondage and My Freedom*, ed. Philip S. Foner. New York: Dover (first published 1855).

Douglass, Frederick (1986). *Narrative of the Life of an American Slave, Written by Himself*, ed. Houston A. Baker Jr. Harmondsworth: Penguin (first published 1845).

Dow, George F. (ed) (1927) *Slave Ships and Slaving*. Cambridge, MD: Cornell Maritime Press.

Doyle, Laura (1994). *Bordering on the Body: The Racial Matrix of Modern Fiction and Culture*. Oxford: Oxford University Press.

Dresser, Madge (2001). *Slavery Obscured: The Social History of the Slave Trade in a Provincial Port*. London: Continuum.

Du Bois, W. E. B. (1965) *The Souls of Black Folk: Three Negro Classics*, ed. John Hope Franklin. New York: Avon, pp. 209–389 (first published 1903).

Duberman, Martin (1989). *Paul Robeson: A Biography*. New York: Random House.

Dundes, Alan (ed.) (1976). *Motherwit from the Laughing Barrell: Readings from the Interpretation of Afro-American Folklore*. Englewood Cliffs, NJ: Prentice Hall.

Dyer, Richard (1997). *White*. London: Routledge.

Dyson, Michael (1998). 'Be Like Mike: Michael Jordan and the Pedagogy of Desire', in Robert G. O'Meally, *The Jazz Cadence of American Culture*. New York: Columbia University Press, 372–80.

Edwards, Paul (ed.) (1967). *Equiano's Travels*. London: Heinemann.

Elder, Melinda (1992). *The Slave Trade and the Economic Development of 18th-Century Lancaster*. Keele, Staffordshire: Ryburn Press.

Elder, Melinda (2001). 'Lancaster and the Slave Trade', *Transatlantic Slave Sites Tour*. Lancaster Maritime Museum, 6 March.

Elliot, E. N. (1969) *Cotton Is King and Pro-Slavery Arguments*. New York: Negro University Press (first published 1860).

Ellison, Ralph (1965). *Invisible Man*. Harmondsworth: Penguin (first published 1952).

Ellison, Ralph (1972). *Shadow and Act*. New York: Vintage.

Ellison, Ralph (1996). *Flying Home and Other Stories*. New York: Vintage (first published 1944).

Epstein, Dena (1977). *Sinful Tunes and Spirituals*. Urbana: University of Illinois Press.

Equiano, Olaudah (1995). *The Interesting Narrative and Other Writings*, ed. Vincent Carretta. Harmondsworth: Penguin (first published 1789).

Eschen, Penny M. Von ((1996). *Race against Empire: Black Americans and Anticolonialism 1937–1957*. Ithaca, NY: Cornell University Press.

Eustace, Revd Chetwode (1991). 'PRO HO 42/191 [10 August 1819],' in Ian McCalman (ed.), *The Horrors of Slavery and Other Writings*. Edinburgh: Edinburgh University Press, pp. 116–17.

Fabre, Genevieve (1999). 'The Slave Ship Dance', in Maria Diedrich, Henry Louis Gates Jr and Carl Pedersen (eds), *Black Imagination and the Middle Passage*. Oxford: Oxford University Press.

Fabre, Genevieve and O'Meally, Robert (eds) (1994). *History and Memory in African American Culture*. Oxford: Oxford University Press.

Fanon, Frantz (1970). *Black Skin, White Masks*. London: Paladin (first published 1952).

Feelings, Tom (1995). *The Middle Passage: White Ships, Black Cargo*. East Rutherford, NJ: Dial.

Ferguson, Moira (1992). *Subject to Others: British Women Writers and Colonial Slavery, 1670–1834*. London: Routledge.

Fisch, Audrey (2000). *American Slaves in Victorian England*. Cambridge: Cambridge University Press.

Fitzhugh, George (1960). *Cannibals All! or Slaves Without Masters*. Cambridge, MA: Harvard University Press (first published 1857).

Floyd, Samuel A. Jr (1995). *The Power of Black Music: Interpreting Its History from Africa to the United States*. New York: Oxford University Press.

Foster, John Wilson (ed.) (1999). *Titanic*. Harmondsworth: Penguin.

Fredrickson, George M. (1971) *The Black Image in the White Mind: The Debate on Afro-American Character and Destiny, 1827–1914*. New York: Harper and Row.

Frey, Sylvia (1991). *Water from the Rock: Black Resistance in a Revolutionary Age*. Princeton, NJ: Princeton University Press.

Frey, Silvia and Wood, Betty (eds) (1999). *From Slavery to Emancipation in the Atlantic World*. London: Frank Cass.

Fryer, Peter (1984). *Staying Power: The History of Black People in Britain*. London: Pluto.

Gaither, Bill (1998). 'Champ Joe Louis', in Patricia Liggins Hill (ed.), *Call and Response: The Riverside Anthology of the African American Literary Tradition*. New York: Houghton Mifflin, p. 811.

Garlake, Margaret (2000). 'Tate Trials', *Art Monthly* 238 (July–August): 6–9.

Gaspar, David Barry (1993). *Bondsmen and Rebels: A Study of Master–Slave Relations in Antigua*. Durham, NC: Duke University Press (first published 1985).

Gates, Henry Louis, Jr (1987). *Figures in Black: Words, Signs and the 'Racial' Self*. Oxford: Oxford University Press.

Gates, Henry Louis, Jr (1988). *The Signifying Monkey: A Theory of Literary Criticism*. New York: Oxford University Press.

Gates, Henry Louis, Jr (1992). *Loose Canons: Notes on the Culture Wars*. Oxford: Oxford University Press.

Gates, Henry Louis, Jr and McKay, Nellie Y. (eds) (1997) *The Norton Anthology of African American Literature*. New York: W. W. Norton.

'The Genius of the Anglo-Saxon' (1999) *Belfast Telegraph* 1 June 1911, quoted in John Wilson Foster (ed.), *Titanic*. Harmondsworth: Penguin, pp. 254–5.

Georgia Writers' Project, Savannah Unit (1986). *Drums and Shadows: Survival Studies among the Georgia Coastal Negroes*. Athens: University of Georgia Press (first published 1940).

Gerzina, Gretchen (1995). *Black England: Life before Emancipation*. London: John Murray.

Gibson-Hudson, Gloria J. (1998) 'The Ties That Bind: Cinematic Representations by Black Women Filmmakers', in Jacqueline Bobo (ed.), *Black Women Film and Video Artists*. London: Routledge, pp. 43–66.

Gilman, Sander L. (1986) *Difference and Pathology: Stereotypes of Sexuality, Race and Madness*. Ithaca, NY: Cornell University Press.

Gilroy, Paul (1988). 'Living Memory: Toni Morrison Talks to Paul Gilroy', *City Limits*, 31 March, pp. 11–12.

Gilroy, Paul (1993a). *The Black Atlantic: Modernity and Double Consciousness*. London: Verso.

Gilroy, Paul (1993b). *Small Acts: Thoughts on the Politics of Black Culture*. London: Serpent's Tail.

Gilroy, Paul (2000). *Between Camps: Nations, Race, Identity and Nationalism at the End of the Colour Line*. London: Allen Lane.

Glissant, Edouard (1989). *Caribbean Discourse: Selected Essays*. trans. J. Michael Dash. Charlottesville: University of Virginia Press (first published in French 1981).

Goldman, Anne E. (1990) ' "I Made the Ink": (Literary) Production and Reproduction in *Dessa Rose* and *Beloved*', *Feminist Studies* 16: 313–28.

Granger, Mary (1986). Introduction, in Georgia Writers' Project, Savannah Unit, *Drums and Shadows: Survival Studies among the Georgia Coastal*

Degrees. Athens: University of Georgia Press, pp. xli–xliv (first published 1940).

Griffith, C. A. (1998). 'Below the Line: (Re)Calibrating the Filmic Gaze', in Jacqueline Bobo (ed.), *Black Women Film and Video Artists*. London: Routledge, pp. 153–73.

Gubar, Susan (1997). *Racechanges: White Skin, Black Face in American Culture*. New York and Oxford: Oxford University Press.

Guerrero, Ed (1993). *Framing Blackness: The African American Image in Film*. Philadelphia: Temple University Press.

Haley, Alex (1976). *Roots*. Garden City, NY: Doubleday.

Hall, Catherine (1992). *White, Male and Middle Class: Explorations in Feminist History*. London: Polity.

Hall, Diana Midlo (1992). *Africans in Colonial Louisiana: The Development of Afro-Creole Culture in the Eighteenth Century*. Baton Rouge: Louisiana University Press.

Hamilton, Cynthia S. (1996) 'Revisions, Rememories and Exorcisms: Toni Morrison and the Slave Narrative', *Journal of American Studies* 30: 429–45.

Hancock, David (1995). *Citizens of the World: London Merchants and the Integration of the British Atlantic Community 1733–1785*. Cambridge: Cambridge University Press.

Harper, Michael (2000). *Songlines in Michaeltree: New and Collected Poems*. Urbana: University of Illinois Press.

Harris, Cheryl (1998). 'Whiteness as Property', in David Roediger (ed.), *Black on White: Black Writers on What It Means to Be White*. New York: Shocken Books, 103–18.

Harris, William J. (1985) *The Poetry and Poetics of Amiri Baraka: The Jazz Aesthetic*. Columbia: University of Missouri Press.

Harris, Wilson (1999). 'History, Fable and Myth in the Caribbean and the Guianas', in Andrew Bundy (ed.), *Selected Essays of Wilson Harris*. New York: Routledge, 152–66.

Hawthorne, Evelyn (1988). 'On Gaining the Double-Vision: *Tar Baby* as Diasporean Novel', *Black American Literature Forum* 22: 97–107.

Hayden, Robert (1962a). *Middle Passage*, in Henry Louis Gates, Jr and Nellie Y. McKay (eds), *The Norton Anthology of African American Literature*. New York: W. W. Norton, pp. 1501–5.

Hayden, Robert (1962b). 'O Daedalus, Fly Away Home', in Henry Louis Gates, Jr and Nellie Y. McKay (eds), *The Norton Anthology of African American Literature*. New York: W. W. Norton, pp. 1505–6.

Henderson, Mae G. (1991) 'Toni Morrison's *Beloved*: Remembering the Body as Historical Text', in Hortense J. Spillers (ed.), *Comparative American Identities: Race, Sex and Nationality in the Modern Text*. New York: Routledge, pp. 62–86.

Henderson, Stephen (1973). *Understanding the New Black Poetry*. New York: Morrow.

Hersh, Blanche Glassman (1978). *The Slavery of Sex: Feminist-Abolition in America*. Urbana: University of Illinois Press.

Himid, Lubaina (1992). *Revenge*. Rochdale, Greater Manchester: Rochdale Art Gallery.

Himid, Lubaina (1999a). *Plan B*. St Ives: Tate Gallery.

Himid, Lubaina (1999b). *Zanzibar*. Llandudno: Oriel Mostyn Gallery.

Himid, Lubaina (2001). 'Revenge: A Masque in Five Tableaux', Transatlantic Slave Sites Tour. University of Central Lancashire, 6 March.

Holiday, Billie (n.d.). *Greatest Hits Vol. 1*. LP. Cleo.

Honour, Hugh (1989). *The Image of the Black in Western Art, Vol. IV, from the American Revolution to World War 1, Part 1, Slaves and Liberators*. Cambridge, MA: Harvard University Press.

hooks, bell and Dash, Julie (1992). 'Dialogue between bell hooks and Julie Dash', in Julie Dash, *Daughters of the Dust: The Making of an American Film*. New York: New Press, pp. 27–67.

Howe, Stephen (1998). *Afrocentrism: Mythical Pasts and Imagined Homes*. London: Verso.

Hughes, Langston (1993). *I Wonder as I Wander: An Autobiographical Journey*. New York: Hill and Wang (first published 1956).

Hugill, Stan (1984). *Shanties from the Seven Seas: Shipboard Work-songs and Songs Used as Work-songs from the Great Days of Sail*. London: Routledge.

Hulme, Peter (1992). *Colonial Encounters: Europe and the Native Caribbean 1492–1797*. London: Routledge.

Hulme, Peter and Whitehead, Neil, L. (1992) *Wild Majesty: Encounters with Caribs from Columbus to the Present Day – An Anthology*. Oxford: Oxford University Press.

Hurston, Zora Neale (1978). *Their Eyes Were Watching God*. Urbana: University of Illinois Press (first published 1937).

Irving, James (1995). Journals and Letters, in Suzanne Schwarz (ed.), *Slave Captain: The Career of James Irving in the Liverpool Slave Trade*. Wrexham: Bridge Books.

J. T. (1822). 'Samboo's Grave', *The Lonsdale Magazine and Kendal Repository*, III: xxix, 31 May, pp. 188–92.

Jackson, Bruce (1974). *Get Your Ass in the Water and Swim Like Me: Narrative Poetry from Black Oral Tradition*. Cambridge, MA: Harvard University Press.

Jacobs, Harriet (1987). *Incidents in the Life of a Slave Girl*, ed. Jean Fagan Yellin. Cambridge, MA: Harvard University Press (first published 1959).

James, C. L. R. (1963) *The Black Jacobins: Toussaint L'Ouverture and the San Domingo Revolution*. New York: Vintage.

James, Winston (1998). *Holding Aloft the Banner of Ethiopia: Caribbean Radicalism in Early Twentieth-Century America*. London: Verso.

The Jazz Singer (1927). Dir. Alan Crosland. Warner Bros.

Jefferson, Thomas (1944). *Notes on the State of Virginia: The Life and Selected Writings of Thomas Jefferson*, ed. Adrienne Koch and William Peden. New York: Random House, pp. 187–288.

Johnson, James Weldon and Johnson, J. Rosamund (1969). *The Books of American Negro Spirituals*. New York: Da Capo Press (first published 1925 and 1926).

Jones, Anne Goodwyn (1999). 'Engendered in the South: Blood and Irony in Douglass and Jacobs', in Alan J. Rice and Martin Crawford (eds), *Liberating Sojourn: Frederick Douglass and Transatlantic Reform*. Athens: University of Georgia Press.

Jones, Gayl (1991). *Liberating Voices: Oral Tradition in African American Literature*. Cambridge, MA: Harvard University Press.

Jones, Howard (1986). *Mutiny on the* Amistad. Oxford: Oxford University Press.

Jordan, Winthrop (1969). *White over Black: American Attitudes toward the Negro 1550–1812*. Baltimore: Penguin.

Joyner, Charles (1986). 'Introduction to the Brown Thrasher Edition', in Georgia Writers' Project, Savannah Unit, *Drums and Shadows: Survival Studies among the Georgia Coastal Negroes*. Athens: University of Georgia Press, pp. ix–xxviii (first published 1940).

Kaplan, Sidney (1969). 'Black Mutiny on the *Amistad*', in Jules Chametzky and Sidney Kaplan (eds), *Black and White in American Culture: An Anthology from the* Massachusetts Review. Amherst: University of Massachusetts Press, pp. 291–5.

Keenan, Sally (1993). ' "Four Hundred Years of Silence": Myth, History and Motherhood in *Beloved*', in Jonathan White (ed.), *Recasting the World*. Baltimore: The Johns Hopkins University Press, pp. 45–81.

Kelley, Robin D. G. (1994) *Race Rebels: Culture, Politics and the Black Working Class*. New York: The Free Press.

Kelner, Martin (2000). 'A Disgusting Freak Show: My Passion for Lemon Puffs', *Manchester Guardian*, Sports Section, 31 January, p. 6.

Kilgour, Margaret (1990). *From Communion to Cannibalism: An Anatomy of Metaphors of Incorporation*. Princeton, NJ: Princeton University Press.

King Kong (1933). Dirs. Ernest B. Schoedsack and Merian C. Cooper. RKO.

Klein, Herbert S. (1999) *The Atlantic Slave Trade*. Cambridge: Cambridge University Press.

Labov, William, Cohen, Paul, Robins, Clarence and Lewis, John (1973). 'Toasts', in Alan Dundes (ed.), *Mother Wit from the Laughing Barrel: Readings in the Interpretation of Folklore*. Englewood Cliffs, NJ: Prentice Hall, pp. 329–47.

Lambidis, Christiana (1995). 'Cannibalism, the Mother and *Beloved*', paper given at CAAR conference, Tenerife, February.

Lazarus, Neil (1994). 'Is a Counter-Culture of Modernity a Theory of Modernity?' *Diaspora* 4: 323–39.

Leadbelly (a.k.a. Huddie Ledbetter) (1998). 'Titanic', in Patricia Liggins Hill (ed.), *Call and Response: The Riverside Anthology of the African American Literary Tradition*. New York: Houghton Mifflin, pp. 814–15.

Lee, Valerie (1996). *Granny Midwives and Black American Women's Literature*. London: Routledge.

Lemisch, Jesse (1993). 'Jack Tar in the Streets: Merchant Seamen in the Politics of Revolutionary America'. In Michael McGiffert (ed.), *In Search of Early America*. Richmond, VA: Institute of Early American History and Culture, pp. 109–37.

Lemisch, Jesse (1999). 'Black Agency in the *Amistad* Uprising: Or, You've Taken Our Cinque and Gone . . . ' *Souls: A Critical Journal of Black Politics, Culture and Society* 1(1) (Winter): 57–70.

Levine, Lawrence W. (1977) *Black Culture and Black Consciousness.* Oxford: Oxford University Press.

Lhamon, W. T. Jr (1998). *Raising Cain: Blackface Performance from Jim Crow to Hip Hop.* Cambridge, MA: Harvard University Press.

Liggins Hill, Patricia. (ed.) (1998). *Call and Response: The Riverside Anthology of the African American Literary Tradition.* New York: Houghton Mifflin.

Lindqvist, Sven (1993). *Exterminate All the Brutes.* New York: The New Press.

Linebaugh, Peter and Rediker, Marcus (2000). *The Many-Headed Hydra: Sailors, Slaves, Commoners and the Hidden History of the Revolutionary Atlantic.* London: Verso.

Lipsitz, George (1990). *Time Passages: Collective Memory and American Popular Culture.* Minneapolis: University of Minnesota Press.

Lock, Graham (1999). *Blutopia: Visions of the Future and Revisions of the Past in the Work of Sun Ra, Duke Ellington and Anthony Braxton.* Durham, NC: Duke University Press.

Lomax, Alan (1994). *The Land Where the Blues Began.* London: Minerva.

Longford, Elizabeth (1979). *A Pilgrimage of Passion: The Life of Wilfred Scawen Blunt.* London: Weidenfeld and Nicolson.

Lott, Eric (1993). *Love and Theft: Blackface Minstrelsy and the American Working Class.* New York: Oxford University Press.

Lott, Tommy (1999). *The Invention of Race: Black Culture and the Politics of Representation.* Oxford: Blackwell.

Lovejoy, Paul E. (ed.) (2000) *Identity in the Shadow of Slavery.* London: Continuum.

Lovelace, Earl (1996). *Salt.* London: Faber & Faber.

Lynch, Eric (2001). Walking Tour of Liverpool Slave Sites, 7 March.

McCalman, Ian (ed.) (1991). *The Horrors of Slavery and Other Writings.* Edinburgh: Edinburgh University Press.

McClintock, Anne (1995). *Imperial Leather: Race, Gender and Sexuality in the Colonial Context.* London: Routledge.

McFeely, William S. (1991) *Frederick Douglass.* New York: W. W. Norton.

McNelly, Cleo (1975). 'Natives, Women and Claude Lévi-Strauss: A Reading of *Tristes Tropiques* as Myth', *The Massachusetts Review* (Winter): 7–29.

Major, Clarence (ed.) (1971). *Black Slang: A Dictionary of Afro-American Talk.* London: Routledge, Kegan and Paul.

Malcolm X (1992). Dir. Spike Lee. Forty Acres and a Mule.

Malone, Jacqui (1996). *Steppin' on the Blues: The Visible Rhythms of African American Dance.* Urbana: University of Illinois Press.

Manning, Patrick (1992). 'Tragedy and Sacrifice in the History of Slavery', in Alan L. Karras and J. R. McNeil (eds), *Atlantic American Societies from Columbus through Abolition 1492–1888.* London: Routledge, pp. 40–72.

Marx, Karl (1990). *Capital, Vol. One*, trans. Ben Fowkes. Harmondsworth: Penguin.

Masilela, Ntongela (1998). 'Women Directors of the Los Angeles School', in Jacqueline Bobo (ed.), *Black Women Film and Video Artists*. London: Routledge, pp. 21–41.

Mason, Peter (1990). *Deconstructing America: Representations of the Other*. London: Routledge.

Mathieson, Barbara Offut (1994). 'Memory and Mother Love: Toni Morrison's Dyad', in Amritjit Singh, Joseph T. Skerrett Jr and Robert E. Hogan (eds), *Memory, Narrative and Identity: New Essays in Ethnic American Literatures*. Boston: Northeastern University Press, pp. 212–32.

Matus, Jill (1998). *Toni Morrison*. Manchester: Manchester University Press.

Meltzer, David (1993). *Reading Jazz*. San Francisco: Mercury House.

Melville, Herman (1984). 'Benito Cereno', *The Piazza Tales*. New York: Library of America (first published 1856).

Mercer, Kobena (1994). *Welcome to the Jungle: New Positions in Black Cultural Studies*. London: Routledge.

Midgely, Clare (1992). *Women against Slavery: The British Campaigns, 1780–1870*. London: Routledge.

Miller, Joseph C. (1988) *Way of Death: Merchant Capital and the Angolan Slave Trade, 1730–1830*. Madison: University of Wisconsin Press.

Miller, Sabrina L. (2000). 'A Museum Exhibit Reveals What Many Don't Know: A Black Family Was on Board', *Chicago Tribune*, 20 February.

Miner, Madonne M. (1985). 'Lady No Longer Sings the Blues: Rape, Madness and Silence in *The Bluest Eye*', in Marjorie Pryse and Hortense J. Spillers (eds), *Conjuring: Black Women, Fiction and Literary Tradition*. Bloomington: Indiana University Press, 176–91.

Mintz, Sidney W. (1986). *Sweetness and Power: The Place of Sugar in Modern History*. Harmondsworth: Penguin.

Monson, Ingrid (1994). 'Doubleness and Jazz Improvisation: Irony, Parody and Ethnomusicology', *Critical Inquiry* 20: 283–313.

Montaigne, Michel de (1928). *The Essays of Michael, Lord of Montaigne*, trans. John Florio, 3 vols, Volume 1. London: Dent.

Montejo, Esteban (1968). *The Autobiography of a Runaway Slave*. London: Bodley Head.

Morrison, Toni (1972). *The Bluest Eye*. 1970. New York: Washington Square Press.

Morrison, Toni (1980a). *Song of Solomon*. 1977. St Albans: Triad Grafton.

Morrison, Toni (1980b). *Sula*. London: Triad Grafton.

Morrison, Toni (1983). *Tar Baby*. 1981. London: Triad Grafton.

Morrison, Toni (1984). 'Memory, Creation and Writing', *Thought* 59: 385–90.

Morrison, Toni (1985). 'Rootedness: The Ancestor as Foundation', in Mari Evans (ed.), *Black Women Writers 1950–1980*. London: Pluto, pp. 339–45.

Morrison, Toni (1988). *Beloved*. London: Picador.

Morrison, Toni (1988b). Personal interview. Edinburgh, 28 February.

Morrison, Toni (1989a). 'A Bench by the Road', *The World* 3(1): 4–5 and 37–41.

Morrison, Toni (1992). *Jazz*. London: Chatto and Windus.

Morrison, Toni (1993). *Playing in the Dark*. 1992. London: Picador.

Mullin, Gerald W. (1975) *Flight and Rebellion: Slave Resistance in Eighteenth-Century Virginia*. Oxford: Oxford University Press.

Mullin, Michael (1992). *Africa in America: Slave Acculturation and Resistance in the American South and the British Caribbean, 1736–1831*. Urbana: University of Illinois Press.

Murray, Albert (1976). *Stomping the Blues*. New York: Da Capo Press.

Myers, Norma (1996). *Reconstructing the Black Past*. London: Frank Cass.

Neal, Larry (1989). *Visions of a Liberated Future: Black Arts Movement Writings*. New York: Thunder's Mouth Press.

Newton, John (1962). *The Journal of a Slave Trader (1750–1754)*, eds B. Martin and M. Spurrell. London: Epworth Press (first published 1788).

Nichols, Grace (1996). *Sunris*. London: Virago.

Nielsen, Aldon L. (1994). *Writing between the Lines: Race and Intertextuality*. Athens: University of Georgia Press.

Niles, Abbe (1928). 'Ballads, Songs and Snatches', *The Bookman* 67(3) (May): 290–1.

Nora, Pierre (1994). 'Between Memory and History: Les Lieux de Mémoire', in Genevieve Fabre and Robert O'Meally (eds), *History and Memory in African American Culture*. Oxford: Oxford University Press, pp. 284–300.

Oliver, Paul (1984). *Songsters and Saints: Vocal Traditions on Race Records*. Cambridge: Cambridge University Press.

Olney, James (1989). 'The Founding Fathers: Frederick Douglass and Booker T. Washington', in Deborah E. McDowell and Arnold Rampersad (eds), *Slavery and the Literary Imagination*. Baltimore: The Johns Hopkins Press.

O'Meally, Robert G. (1989) 'The Black Sermon: Tradition and Art', *Callaloo* 11: 198–200.

O'Meally, Robert G. (1994) 'On Burke and the Vernacular: Ralph Ellison's Boomerang of History', in Genevieve Fabre and Robert O'Meally (eds), *History and Memory in African American Culture*. Oxford: Oxford University Press, pp. 244–60.

The Original Kings of Comedy (2000). Dir. Spike Lee. Forty Acres and a Mule.

Osagie, Iyunolu Folayan (2000). *The Amistad Revolt: Memory, Slavery and the Politics of Identity in the United States and Sierra Leone*. Athens: University of Georgia Press.

'Packwood's Superior Razor Strop' (1794). Advertisement, *Morning Chronicle*, 3 November, p. 3.

Palmer, Colin A. (1997) 'The Slave Trade, African Slavers and the Demography of the Caribbean to 1750', in Franklin W. Knight (ed.), *General History of the Caribbean: Volume III – The Slave Societies of the Caribbean*. London: Unesco/Macmillan.

Park, Mungo (1954). *Travels in the Interior Districts of Africa*. London: J. M. Dent (first published 1799).

Parrish, Timothy L. (1997). 'Imagining Slavery: Toni Morrison and Charles Johnson', *Studies in American Fiction* 25: 81–100.

Parsons, Neil (1998). *King Khama, Emperor Joe and the Great White Queen: Victorian Britain through African Eyes*. Chicago: Chicago University Press.

Pettinger, Alasdair (1998). *Always Elsewhere: Travels of the Black Atlantic*. London: Cassell.

Pettinger, Alasdair (1999). 'Send Back the Money: Douglass and the Free Church of Scotland', in Alan J. Rice and Martin Crawford (eds), *Liberating Sojourn: Frederick Douglass and Transatlantic Reform*. Athens: University of Georgia Press.

Philbrick, Nathaniel (2001). *In the Heart of the Sea*. London: HarperCollins.

Philip, M. Nourbese (1997). 'Trying Her Tongue', in Yopie Prins and Maeera Shreiba (eds), *Dwelling in Possibility: Women Poets and Critics on Poetry*. Ithaca, NY: Cornell University Press, pp. 116–25.

Phillips, Caryl (2000). *The Atlantic Sound*. London: Faber.

Phillips, Jerry (1998). 'Cannibalism Qua Capitalism: The Metaphorics of Accumulation in Marx, Conrad, Shakespeare and Marlowe', in Francis Barker, Peter Hulme and Margaret Iverson (eds), *Cannibalism in the Colonial World*. Cambridge: Cambridge University Press, pp. 183–203.

Piersen, William D. (1993) *Black Legacy: America's Hidden Heritage*. Amherst: University of Massachusetts Press.

Pieterse, Jan Nederveen (1992). *White on Black: Images of Africa and Blacks in Western Popular Culture*. 1990. New Haven, CT: Yale University Press.

Piper, Adrian (1996). *Out of Order, Out of Sight: Volume 1: Selected Writings in Meta-Art 1968–1992*. Cambridge, MA: Massachusetts Institute of Technology Press.

Pollock, Griselda (1999). *Differencing the Canon: Feminist Desire and the Writing of Art's Histories*. London: Routledge.

Pratt, Mary Louise (1992). *Imperial Eyes: Travel Writing and Transculturation*. London: Routledge.

Prince, Mary (1986). *The History of Mary Prince, A West Indian Slave*, ed. Moira Ferguson. London: Pandora Press (first published 1831).

Ras Michael and the Sons of Negus (1998). 'Nyah Man Say', *Nyahbinghi*. Trojan Records.

Raynal, Guillaume (1776). *A Philosophical and Political History of the Settlements and Trade of the Europeans in the East and West Indies*. London: T. Caldwell.

Read, Alan (ed.) (1996). *The Fact of Blackness: Frantz Fanon and Visual Representation*. London and Seattle: Institute of Contemporary Arts/Bay Press.

Rediker, Marcus and Linebaugh, Peter (1993). 'The Many-Headed Hydra: Sailors, Slaves and the Working Class in the Eighteenth Century', in Ron Sokalsky and James Koehnline (eds), *Gone to Croatan: Origins of North American Dropout Culture*. Edinburgh: AK Press.

A Respectable Trade? Bristol and Transatlantic Slavery (1999). Curator Sue Giles. City Museum and Art Gallery, Bristol.

Rice, Alan J. (1994a) ' "Fear of White Cannibals": An Essay Review', *Times Higher Education Supplement*, Issue 2110 (11 February), pp. 18–19. Reprinted in *The Australian*, 3 March.

Rice, Alan J. (1994b) 'Finger-snapping to Train-dancing and Back Again: The Development of a Jazz Style in African American Prose', *Yearbook of English Studies* 24: 105–16.

Rice, Alan J. (1994c) 'Jazzing It up a Storm: The Execution and Meaning of Toni Morrison's Jazzy Prose Style', *Journal of American Studies* 28: 423–32.

Rice, Alan J. (1998) ' "Who's Eating Whom": Cannibalism in the Writing of the Black Atlantic from Equiano to Toni Morrison', *Research in African Literatures* Winter: 107–20.

Rice, Fred (1993). *Chestnuts, Greys and Rodeo Days*. Crawley: Oran's Paddock.

Rigney, Barbara Hill (1991). *The Voices of Toni Morrison*. Columbus: Ohio State University Press.

Roach, Joseph (1996). *Cities of the Dead: Circum-Atlantic Performance*. New York: Columbia University Press.

Roberts, John W. (1989) *From Trickster to Badman: The Black Folk Hero in Slavery and Freedom*. Philadelphia: University of Pennsylvania Press.

Robeson, Paul (1978). *Paul Robeson Speaks: Writings, Speeches, Interviews*, ed. Philip S. Foner. London: Quartet.

Robinson, Cedric (1983). *Black Marxism: The Making of the Black Radical Tradition*. London: Zed Press.

Roediger, David (ed.) (1998). *Black on White: Black Writers on What It Means to Be White*. New York: Shocken Books.

Rogin, Michael (1998). *Blackface, White Noise: Jewish Immigrants in the Hollywood Melting Pot*. London: University of California Press.

Ross, Leonard Q. (1993) 'The Strangest Places', 1939. In David Meltzer (ed.), *Reading Jazz*. San Francisco: Mercury House, pp. 147–55.

Rushdy, Ashraf H. A. (1990). ' "Rememory": Primal Scenes and Constructions in Toni Morrison's Novels', *Contemporary Literature* 31: 300–23.

Sale, Maggie Montesinos (1997). *The Slumbering Volcano: American Slave Ship Revolts and the Production of Rebellious Masculinity*. Durham, NC: Duke University Press.

Sanders of the River (1935). Dir. Zoltan Korda. London Film Productions.

Sartin, Stephen (2001). 'Guided Tour of the Judge's Lodgings', *Transatlantic Slave Sites Tour*. Lancaster Judges Lodgings, 6 March.

Schwarz, Suzanne (1995). *Slave Captain: The Career of James Irving in the Liverpool Slave Trade*. Wrexham: Bridge Books.

Scotland and Africa (1997). Curator Polly Rewt. City Art Centre, Edinburgh.

Send Back the Money (1996). Dir. Vicki Davidson. Edinburgh: BBC Radio Scotland, 11 December.

Shepperson, George (Sam) (1953). 'Frederick Douglass and Scotland', *Journal of Negro History* 38 (July): 307–21.

Shepperson, George (Sam) (1998). 'Paul Robeson in Edinburgh', *University of Edinburgh Journal* (Graduates Association) 38(4) (December): 233–8.

Shepperson, George (Sam) and Price, Thomas (1987). *Independent African: John Chilembwe and the Nyasaland Rising of 1915.* Edinburgh: Edinburgh University Press.

Shyllon, F. O. (1974) *Black Slaves in Britain.* London: Oxford University Press.

Simpson, A. W. Brian (1986). *Cannibalism and the Common Law.* Harmondsworth: Penguin.

Singleton, Theresa A. (1999) 'The Slave Trade Remembered on the Former Gold and Slave Coasts', in Sylvia Frey and Betty Wood (eds), *From Slavery to Emancipation in the Atlantic World.* London: Frank Cass, pp. 150–69.

Skerrett, Joseph T. Jr (1985). 'Recitation to the Griot: Storytelling and Learning in Toni Morrison's *Song of Solomon*', in Marjorie Pryse and Hortense J. Spillers (eds), *Conjuring: Black Women, Fiction and Literary Tradition.* Bloomington: Indiana University Press, pp. 192–203.

Slavery: A Global Investigation (2000). London: Channel 4, September.

Small, Christopher (1987). *Music of the Common Tongue.* London: John Calder.

Smith, J. T. (1874) *Vagabondiana or, Anecdotes of Mendicant Wanderers through the Streets of London; with Portraits of the Most Remarkable.* London: Chatto and Windus (first published 1815).

Smitherman, Geneva (1985). *Talkin and Testifyin.* Detroit: Wayne State University Press.

Snead, James (1994). *White Screens, Black Images: Hollywood from the Dark Side.* London: Routledge.

Softing, Inger-Ann (1995). 'Carnival and Black American Music as Counterculture in Toni Morrison's *The Bluest Eye* and *Jazz*', *American Studies in Scandinavia* 27: 81–102.

Spillers, Hortense (1994). 'Mama's Baby, Papa's Maybe: An American Grammar', in Angelyn Mitchell (ed.), *Within the Circle: An Anthology of African American Literary Criticism from the Harlem Renaissance to the Present.* Durham, NC: Duke University Press, pp. 454–81.

Spivak, Gayatri (1988). 'Can the Subaltern Speak?' in Cary Nelson and Lawrence Grossberg, *Marxism and the Interpretation of Culture.* London: Macmillan.

Splawn, P. Jane (1998). 'An Intimate Talk with Ntozake Shange: An Interview', in Jacqueline Bobo (ed.), *Black Women Film and Video Artists.* London: Routledge, pp. 189–206.

Stark, Suzanne (1999). 'Female Tars: Women Aboard Ship in the Age of Sail', *Black and Asian Studies Association Newsletter* 25 (September): 10–12.

Stearns, Marshall (1956). *The Story of Jazz.* Oxford: Oxford University Press.

Stedman, John Gabriel (1988). *Narrative of a Five Years' Expedition against the Revolted Negroes of Surinam Transcribed from the Original 1790 Manuscript*, ed. Richard Price and Sally Price. Baltimore: The Johns Hopkins Press.

Stuckey, Sterling (1987). *Slave Culture: Nationalist Theory and the Foundations of Black America.* Oxford: Oxford University Press.

Sulter, Maud (1992). 'Without Tides, No Maps', *Revenge*. Lubaina Himid. Rochdale: Greater Manchester Rochdale Art Gallery, 27–35.

Sun Ra (1990a). 'Let's Go Fly a Kite'. Concert performance, Edinburgh International Jazz Festival, August.

Sun Ra (1990b). 'Space Chants: A Medley', *Live in London*. LP. Blast First.

Szwed, John (1997). *Space Is the Place: The Lives and Times of Sun Ra*. New York: Pantheon.

Tabili, Laura (1996). '"A Maritime Race": Masculinity and the Racial Division of Labour in British Merchant Ships 1900–1939', in Margaret S. Creighton and Lisa Norling (eds), *Iron Men, Wooden Women: Gender and Seafaring in the Atlantic World, 1700–1920*. Baltimore: The Johns Hopkins University Press.

Taylor, Clare (ed.) (1974). *British and American Abolitionists: An Episode in Transatlantic Understanding*. Edinburgh: Edinburgh University Press.

Taylor, Helen (2001). *Circling Dixie: Contemporary Southern Culture through a Transatlantic Lens*. New Brunswick, NJ: Rutgers University Press.

Thomas, Helen (2000). *Romanticism and Slave Narratives*. Cambridge: Cambridge University Press.

Thomas, Hugh (1997). *The Slave Trade: The Story of the Atlantic Slave Trade, 1440–1870*. London: Picador.

Thompson, Robert Farris (1983). *Flash of the Spirit*. New York: Vintage.

Thornton, John K. (1992). *Africa and Africans in the Making of the Atlantic World, 1400–1680*. Cambridge: Cambridge University Press.

Tibbles, Tony (1999). '*Slave Passages and Liberating Sojourns. The Black Atlantic in the Museum*' – A Colloquium. University of Central Lancashire, Preston, 10 May.

Tibbles, Tony (2000). Personal conversation, May.

Tibbles, Tony (2001). Personal correspondence, May.

Torgovnick, Marianna (1990). *Gone Primitive: Savage Intellects, Modern Lives*. Chicago: University of Chicago Press.

Turley, David (1999). 'British Unitarian Abolitionists, Frederick Douglass and Racial Equality', in Alan J. Rice and Martin Crawford (eds), *Liberating Sojourn: Frederick Douglass and Transatlantic Reform*. Athens: University of Georgia Press.

Ugwu, Catherine (ed.) (1995). *Let's Get It On: The Politics of Black Performance*. London: ICA.

Ulanov, Barry (1998). 'The Ellington Programme', in Robert G. O'Meally (ed.), *The Jazz Cadence of American Culture*. New York: Columbia University Press, pp. 166–71.

Vasili, Phil (1998). *The First Black Footballer: Arthur Wharton 1865–1930*. London: Frank Cass.

Verges, Françoise (1996). 'Chains of Madness, Chains of Colonialism: Fanon and Freedom', in Alan Read (ed.), *The Fact of Blackness: Frantz Fanon and Visual Representation*. London and Seattle: Institute of Contemporary Arts/ Bay Press.

Warner, Marina (1994) *Managing Monsters*. New York: Vintage.

Warner, Marina (1998). 'Fee Fie Fo Fum: The Child in the Jaws of the Story', in Francis Barker, Peter Hulme and Margaret Iverson (eds), *Cannibalism in the Colonial World*. Cambridge: Cambridge University Press, pp. 158–82.

Watkins, James (1860). *Struggles for Freedom; or The Life of James Watkins, Formerly a Slave in Maryland U.S.; in Which Is Detailed a Graphic Account of His Extraordinary Escape from Slavery* ... nineteenth edn. Manchester: James Watkins.

Watkins, Mel (1995). *On the Real Side: Laughing, Lying, and Signifying – The Underground Tradition of African American Humour* ... New York: Touchstone.

Wedderburn, Robert (1991a). *The Axe Laid to the Root, or a Fatal Blow to Oppressors, Being an Address to the Planter and Negroes of the Island of Jamaica. No 2 [1817]*. 1817, in Ian McCalman (ed.), *The Horrors of Slavery and Other Writings*. Edinburgh: Edinburgh University Press, pp. 89–95.

Wedderburn, Robert (1991b). *The Horrors of Slavery; Exemplified in the Life and History of the Rev. Robert Wedderburn*. 1824, in Ian McCalman (ed.), *The Horrors of Slavery and Other Writings*. Edinburgh: Edinburgh University Press, pp. 43–61.

West, Hollie (1990). 'Travels with Ralph Ellison through Time and Thought', in Kimberly W. Benston (ed.), *Speaking for You: The Vision of Ralph Ellison*. Washington, DC: Howard University Press, pp. 37–44.

White, Shane and White, Graham (1999). *Stylin': African American Expressive Culture from Its Beginnings to the Zoot Suit*. Ithaca, NY: Cornell University Press.

Whitehead, Neil L. (1997) 'Monstrosity and Marvel: Symbolic Convergence and Mimetic Elaboration in Trans-Cultural Representation – An Anthropological Reading of Ralegh's *Discoverie* ... ', *Studies in Travel Writing* 1: 72–95.

Wiegman, Robyn (1995). *American Anatomies: Theorizing Race and Gender*. Durham, NC: Duke University Press.

Wilkins, Frances (1999). *Manx Slave Traders*. Kidderminster, Hereford and Worcester. Wyre Forest Press.

Willis, Susan (1984). 'Eruptions of Funk: Historicizing Toni Morrison', in Henry Louis Gates Jr. (ed.), *Black Literature and Literary Theory*. New York: Methuen, pp. 263–80.

Willis, Susan (1987) *Specifying: Black Women Writing the American Experience*. London: Routledge.

Willis, Susan (1994). 'Memory and Mass Culture', in Genevieve Fabre and Robert O'Meally (eds), *History and Memory in African American Culture*. Oxford: Oxford University Press, pp. 178–87.

Wilson, Olly (1998). 'Black Music as an Art Form', in Robert G. O'Meally (ed.), *The Jazz Cadence of American Culture*. New York: Columbia University Press, 82–101.

Wong, Shelley (1990). 'Transgression as Poesis in *The Bluest Eye*,' *Callaloo* 13: 471–81.

Wonham, Henry B. (ed.) (1996) *Criticism and the Color Line: Desegregating American Literary Studies*. Rutgers, NJ: Rutgers University Press.

Wood, Marcus (2000). *Blind Memory: Visual Representations of Slavery in England and America 1780–1865*. Manchester: Manchester University Press.

Wood, Nancy (1999). *Vectors of Memory: Legacies of Trauma in Postwar Europe*. Oxford: Berg.

Wright, Richard (1954). *Black Power*. London: Dennis Dobson.

Young, James E. (1992) 'Holocaust Memorials in America: Public Art as Process', in Harriet F. Senie and Sally Webster (eds), *Critical Issues in Public Art: Content, Context and Controversy*. New York: HarperCollins, pp. 57–70.

Young, Robert J. C. (1995). *Colonial Desire: Hybridity in Theory and Practice*. London: Routledge.

INDEX

Page numbers in italics refer to illustrations.

Lightning Source UK Ltd.
Milton Keynes UK
UKHW011524210119
335938UK00003B/182/P